25.00

P9-DWU-618

Prayer, Patronage, and Power

Capital on attached column of northeastern pier, la Trinité, Vendôme (eleventh century)

Prayer, Patronage, and Power

The Abbey of la Trinité, Vendôme,
1032–1187

by

PENELOPE D. JOHNSON

New York University Press · New York and London · 1981

Library of Congress Cataloging in Publication Data

Johnson, Penelope C. (Penelope Delafield), 1938–
    Prayer, patronage, and power.

Bibliography: p. 194–207.
Includes index.
1. Abbaye de la Trinité (Vendôme, France)
I. Title.
BX2615.V462J63   271′.1′04453   81-3955
    ISBN 0-8147-4162-2   AACR2

Manufactured in the United States of America

To
Rollin,
Wade,
and
Kate

Preface

FOR THIS STUDY I have consulted both published and archival sources. The five-volume collection of documents made by Abbé Métais has proved exceedingly useful, and I have used his numbering of charters for easy reference. As his printed edition is not exact in specifying the document from which he has drawn his text, I have used originals or the earliest reliable copies in questionable cases. All translations are my own.

Research in France has been helped by the excellent professional assistance of Monsieur Dupont and his staff of the municipal library of Vendôme. In addition, the warm friendships forged with Jane and Geoffrey Grigson, Adey Horton, and Jean-Sebastien Stehli have made of the Vendômois *un pays accueillant*.

I have been extremely fortunate during the course of this research to have received help and advice from a number of generous scholars. I wish to thank Dean Norman Cantor of New York University; Professors Giles Constable, Director of the Dumbarton Oaks Center; Jaroslav Pelikan, Jeffrey Merrick, and Walter Cahn of Yale; John Beckerman of Haverford College; Jean-François Lemarignier, of the Université de Paris; Olivier Guillot of the Université de Rouen; and Jeremy Adams of Southern Methodist University. Above all, it is to Professor John Boswell of Yale that I owe an inestimable debt of gratitude for his unfailing interest, insights, and guidance—like the greatest of the twelfth-century teachers, he is "clarus doctor, et admirabilis omnibus. . . ." (John of Salisbury, *Metalogicon* 2:10).

Abbreviations

Bull. Vend. *Bulletin de la société archéologique, scientifique et littéraire du Vendômois.*

CM *Cartulaire de Marmoutier pour le Vendômois*, ed. de Trémault (Paris, 1893).

CS *Cartulaire saintongeais de la Trinité de Vendôme*, ed. Charles Métais, *Archives historiques de la Saintonge et de l'Aunis* 22 (1893), 1–431.

CT *Cartulaire de l'abbaye cardinale de la Trinité de Vendôme*, ed. Charles Métais, 5 vols. (Paris, 1893–1904).

JL Philip Jaffé, *Regesta pontificum romanorum ab condita ecclesia ad annum post Christum natum 1198,* 2d ed., ed. F. Kaltenbrunner, P. Ewald, S. Loewenfeld, 2 vols. (Leipzig, 1885–88).

PL Jacques Paul Migne, *Patrologia Latina* (1878–90).

B.N. Bibliothèque Nationale.

B.D. Bibliothèque Départementale.

B.M. Bibliothèque Municipale

Contents

Maps and Figures

Maps

Figures

Plates

Prayer, Patronage, and Power

Introduction

THE PROFOUND influence of monasticism on Western culture is a commonplace of historical scholarship; scholars regularly cite Benedictine monks as peacekeepers, preservers of the cultural heritage of the West, and as the arbiters and embodiment of Western spiritual ideals.[1] Some have even gone so far as to name the monks as early promoters of the work ethic.[2] Specific studies have dealt topically with monasticism, and monographs have examined individual houses. But the subject continues to elude a wholly satisfactory treatment. One can read extensively in the literature and still have difficulty in answering such fundamental questions as: How did medieval monasteries reflect their society, and how did they affect their environment? This problem exists because monastic historians have usually taken one of two distinct routes that circle the central issue of the monastery as a social institution. The most venerable approach has been to focus on the religious life within the monastic enclosure, concentrating on hagiographical sources so that the historian depicts monastic life primarily as a spiritual pilgrimage. The more recent tendency is to scrutinize the economic and agricultural activity of abbeys, utilizing the often extensive monastic records of land alienation and exploitation. The first avenue leads past most of the monastery and straight to the church at the north side of the enclosure, while the second remains outside the monastic walls winding among the abbey's fields. Both areas were critical to monastic life, but there was much more to a monastery than its sanctuary and farmland. The gates that pierced the enclosure wall admitted travelers; the sick, angry or needy neighbors; oblate children and adults; powerful lords; visiting ecclesiastical dignitaries—a

host of varied entrants. The gates symbolized "the mutual relations between monasteries and their environment,"[3] and in the
mind of the historian seeking to move beyond the traditional
resting places of monastic history, they prompt a multitude of
questions about the real social significance of the monastery and
its relations with its neighbors.

This study, limited to one house during a century and a half
of its early life, cannot flesh out the whole body of medieval
monasticism.[4] It can and does attempt to recapture the reality of
monastic life by viewing one abbey holistically, as a many-fac-
eted institution with not only a lively religious life but also extensive and significant economic and legal influence; networks of
patrons, friends, and clients; and substantial input into the social,
economic, and spiritual welfare of its county.

The subject is the Benedictine abbey of la Trinité, Vendôme,
chosen because research on its political and social history can rely
on surviving primary sources (early documents, much of the library, and some of the original buildings) and because its foundation connected it with important families during a crucial
struggle for power in the county. Since this sort of detailed investigation of a single monastic institution and its environment
is either not possible or has not been attempted for many comparable institutions, it has not been possible to provide the sort
of comparative data one naturally hopes for in such an undertak-
ing. A few other studies have been used more or less systemati-
cally, and others have been consulted for specific points, but it is
simply not possible at present to sustain a thorough comparison
with any other such institution.[5]

For la Trinité itself the investigation is limited to the monastery's first century and a half, roughly 1032 to 1187. This time
span comprises the period of its early growth, a transitional stage
in the three decades around 1100, and the beginning of the later
monastic period. Because the documents are most numerous for
the eleventh century and dwindle during the twelfth, some
means of comparison must be used to offset documentary dis-
proportion and distortion of the evidence; the 150-year period
provides easily distinguishable fifty-year intervals that can be

compared to produce significant comparative figures. (So few charters survive from the last five years that the last interval of actually fifty-five years is treated as equivalent to the first two fifty-year spans.) The terminal date is that of the death of Abbot Girard in 1187.

Since the history of the abbey of la Trinité is inexorably linked with that of its county, the historical background for the abbey's beginnings needs to be sketched. In the late tenth century the county of Vendôme was dependent on the cathedral of Chartres, and since the bishop of Chartres was vassal to the French king, Vendôme fell within the sphere of influence of the Capetians.[6] Burchard the Venerable (fl. 985–1005), a supporter and close companion of Hugh Capet, was the founder of the comital family of Vendôme, and the grant of Vendôme to Burchard may well have been made by the bishop at the instigation of the Robertians.[7]

In the early days of the Capetian dynasty when Hugh Capet and Robert the Pious were struggling to establish effective control over the royal domain, one of their most obstreperous barons was Odo II, count of Blois, whose lands lay immediately southeast of Vendôme. To the southwest of Vendôme another powerful fief, the county of Anjou, remained loyal to the Robertians. Vendôme allied with Anjou in the late tenth century, creating with the royal domain and Chartres a power constellation to block Blois. (See Map 1.) The alliance was cemented in the early years of the eleventh century by the marriage of Burchard's daughter, Elizabeth, to Fulk Nerra of Anjou. (See genealogies in Appendix III.) In recognition of Vendôme's loyalty to the Capetians, Burchard's son Rainald was rewarded with the bishopric of Paris.

Upon Burchard's death (c. 1005), Rainald became count of Vendôme. The bishop had no legitimate heir, and the county passed to the offspring of his sister Elizabeth. Her heir was the only child of her marriage to Fulk Nerra—a daughter, Adele; when Adele reached maturity, she married Odo of Nevers and produced four sons.[8] At the death of Bishop Rainald around 1016, Adele seems to have entrusted her eldest son, Burchard, to

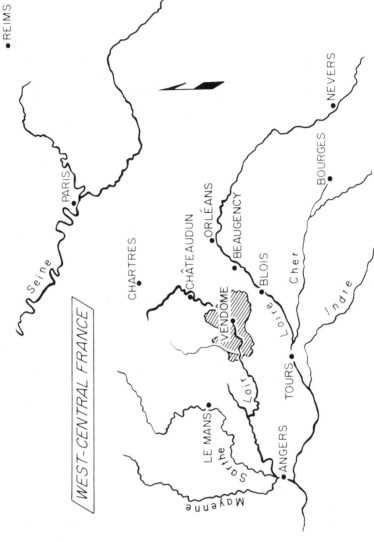

Map 1. Detail of west-central France.

WEST-CENTRAL FRANCE

REIMS

PARIS

Seine

CHARTRES

CHÂTEAUDUN

ORLÉANS

BEAUGENCY

BLOIS

VENDÔME

Loir

Loire

Cher

Indre

NEVERS

BOURGES

TOURS

ANGERS

LE MANS

Sarthe

Mayenne

UMBERTO AMODIO

4

her father, Fulk Nerra, who then held the wardship both of the boy and of the county of Vendôme. As late as 1021–22, Fulk still controlled Vendôme.[9]

A few years later, the crisis inaugurated in 1027 by the anticipation of Prince Henry's consecration began to work to the advantage of the count of Blois, for Odo II of Blois issued a charter as lord of Vendôme in 1029.[10] Bishop Fulbert of Chartres had died the year before, and it is probable that Odo had seized the episcopal position as overlord of Vendôme. Shortly thereafter, to counter the growing power in Blois, King Henry urged Fulk Nerra to cede Vendôme's wardship to his son, Geoffrey Martel. Thus, in 1031 Geoffrey Martel received the title of Count of Vendôme and regranted the lands to Adele and her son Burchard to hold as his *fideles*.[11] Young Burchard died soon after,[12] and Geoffrey regranted the honor to Adele, who gave Burchard's half to her second son, Fulk Oison. Fulk resented sharing the inheritance with his mother and unwisely attacked her half of the county. His aggression gave Geoffrey an excuse to chase out his nephew and claim the honor. Thereupon Adele ceded the remaining half of the county to Geoffrey, who could then exercise full comital power. The story of the abbey begins after this complex political maneuvering had left Geoffrey as lord of the county of Vendôme.

As important as the political background for la Trinité was its religious constitution. The abbey followed the Rule of St. Benedict, according to which the individual monk is to tread the road of obedience and humility to reach his Creator. This journey is made possible by the legislation of the Rule, establishing a monastic organization and administration. The Rule seems to embody a contradiction: the monk is to seek spiritual perfection by withdrawing from the world, but at the same time is to follow the example of Christ by involving himself in the needs of secular society. It is in Christ's name that the religious should offer hospitality to all travelers as well as charity for the needy, care and consolation for the suffering, and burial for the dead (*RB:* 53 and 4).

The foundation of and subsequent donations to a monastery entailed further paradoxes. Endowments emphasized the importance of material goods, which were, however, given in recognition of the otherworldliness of the cloistered life. Lay people desired to share in the monks' spirituality by donating property to monastic houses. This property increased a monastery's involvement in secular affairs and lessened its separation from the world. All the forces that generated and organized the abbey produced tension between spiritual goals and social and material responsibilities.

La Trinité was both affected by and involved in the rapid changes of the central Middle Ages. The interaction of population increase, a warmer and drier climate, and better crop yields led to expansion into new areas, an increase in manpower available to exploit land, and an acceleration of the commercial revolution. In the second half of the eleventh century these interlocking changes benefited la Trinité, while the abbey's prosperity contributed locally to the upswing. In the same period, western Europe experienced a powerful new spirituality and an ecclesiastic reform movement, both of which also affected the abbey. The growth in power and possessions of the great feudatories had a resounding impact on the monastery, making monastic patronage an important political tool but changing Angevin patronage during the twelfth century. The history of la Trinité can be considered only against the backdrop of such political, social, and economic changes; the monastery, no less than the forces around it, was an organic part of its environment.

Notes

1. Richard W. Southern, *The Making of the Middle Ages* (New Haven, Conn., 1953), p. 155. "The monasteries were a force making for peace in a world which was rudely shaken by the controversies of the Hildebrandine age." Norman Cantor, "The Crisis of Western Monasticism, 1050–1130," *American Historical Review* 66, no. 1 (1960), 47, writes that it was in the eleventh and twelfth centuries that "the fate not only of religion but also of culture and civilization in Western Europe was in large part determined by the work of the black monks." Southern, *Western Society and the Church in the Middle Ages* (Harmondsworth, England, 1970), p. 230, adds that "By about 1050 it must have seemed that the Benedictine Order had established itself forever as the prime expression of the Christian religion throughout western Europe. Its position in the hearts and minds of men and in the social order seemed unshakeable."

2. J. A. Raftis, "Western Monasticism and Economic Organization," *Comparative Studies in Society and History* 3, no. 4 (1961), 456.

3. Giles Constable calls for "a sociological and comparative approach" to the study of monastic history in "The Study of Monastic History Today," *Essays on the Reconstruction of Medieval History*, ed. Vaclav Mudroch and G. S. Couse (Montreal, 1974), p. 29.

4. Jacques Dubois urges scholars to concentrate on editions of texts and individual studies, since a synthetic treatment is not possible for such a complex subject. "Les Moines dans la société du moyen âge, (950–1350)," *Revue d'histoire de l'église de France* 60 (1974), 37.

5. Nine major monasteries that lend themselves well in one way or another to comparisons with la Trinité: Eleanor Searle, *Lordship and Community: Battle Abbey and Its Banlieu, 1066—1538* (Studies and Texts, 26) (Toronto, 1974); Edmund King, *Peterborough Abbey, 1086—1310: A Study in the Land Market* (Cambridge, England, 1973); F. S. Hockey, *Quarr Abbey and Its Lands, 1132—1631* (Leicester, 1970), and *Beaulieu: King John's Abbey* (Old Woking, Surrey, 1976); Charles Seymour Jr., *Notre-Dame of Noyon in the Twelfth Century* (New York, 1968); Jacques Dubois, *Un Sanctuaire monastique au moyen âge: Saint-Fiacre-en-Brie* (Geneva, 1976); Pierre-Roger Gaussin, *L'Abbaye de la Chaise-Dieu (1043—1518)* (Paris, 1962); Marcel Garaud, *L'Abbaye Sainte-Croix de Talmond en Bas-Poitou c. 1049—1250* (Poitiers, 1914); Noreen Hunt, *Cluny under Saint Hugh, 1049—1109* (Notre Dame, Ill., 1967).

6. Olivier Guillot, *Le Comte d'Anjou et son entourage au XIᵉ siècle*, 2 vols. (Paris, 1972), 1:28.

7. J. de Pétigny, *Histoire archéologique du Vendômois* (Vendôme/Blois, 1882), pp. 196–97. The author rejects one theory that Burchard was a son of Fulk the Good, tenth-century count of Anjou. Dhondt emphasizes the loyalties between Burchard and the Capetians. J. Dhondt, *Etudes sur la naissance des principautés territoriales en France, (IX—Xᵉ siècle)* (Bruges, 1948), p. 114, footnote 4. Guillot, *Le Comte d'Anjou*, 1:31, suggests Capetian pressure lay behind the grant to Burchard.

8. *Cartulaire de l'abbaye cardinale de la Trinité de Vendôme*, ed. Charles Métais, 5 vols. (Paris, 1893–1904), 1:15, no. 6, footnote 3, hereafter cited as CT.

9. Guillot, *Le Comte d'Anjou*, 2:41.

10. Ibid., 1:37; see footnote 183.

11. CT 1:16, no. 6. "Eo quidem pacto Gaufredus comes a Rege percepit honorem, quatenus et mater et puer ejus ab eo tenerent." No date is given for when Robert the Pious made Geoffrey overlord of the Vendômois, but Geoffrey was not designated as count before Easter of 1031 (see Guillot, *Le Comte d'Anjou*, 1:45); yet by the time of his marriage (January 1, 1032) he bore the comital title: *Receuil d'annales angevines et vendômoises*, ed. Louis Halphen (Paris, 1903), "Obituaire de Saint-Serge," p. 107. It must have been in 1031 that Geoffrey received the honor of Vendôme.

12. CT 1:17, no. 6, "et factum est quandiu vixit isdem puer. Cumque mortuus esset. . . ." This is the only evidence for the death of young Burchard.

CHAPTER ONE

Foundation and Fabric

G EOFFREY MARTEL and Agnes of Burgundy founded la Trinité, Vendôme, "monasterium in honorem sanctae atque individuae Trinitatis," in the third decade of the eleventh century (CT 1:56, no. 35). From the moment of its conception, tension existed between the ideal of the spiritual life and the reality of the abbey's secular involvements. A powerful lay couple had founded the house—yet it was to be a sanctuary for the most unworldly of men; the monastery's patrons had endowed it with lands and revenues that had to be managed—but the monks were supposed to concentrate all their energies on the contemplation of God by turning away from the cares of the world; the abbey was to be a place for withdrawal from the world behind a "murus silentii"—yet it was situated in a busy and noisy location; the monastery became rich and powerful—but worldly success could lead to the terrible sin of pride.[1]

Such tensions were inherent in medieval monasticism. A strong worldly impulse was frequently at odds with other-worldly goals, although from time to time the two motivating forces worked in harmony. The history of the abbey of la Trinité, Vendôme, is no exception to this pattern. Its foundation set two masters over the monastery: God, for whose service and praise the abbey was created, and its founders and protectors. The early abbots managed to find ways to balance the resulting divergent spiritual and secular interests, a process that became, however, increasingly difficult during the twelfth century.

Geoffrey and Agnes' complex motives for founding la Trinité and their distinctive styles of patronage provide evidence for the interlocking relationships between the abbey and its environ-

8

ment. The extent and composition of the founders' endowment, the ties between them and other patrons, their choice of a site, and the buildings erected—all attest to the impact of the count and countess on la Trinité.

The Foundation

According to the legend of the abbey's foundation, Geoffrey Martel and his new bride, Agnes of Burgundy, were standing at their bedroom window in the castle of Vendôme just before daybreak one Sunday morning. While admiring the beauties of nature, they were startled by the fall of three stars in rapid succession into a spring in the broad fields below the castle. (See Map 2.) Dressing quickly in their most elegant clothes, they hurried to the church of Saint-Martin to have a mass celebrated in honor of the Trinity. When the count told his ecclesiastical advisers of the event, they urged him to build a monastery dedicated to the Trinity over the spring where the stars had fallen.

This tale was recorded about one hundred years after the supposed events took place by Odo, abbot of Marmoutier.[2] It was probably circulated orally in the Vendômois by a member of Geoffrey and Agnes' court before Odo's redaction, for it seems unlikely that the abbot of Marmoutier would have created such a flattering tale for la Trinité—Marmoutier's greatest rival.[3] Although the story is probably apocryphal, it evokes the significance and solemnity that the author detected in the abbey's foundation. There are no light or adventuresome touches to the legend; it is a straightforward account emphasizing the piety and obedience of Agnes and Geoffrey.[4]

Exact dating of the decision to found la Trinité is not possible, although Agnes and Geoffrey issued the foundation charter of the abbey on May 31, 1040 (CT 1:55–60, no. 35). This was the formal document recording all the donations to the abbey and conforming all its possessions. V. H. Galbraith argues persuasively that a monastery's existence must be dated from the time of its verbal *donatio,* often years before the foundation charter was issued.[5] From a practical point of view, land had to be pur-

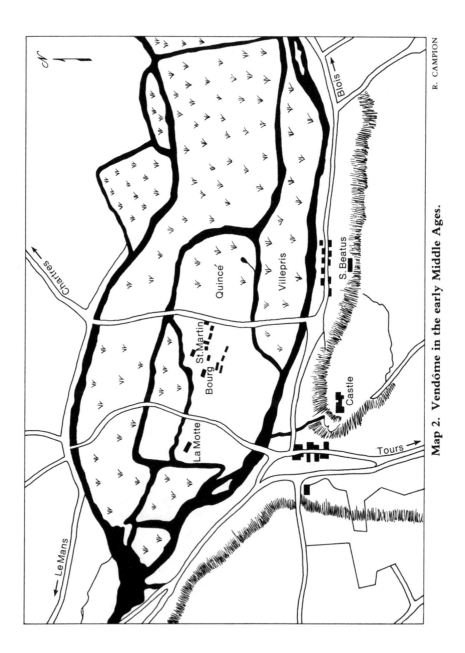

Map 2. Vendôme in the early Middle Ages.

Chartres

Le Mans

La Motte

St. Martin
Bourg

Quincé

Villepris

S. Beatus

Castle

Tours →

Blois →

R. CAMPION

10

chased and cleared and buildings erected before a monastery could be dedicated. Although the exact moment of the *donatio* to la Trinité can not be identified, it must have fallen between the marriage of Geoffrey and Agnes on January 1, 1032, and the formal dedication of the abbey in 1040.[6] The first evidence of a plan to build an abbey in Vendôme appears in an undated charter issued by Leudon confirming the sale by his vassal, Archembald, of the lands of Quinçay and Villepeis to Geoffrey and Agnes "for constructing the place founded in honor of the Holy Trinity. . . . "[7] This sale probably occurred soon after the *donatio,* as the purchase of a site is the first order of business for a building program. Construction of the monastery proceeded rapidly, so that in 1038 it is referred to as "recently constructed," and in two charters from 1039 as the abbey "which Count Geoffrey and his wife Agnes built in the town of Vendôme," and "which had been built next to the town of Vendôme. . . ."[8]

The monastery's origins then can be fixed within the span of six years between January 1, 1032, and the point in 1038 when Bishop Gervais gave the first donation to the "recently constructed" house. By May 31, 1040, the abbey was at least partially built, richly endowed, and ready to play its part in its founders' wider plans.

The foundation instrument for la Trinité cites both Geoffrey and Agnes as cofounders and lists property with which they endowed the abbey. Scholars who have studied la Trinité's history have, however, tended to assume that Geoffrey was the real founder of the abbey and that Agnes was included out of courtesy and to bind her legally to respect her husband's actions.[9] Sufficient evidence exists to challenge this view of Agnes as a passive participant in the abbey's establishment. Charter no. 35 specifically records a direct first-person grant by Agnes of two churches and their appurtenances in Saintonge. The rest of the charter's inventory is not so helpful, as it simply lists possessions without specifying their provenance. However, at least seven items in this catalogue can be identified by means of other documentary evidence as gifts or sales to the abbey made prior to 1040 by persons other than the count and countess. This would suggest that as well as listing the founders' direct endowment, no. 35 itemizes property given by others at the founders' request or in order to win their approval. Both male and female magnates sometimes employed subtle coercion in the Middle Ages to bring their *fideles* into line with their plans. In the case of Agnes and Geoffrey, it was a standard method employed only by Agnes. Agnes pressured both castellans and lords to endow the abbey by appealing to their piety and their affection for her (CT 1:135–36, no. 74). She maneuvered the provost Archembald, the Lady Aremburga, and even her own husband, the redoubtable Geoffrey Martel, all to actions which enriched the monastery.[10]

Agnes also played an active role as one of the abbey's benefactors. Over the years she carried out a program of purchases designed to augment the abbey's holdings, buying churches, mills, a fishery, and lands for the abbey which included a meadow conveniently located next to the monastery's garden; for "a great price," she purchased a book of homilies for la Trinité that still survives in the abbey's collection in Vendôme.[11] Her total expenditures for la Trinité exceeded 385 pounds in coin, as well as 200 sheep and valuable marten skins and measures of grain. She acted also as joint donor of property to la Trinité on several occasions; in one case, she and Geoffrey gave a toll across the Loire to the abbey (CT 1:160, no. 88). As the toll had been shared by Agnes and the abbey of Saint-Florent, Geoffrey must have been named only out of courteous recognition of his presence in Angers when the charter was drawn up. Indeed, Agnes' contributions to la Trinité seemed so notable to her contemporaries that in two cases it was she alone who was referred to as the founder.[12] Agnes' money was, like Bishop Ethelwold's for Peterborough Abbey, critical in shaping and consolidating la Trinité's holdings.[13] It therefore seems appropriate to recognize Agnes as cofounder of the abbey and to acknowledge her influence in the abbey's formation.

Geoffrey's style of liberality to la Trinité provides a striking comparison with that of his wife. He gave the abbey property forfeited by one of his men convicted of murder, land given him as ransom by the count of Blois, and property forfeited by traitors and banlieu offenders; on the occasions of a donation to the abbey, Geoffrey sometimes resigned his overlord's right to customary taxes on the property.[14] In one case only does a record survive of Geoffrey making an outright donation of property to the monastery's new priory in Angers, and therefore to la Trinité indirectly (CT 1:133–35, no. 73). In short, Geoffrey utilized his economic perquisites of banal and juridical lordship to enrich the abbey with little or no immediate cost to himself. As Agnes exercised lordship as regent, she did not have the opportunities open to Geoffrey. However, she did have income or property of her own which she could and did translate into capital for donations. The contrast in Agnes and Geoffrey's styles of patronage—the personal versus the official—reflects the types of power available to prominent women as opposed to that wielded by important men in the eleventh century.

At the time of the decision to found the abbey, the founders were adjusting to recent changes in their lives. Geoffrey was no longer a landless bachelor but had become count of Vendôme in 1031 and had married Agnes of Burgundy a few months later. He was twenty-six years old at the time of his marriage and was eager for independence from his flamboyant father, Fulk Nerra, with whom he had clashed repeatedly.[15] Vendôme beckoned as the potential power base from which Geoffrey might contest his father's authority, and Agnes seemed the perfect ally. She had abandoned widowhood to marry Geoffrey but remained deeply concerned with the well-being of her three children from her first marriage. She nourished the ambition to see her sons by her first husband, William of Aquitaine, enjoy their patrimony—an unlikely aspiration without armed intervention to remove their older half brothers who had inherited Poitou and Aquitaine.[16] Agnes may also have wanted to regain control of her daughter and namesake, Agnes, who seems to have been in the custody of her half brother, William the Fat (ruler of Poitou and Aquitaine after his father's death).[17] Geoffrey supported and helped implement his wife's schemes on behalf of her children, since advancing his stepchildren helped extend his own influence.

In addition to these family concerns, both Agnes and Geoffrey were aggressive and capable people who may well have been considering an attempt to extend their power beyond Vendôme.

Geoffrey was a leader of considerable potential and heir to the county of Anjou; Agnes was the daughter of Otto William, duke of Burgundy, and granddaughter of Adalbert, the last native king of Italy.[18] Agnes and Geoffrey had only the small county of Vendôme from which to launch their larger schemes, and Geoffrey's claim to its overlordship looked shaky. It had been a common practice on the part of the counts of Anjou to bolster their political authority through monastic foundations, a tradition that at this crucial moment Geoffrey and Agnes skillfully continued with the founding of la Trinité.[19]

A religious house imparted to its founders some of its sanctity and splendor and insured them a place in the unceasing prayers of the *Opus Dei*.[20] La Trinité also helped to legitimize its founders: from the moment of the *donatio,* Agnes and Geoffrey were seen to be carrying out a divine directive in establishing a house of monks in Vendôme—a foundation in whose good reputation they subsequently shared. Their position as patrons of a Benedictine abbey in Vendôme increased their respectability and prestige in the county, thereby serving not only to bolster Geoffrey's questionable position of authority after his ousting of the young count of Vendôme but also to counter clerical opposition to his marriage, viewed by the church as incestuous.[21] The foundation drew support from both lay and clerical donors; gifts flowed in from artisans and bishops, knights and priests—often at the urging of the founders or in order to win their approval. The new house was a focus for attention in the Vendômois, culminating in the ceremony of 1040 when lords temporal and spiritual witnessed the solemn granting by Agnes and Geoffrey of the formal diploma to la Trinité. If, indeed, the eleventh-century monastery was "the expression of the corporate religious ideals and needs of a whole community," or if as the foundation document puts it, an abbey contributed "to the general advantage of many," then the founders and major benefactors merited the position of lay leaders in the community.[22]

The site chosen for the abbey suggests other motives of the founders. In 1032 the *castrum Vindocinum* consisted of a primitive fortification on an abrupt, rocky bluff just south of a 90-degree bend in the Loir. At this point, the river dwindled into numerous, shallow branches and bogs, and a small collection of houses huddled at the base of the hill. (See Map 2.) One logical site for a monastery would have been south of the Loir next to the castle on the hill. This location would have enjoyed the protection of the castle's garrison as well as allowing the abbey to exploit excellent fields to the southeast. The site chosen, however, was not on the high, safe ground but right in the midst of the marshy network of the Loir below the castle.

The siting of monasteries is a fascinating and potentially illuminating topic.[23] Most directly, the site affected the development of a house while the presence of a monastery tended to spur the growth of an area. Thus, Noyon's position at the juncture of major routes contributed to the abbey's importance which then helped the development of its burg. In the same vein, by investigating the reasons behind the choice of a site, we may add to our understanding of the founder. For instance, from time to time a monastery was resituated either to suit the patron or (less often) to suit the monks. It would be interesting if one could discover the reason for the movement of the monks of Beaulieu from Berkshire to New Forest, since the rationale behind the move might aid our comprehension of the abbey's enigmatic founder, King John of England. Often a founder's wishes were clearly the paramount reason for picking a site; William the Conqueror insisted that Battle Abbey be situated exactly on the battlefield of Hastings. The inhospitable terrain and lack of water daunted the contingent of monks from Marmoutier but failed to deter William. Richard I of England established the abbey of Bonport on the spot where, legend related, he had been saved from drowning, although he probably had other more pragmatic reasons for his choice. Legends of miraculous events, such as Richard's deliverance in response to his prayers, may have developed to add to a monastery's pious reputation while cloaking the founder's more mundane motives.

The foundation legend of la Trinité explaining the choice of location in miraculous terms is lent some credibility by the discovery of an enclosed spring under the floor of the northern ambulatory of the abbey.[24] A more pragmatic explanation for the founders' choice of location might be that it allowed the monastery to dominate traffic across the Loir for both defensive and economic purposes. Also, since this marshy land was of marginal agricultural value, the donors had little to lose and much to gain if the monks could harness the river and drain the fields. The Loir remained the monastery's *bête noire* whose repeated floodings disrupted the abbey and on one occasion even forced evacuation of the library to l'Evière.[25] This drawback was, however, offset by the river's value, which the monks exploited for transportation, fish, water for crops and flocks, power for mills, and income from tolls. At the same time, the Loir served defensive purposes after the area was drained and its waters diverted into two branches encircling the town and abbey (work that may well have been carried out by the eleventh-century monks).[26]

The new house in Vendôme also served as part of a defiant gesture by Geoffrey toward his father, Fulk Nerra, count of Anjou, with whom Geoffrey was competing. The endowment of la Trinité was definitely bigger and richer than for one of Fulk's abbeys: Beaulieu-lès-Loches, or Saint-Nicolas and Ronceray both in Angers.[27] Geoffrey's competitive spirit shows in the choice of a patron for the new abbey. Like Fulk's favorite abbey of Beaulieu, Geoffrey dedicated his foundation to the Holy Trinity, but his monastery was a far grander abbey than his father's.[28] Nor did the challenge to Fulk end with the dedication and endowment; it culminated in the reception by Geoffrey of the fugitive monk, Rainald, to serve as abbot of la Trinité after escaping Fulk's presumably heavy-handed treatment at Saint-Nicolas in Angers.

During the eleventh century, widespread belief existed in the efficacy of monastic prayers to avert divine retribution for a sinful life. Agnes and Geoffrey's foundation was intended "for the care of our souls as well as for the salvation of our relatives both living and dead. . . ."[29] This overt concern for their spiritual health was probably just as sincere as their covert political ambition. It is not, however, possible to rank the founders' mixed motives into a hierarchy of importance. It must suffice to recognize that pious sentiments reinforcing family interests and competitive ambitions had brought Agnes and Geoffrey to the decision to establish the abbey of la Trinité.

The foundation instrument's inventory and witness list reveal some of la Trinité's interdependency with its social and political milieu. The inventory records the possessions of the new house in Vendôme, Maine, and Saintonge, and is signed by the forty-three magnates present in Vendôme at the dedication of May 31, 1040. Of the thirty-two discrete inventory entries in the charter, eleven are gifts or sales made to the abbey prior to 1040 by persons other than the founders. This is probably also the case for most of the other grants in the Vendômois and Maine enumerated in the charter, since the founders had little property of their own in these counties. Agnes and Geoffrey had either to motivate other benefactors or to buy property for the endowment themselves.

Agnes and Geoffrey's only joint purchase specifically mentioned in the foundation charter was land for the monastery's site.[30] Their one other gift situated in Vendôme comprised the great forest of the Gâtines and half its pannage (the right to pasture swine in the forest). The Gâtines had been held by the second count of Vendôme, Bishop Rainald, who had begun to clear the woods; later his young nephew and successor, Count Burchard, had evicted all the assarters and burned their houses (CT 1:3, no. 1, and 1:16, no. 6). After Burchard's death and the disgrace and ousting of his brother, Fulk Oison, his uncle, Geoffrey Martel, held the honor of Vendôme and controlled the Gâtines Forest. (See Map 3). Following this tumultuous period, the tenure of lands in the forest had become so hopelessly confused that Geoffrey called a meeting of his foresters and ordered the return of all property in the woods to the tenants who had held seisin in the time of Bishop Rainald (CT 1:20, no. 7). After this reinstatement, he turned over all the unauthorized clearings to la Trinité. It is this donation which is itemized in charter 35 as the gift of all the Gâtines and half the pannage to the monks.

Agnes gave two churches in Saintonge to la Trinité, which were either part of the dower from her first marriage or ecclesiastical properties she had purchased.[31] The rest of the endowment in the Saintonge probably came from land acquired by Geoffrey during his successful military campaigns against Agnes' stepsons, William the Fat and Odo.[32]

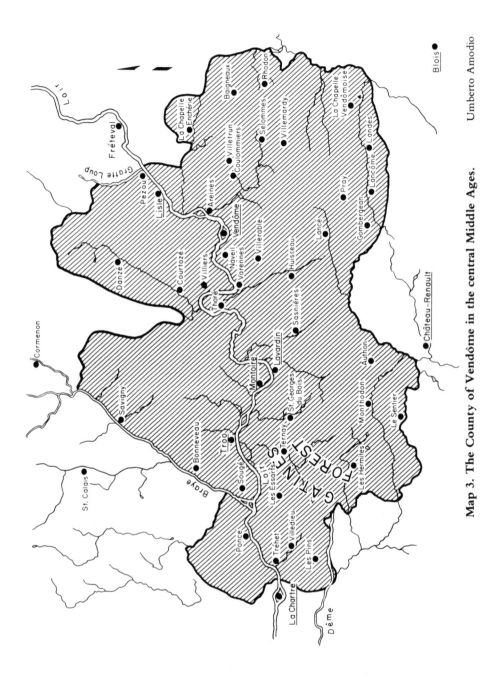

Map 3. The County of Vendôme in the central Middle Ages.   Umberto Amodio

18

Only one donation listed in the inventory derived from a major figure: Bishop Gervais of le Mans, who endowed the abbey with Notre-Dame in Villedieu and a nearby stream (CT 1:30–34, nos. 14 and 15). His endowments were made in 1038 and 1039, after the cessation of hostilities between Geoffrey and Gervais in 1038.[33] Gervais may well have been trying to improve his relations with his formidable opponent by a generous gesture to Geoffrey's new protégés.

Benefactors from the other end of the social scale included a number of peasant women and men, designated as *villani,* who sold and donated small parcels of land to the abbey.[34] Individual charters of alienation survive for a number of these grants. Charter no. 30 (CT 1:50–52) lists a dozen gifts and five sales, primarily of alodial farmland, transferred to la Trinité in small parcels ranging in size from one half an arpent to thirty-three arpents. This land is in Viviers (*Villa Viveris*), a town whose location in the Vendômois is no longer known. Two other charters describe small transfers to la Trinité of other peasants' property in Viviers: the gift of one arpent and one carrucate (CT 1:52, 54–55, nos. 31 and 34). Another pair of documents records larger sales of land in Viviers to the monastery: Testa sold the monks her alod consisting of an island with a mill, part of a meadow, a house, and four arpents of vines, while Fulbert of Viviers received twenty-two solidi for his sale of a homestead, twenty-three arpents, and two parts of a meadow (CT 1:50 and 54, nos. 29 and 33). Later, when the monks accepted him into their confraternity, he endowed them with twelve more arpents of land. Testa and Fulbert were more substantial landholders than the men and women recorded in charter 30. Whether or not they are subtended in the inventory's designation of the *villani* of Viviers remains unclear, although all these men and women of Viviers could be fairly described as peasant farmers of greater or lesser means.

The foundation endowment itemized in charter 35 consists almost exclusively of real estate unlike some endowments of the period. Sainte-Croix, for example, enjoyed a much wider variety of banal and economic rights in its endowment, reflecting the more advanced commercial life of its region in the mid-eleventh century.[35] Some of la Trinité's parcels of land were newly cleared for farming, while other tracts were established farmland often described as *mansi* and *manufirmae;* there are also six forest areas and eight churches listed in the inventory (CT 1:57, no. 35). In 1040, these counted as two extremely valuable types of property, and both were or were soon to be involved in controversy. Woodlands supplied fuel, construction materials, honey, wax for candles, and forage for swine, while also serving as hunting preserves. Forested areas could also be cleared and used for farming. As population rapidly expanded in the eleventh and twelfth centuries, pressure grew to assart more and more wooded land. Some overlords (like Bishop Rainald) viewed this as a positive development that would increase income from assarters' rents and dues. Other lords, like the young Count Burchard, were hostile to the clearing of forests. But there was no stopping the movement of *défrichement* in the Vendômois. In 1040 la Trinité's endowment included newly assarted areas in Ville-Evêche and Monthodon, as well as the woods of Houssay, which had been specifically given to be cleared and farmed; as the years passed, la Trinité continued a quiet but steady policy of felling woods and planting new fields to expand its arable.[36]

The eight churches enumerated in the endowment are in the three counties of Vendôme, Maine, and Saintonge. Although half were only partial shares, these still produced excellent income for the monks from *donationes altaris* (parishioners' thank-offerings for the sacraments), tithes, and rents. Accelerated at least partly by the Gregorian Reform, sentiment for the return of proprietary churches to ecclesiastical hands was growing during the eleventh century.[37] Hence, the donation of a church to an abbey redounded doubly to the credit of a lay benefactor.

The only item in the inventory that hints at the existence of a nascent mercantile—rather than wholly agricultural—economy is the gift of one half the tax (*cens*) on all the cuttlefish harvested in Saintonge. Cuttlefish were sold for consumption as well as for the production of inks. In the rapidly expanding society of the eleventh century, the ink industry gew in increasing importance, and this tax may have been a valuable source of income for the abbey.

A large group of laymen had gathered in Vendôme in 1040 to witness the pivotal moment of la Trinité's consecration. The witness list records forty-three names and is at once crowded with many illustrious men and notable for the omission of many of those whose close interest would sustain and protect the abbey in its day-to-day affairs. Among those present were: Count Thibald of Blois (soon to be Geoffrey's enemy and prisoner); Lord William of Parthenay from Poitou, a great friend and supporter of Agnes; Agnes' son, Duke William of Aquitaine; and Helias of Vouvant in the Saintonge. All counted as important men but did not figure significantly in la Trinité's history after the dedication. This is understandable, since they were probably invited by Agnes and Geoffrey to be impressed by the founders' lavishness and power rather than because they were themselves benefactors. Some of the local men of note who constantly affected the abbey's life were present: the castellans of Lavardin, Montoire, Beaugency, and Fréteval. However, no representative is recorded from one of the most unfailingly supportive families of castellans: that of Montdoubleau. Also conspicuously absent were any members of the loyal knightly families of Burchard of Caresmot, Joscelin Bodell, Ingelbald Brito, Odo Rufus, or the provosts of Vendôme.

These knights who formed the core of supporters for the new house had all been simple officials for Geoffrey when he first had begun to administer the honor of Vendôme. A partial list survives of those foresters and counselors who had been called together by Geoffrey when he was endeavoring to sort out the confused tenures in the Gâtines (CT 1:20, no. 7). Some of these names can not be identified, but among those specifically mentioned are: Nihard, Salomon, Joscelin the huntsman, the brothers Matthew and Drogo of Montoire, Odo Rufus, Ingelbald Brito, Hamelin of Langeais, and unfortunately for the historian, "many others whom it is not necessary to name. . . ."[38] Odo Rufus, Ingelbald Brito, and Hamelin of Langeais numbered among the most steadfast of the abbey's benefactors; Nihard and Salomon were, most likely, the first castellans, respectively, of Montoire and Lavardin, and Joscelin may well have been Joscelin Bodell. The other major patron of the abbey who had an official tie to

Geoffrey came from the family who served as provosts of Vendôme.[39] All these men began their careers as appointed foresters,
castellans, and provosts wholly dependent on Geoffrey's favor.
By the second half of the century, however, most of their positions had become hereditary, and they were being designated as
milites, or knights. Geoffrey's officials had risen into the ranks of
the privileged; they were supporting his abbey both out of loyalty to their lord and to demonstrate their position among the
nobility. Their patronage of la Trinité helped it to grow while
the aggrandizement of the monastery in turn added luster to its
supporters. In this way the cycle of rapid upward social and economic mobility in Vendôme was closely linked to the steady
growth in importance of the abbey of la Trinité.

The foundation of la Trinité received confirmation from a
group of bishops, King Henry I of France, and Pope Benedict
IX. However, only the incipits of these documents survive in the
table of contents from the earliest cartulary manuscript.[40] The
papal charter may have granted privileges to the new abbey, but
it is unlikely that these were anywhere near as extensive as those
outlined in the patent forgeries, charters 36 through 40. (See Appendix I.) Although not authentic, these documents constitute a
valuable source for understanding the history of the abbey, as
they were considered genuine from the late eleventh century on
and were used as proof texts. The concessions granted in these
forgeries will be considered in a later chapter.

The foundation document ends with a *sanctio* that is closely
related to that of the foundation document for Notre-Dame of
Saintes.[41] It sums up the founders' desire that all those properties
with which they or their followers had endowed la Trinité are to
be securely held by the abbey without interference from the
claims of relatives or any others. Moreover, the monks have absolute rights of usage over all this property so that it can be fully
exploited by the abbey. Finally, anyone ill advised enough to
threaten the monastery with claims against this endowment will
have to pay the enormous fine of one hundred pounds in gold—
a symbolic sum—to "the venerable monastery." The founders
close with the signatures of their men and other nobles present,
who lend their authority and power to preserve and maintain the

foundation in all its wealth and power—exceeding that of even many a royal abbey of the period—for all time.[42]

The mixed motives of the founders, feudal loyalties of area barons, larger political pressures, and economic upswing of the eleventh century all contributed to the shaping of la Trinité within its larger lay society. The abbey acquired distant lands in the Saintonge and Poitou as a by-product of Agnes' first marriage; it received the Gâtines woodlands, which would prove both a source of potential wealth in a period of expansion and a bone of contention due to its early, unclear title. Since land formed the basis of the monastery's endowment, the monks were required to assume the position of agrarian overseers, and since the property was dispersed over a large area, they had to arrange a system to administer these holdings. In a variety of ways, the foundation of the abbey planted the monks firmly within the world from which they were supposed to withdraw, necessitating some compromise to balance the spiritual aims of the Rule with the worldly realities as Geoffrey and Agnes had initiated them. This duality—the spiritual and the worldly concerns of the monks—can be seen in the abbey's buildings.

Monastic Fabric

La Trinité's walls excluded the mundane at the same time that the abbey's richly decorated buildings proclaimed its wealth and prestige. The abbey's site, enclosure, church, and conventual buildings embodied a vision not only of the monastery's mission but also of its importance. The physical plant shaped the lives of the monks who moved within the monastic confines while also affecting the abbey's neighbors. At the same time, the abbey was an expression of its founders' generosity and their intentions. We can gather an impression of la Trinité at the time of its dedication and in the 150 years following through a consideration of the existing buildings, the archaeological work of Abbé Plat, and documentary evidence.

La Trinité's location in the Vallée du Loir placed the monastery in a fertile river valley blessed with a mild climate. Its site—the most fundamental element of the monastic environment—has changed little over the centuries. The low-lying land is marshy and crisscrossed by shallow branches of the Loir, whose repeated floodings forced the abbey to struggle with river control and marsh drainage from its earliest days. The river also affected the tenor of the monks' lives by situating them halfway along the busy line of communication that connects Bonneval, Châteaudun, Cloyes, Vendôme, la Chartre, le Lude, Angers, and Nantes. North-south traffic crossed the ford and clattered past the monastery's gates, while westbound goods floated by the encircling walls of the abbey. Pilgrims bound for Compostella found the abbey a convenient way station, as did travelers moving north to Chartres and Paris. La Trinité's location set a worldly stage on which the abbey would play its part, unable to withdraw from temporal concerns. The religious of Vendôme were destined to fall into the group of "those monks who live in cities and villages and are seen often to deal with secular matters"—the categorization of an early-twelfth-century canon who worried that monks living in such a fashion would be involved in worldly activity "which seems secular and hardly religious."[43] La Trinité's site predisposed the abbey to interaction with the secular world, and its buildings reflected this involvement.

The three monastic annals of Saint-Aubin and Saint-Serge (both in Angers) and la Trinité comment that in 1040 the *monasterium* of la Trinité in Vendôme was dedicated, but although they do not specify whether this meant the church or conventual buildings or both, it probably referred to the church itself.[44] There are extant only two unequivocally eleventh-century structures that could have been part of the original building campaign: the transept of the church and a small chapel situated south of the apse and just east of the cloister.

The transept (discounting its later Angevin vaulting) is the only section of the surviving church that was part of the first structure for which there is a *terminus ad quem;* the completed Romanesque church must have been finished and dedicated by February 26, 1096, when Pope Urban II visited. If the church had been under construction, the monks would probably have requested a papal blessing on the building materials (as was done for the new cathedral of Carcassonne). As it was, Urban blessed a new altar, which implies that the church in which the altar would stand was already completed.[45]

The general plan of the Romanesque church is known to us from Abbé Plat's archaeological research, which indicates that the bulk of the present church is built on the earlier building's foundation.[46] (See Figure 1). The Romanesque church was seventy meters long and fifteen meters wide. It had eight bays with circular pillars and flanking aisles. There was an ambulatory with five radiating chapels that were all smaller than the Gothic chapels existing today. Plat deduced from its size and the massive hinges and door (which could close it off) that the axis chapel was the most important. This chapel was probably the site of the altar of the cross dedicated by Urban II. The first church was not vaulted, as can be seen from the low positioning of the original windows still visible in the walls of the transept. The floor of the building, composed of pebbles set in cement, was lower than the present level, which partly obscures the bases of the four massive crossing piers of the transept.[47] These piers bear four extraordinary Romanesque capitals that remain from the earliest building campaign. (See Frontispiece.) They serve as evidence of the elegance and grandeur of the first abbey's church. About ten years after the foundation, there was already a wooden three-storied bell scaffold (*tristega signorum*) from which to ring the hours and regulate monastic prayers and activities (CT 1:109, no. 54). By the early twelfth century, a single, magnificent stone bell tower was built in front of the western facade.[48] Plat's excavations indicate that there was a structure connecting the tower to the facade of the church; this structure he interprets as having been a great porch similar to the early western porch at Chartres. René Crozet challenges this theory and suggests instead that a low vestibule or atrium stood before the western facade with the tower next to one corner.[49] In any event, it served as the galilee or porch for the Romanesque church.

Not only the form of the galilee but also the date of its construction have been subjects of scholarly controversy. The structure is mentioned in charter no. 9, part one, and no. 10, both dated 1033 (CT 1:23–26, nos. 9 and 10). There is a strong pre-

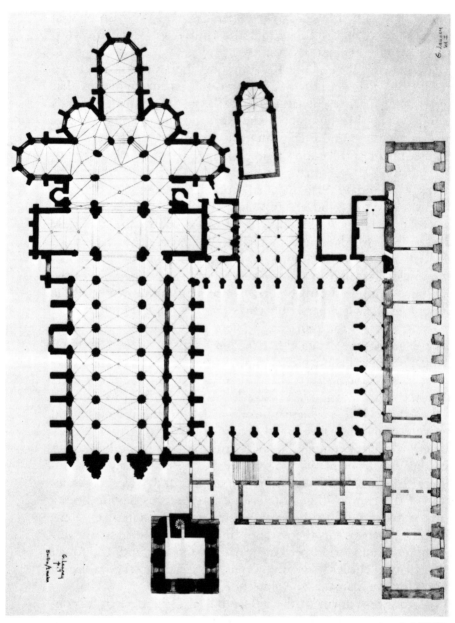

Figure 1. Architectural plan of la Trinité, Vendôme.   G. LAUNAY

26

sumption that these charters are not authentic, based partly on the unlikelihood that any part of the church was built as early as 1033. (See Appendix I for discussion of the forgeries.) The situation becomes further complicated by Abbé Simon's definition of the galilee as serving as the cemetery for seculars in 1033.[50] He may have based this attribution on a charter from the late twelfth century, in which a dying layman gives the abbey a gift for the privilege of burial in the monastic galilee.[51] Certainly by the end of the twelfth century it was not unusual for a lay patron to be buried within the monastery in the cloister itself or even in one of the chapels.[52] Nevertheless, this does not prove that a galilee existed in 1033 or that it served then as a cemetery for secular people. The first impeccable evidence for the existence of a galilee comes from the year 1047, when a family's commendation to the abbey took place "in the galilee of the abbey of Vendôme", and by the mid-twelfth century or earlier, it was dedicated to the Holy Sepulcher.[53]

The second extant eleventh-century structure is the chapel, known locally as *l'église primitive,* which has been extensively rebuilt except for the original north wall, in which there are three simple Romanesque windows. Although they are walled up now, their round arches, splayed jambs, and depth all indicate an eleventh-century origin. On the exterior of the north wall is a round attached column whose capital is mostly destroyed except for a small remaining portion of an early Romanesque checkerboard pattern around the base of the capital. The apse was rebuilt in the thirteenth century and vaulted with slender ribbed vaults springing from delicate acanthus leaf capitals.[54] The south wall was pierced with modern windows and the original western door was dismantled at some unknown date.

Charter no. 134 records that a chapel was begun within the monastery's walls in 1060 (CT 1:237). Another charter, no. 222, indicates that the bishop of Chartres dedicated a chapel on December 5, 1070, to the Virgin, Pope Leo, Bishops Eutropus and Léonce both of Saintes, St. Columba, and St. Brigid (CT 1:355–56). It was built for "the poor and the domestics of the Holy Trinity in whose cemetery it was situated. . . ."[55] These two charters refer to the same chapel whose dedication lagged a decade behind its construction. Charter 222 names the builder as Prior Albert, who held that office in 1058 to 1061 at the latest, neatly agreeing with the date from no. 134. Thus, the information suggests that the building begun in 1060 was completed within a year, as it "was built from its foundations by the hand of the same Brother Albert. . . ."[56] The documentary evidence fits the chapel existing today, but misnamed locally *l'église primitive*.[57] The chapel's original north wall accords stylistically with a date of 1060, and the building's size (7.8 by 18.6 meters) is consistent with a short building campaign of about a year's time. The present chapel is located next to the church just south of the apse where it would have been in the cemetery lying to the east of the cloister but within the monastery's walls. Its size, simplicity, and location are all appropriate for a lady chapel serving the abbey's servants and poor charity cases. Both this lady chapel and the burial grounds serve as reminders of services the monastery performed for its larger Christian community.

None of the original eleventh-century conventual buildings survive. A cloister, however, takes its dimensions from the shape and length of its church, and as excavations reveal that the original plan of the church of la Trinité is closely followed by the later building, the present cloister probably reproduces the form of the original. (See Figure 2.) Within this square we can reconstruct some of the abbey from the documents. As early as 1043 there was a chapter house for the monks where important acts were witnessed by all the brothers (CT 1:113, no. 57). The chapter house surviving today is predominantly thirteenth-century; however, its south wall dates from at least the twelfth century and could be older.[58] The chapter house is located on the ground floor of the cloister's east range, separated from the church's south transept by only the small ancien-régime sacristy. As this is the traditional location for a Benedictine chapter house, the original probably stood on the same spot.[59] The dormitory occupied the second story probably over the chapter house, and the refectory would have been situated in the south range (positions occupied by these two rooms in the seventeenth century: see Figure 2).[60] Next to the chapter house was a *locutorium* or small parlor, probably located where there is now a passageway (CT 1:217, no. 120).

The monastery was encircled by a wall enclosing gardens, cemeteries, orchards, and fields. On the west side, this wall was made up of buildings, of which two twelfth-century Romanesque sections survive. The building on the northwestern wall must have been used as a granary or storehouse, as there is only one window piercing a long stretch of stone wall; Plat dates the window stylistically c. 1125.[61] The surviving southwestern section has a row of elegant second-story Romanesque windows and may have been the site of the hospice.

By 1074 there was mention of an *auditorium* in which mass was sung and the poor were fed (CT 1:386, no. 244). It is described as an outer chamber, which may therefore have been located in the western wall of the forecourt, making it accessible to the poor who waited outside the abbey for alms.[62] It was also a suitable room to which the prior hurried the irate count of Vendôme when the latter stormed in prepared to make a scene, and to which a woman could gain access when barred from entering the chapter house.[63] As the *auditorium* was used for almsgiving and interviews with lay people, its functions would suggest that it was part of the hospice buildings traditionally located in the abbey's outer walls.[64] The *hospitium* is first mentioned in 1097 but must have existed before that date when it was the meeting place for a large and illustrious gathering of barons presided over by Bishop Ivo of Chartres (CT 2:98–99, no. 356). If the major room of the hospice was able to accommodate a large crowd of barons, it may have been rather like the central chamber of the hospital of Saint-Jean in Angers.

The last building of the early years for which we have any record is the round kitchen located at the southwestern corner of the cloister. No structure survives: only a sketch by Violet-le-Duc that is so like the kitchen at Fontevrault that a twelfth-century date is appropriate, and some influence between the two seems likely.

The size and elegance of the church must have given passers-by an impression of wealth and importance. This is not surprising, as a comparison of the plans of la Trinité and Cluny in the mid-eleventh century suggests that la Trinité could have used the great Burgundian abbey as a model.[65] La Trinité had no formal filiation with Cluny but did owe some debt to Marmoutier, which had been influenced by Cluny. On the one hand, the transept and general proportions of the church tell of la Trinité's prestige; on the other, the lady chapel reminds us of the monks' commitment to caring for simple people. Penetration within the conventual buildings by donors, servants, the poor, and travelers, as well as the burial of lay folk within the abbey's walls give the impression that la Trinité was a house open to and affected by the secular world. Indeed, a cross section of medieval society entered the abbey's gates. The abbey was founded and financed by worldly men and women, and to a large extent it came to

Legend for the 1677 plan of la Trinité

A Entrance
B First courtyard of abbey
C Church
D Rooms, storerooms, prison, stables, and granaries on top two floors
E Gatekeeper's lodging
F First courtyard
G Entrance to monastery
H Guesthouses
I Bell tower
K Refectory for servants and bakery
L Courtyard
M Kitchen and refectory for religious
N Large storeroom and common room on second floor
O Cloister
P Stairway from dormitory
Q Parlor, common rooms, woodshed, dormitory on second floor
R Little courtyards
S Storerooms and library on second floor
T Garden for sacristy
V Sacristy
Y Tower of the washhouse
Z Woodsheds, storerooms, and infirmary on second floor

1 Large garden
2 Reservoir
3 Gardener's house
4 Bridge to little woods
5 Dovecote
6 Infirmary garden
7 Allée
8 Abbot's lodging
9 Abbot's courtyard
10 Abbot's garden
11 Abbot's dovecote
12 Abbot's stables
13 Sacristan's lodging
14 Passage to abbot's lodging
15 Almoner's lodging
16 Chapel of Notre Dame of Pity
17 Cellar
18 Cellars on ground floor and great granary of abbot on second floor

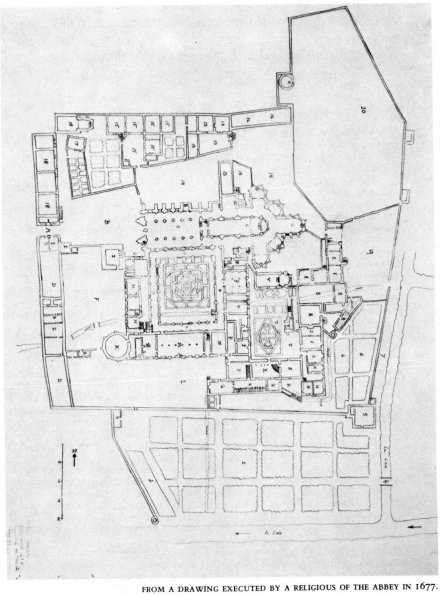

FROM A DRAWING EXECUTED BY A RELIGIOUS OF THE ABBEY IN 1677.

Figure 2. Plan of the Abbey of la Trinité

31

serve the world: its founders, patrons, and neighbors. The wall of silence behind which men had sought to purify their souls in order to serve God was breached by the proximity and stridency of worldly affairs as they impinged on the cloister.

Notes

1. Vendôme B.M., MS 203, Abbot Oderic of Vendôme, *De virtutibus et vitiis*, fol. 42r and v; fols. 19r and 37v; fol. 14v; fols. 17v and 32v.

2. *Chroniques des comtes d'Anjou et des seigneurs d'Amboise*, ed. Louis Halphen and René Poupardin (Paris, 1913), pp. 150–56.

3. Luc Compain, *Etude sur Geoffroi de Vendôme*, Bibliothèque de l'Ecole des Hautes-Etudes fasc. 86 (Paris, 1891), p. 66.

4. Many foundation legends deal with exciting hunting or sailing mishaps, unusual animal activity, or the marvelous discovery of a lost object in an unexpected place. A contemporary Angevin legend of this type is recorded in "Chronicon Sancti Florentii Salmurensis," *Chroniques des églises d'Anjou*, ed. Paul Marchegay (Paris, 1869), p. 275. Other legends glorify the holiness of the saintly founder. For a brief collection of some Cistercian examples, see: Marie-Anselme Dimier, "Quelques légendes de fondation chez les cisterciens," *Studia Monastica* 12 (1970), 97–105.

5. Vivian H. Galbraith, "Monastic Foundation Charters of the Eleventh and Twelfth Centuries," *Cambridge Historical Journal* 4 (1934), 221–22.

6. See "Annales de Saint-Aubin," pp. 3 and 46, and "Annales de Saint-Serge," p. 107, for the marriage date.

7. CT 1:22, no. 8, "ad construendum edificandumque locum in honore Sancte-Trinitatis fundatum. . . ."

8. CT 1:31, no. 14, "nuper constructum est." The date 1038 is recorded in B.N. MS Baluze 47, fol. 236, as well as in B.N. MS nouv. acq. français 7433, fol. 124, and corresponds to the sixth indiction year. Métais has recorded 1037 from B.N. MS Collection Touraine 2, no. 433, fol. 108, which, however, does not accord with the indiction. CT 1:33, no. 15, "quod comes Gaufridus et Agnes ejus conjux apud castrum Vindocinum construunt. . . ."; 1:36, no. 17, "quod . . . juxta Vindocinum castrum constructum est. . . ."

9. To cite two examples: Compain, *Etude sur Geoffroi de Vendôme*, pp. 13 and 115; Southern, *The Making of the Middle Ages*, p. 85.

10. Agnes functioned from behind the scenes in her dealings with other religious houses. See *Archives d'Anjou, recueil de documents et mémoires*, ed. Paul Marchegay, 2 vols. (Angers, 1843), 1:377, no. 33, for Saint-Maur sur Loire, and *Cartulaire de l'abbaye du Ronceray d'Angers*, ed. Bernard de Broussillon (Paris, 1900), p. 7, no. 5, for two examples. Odo Dublell and Lancelin of Beaugency responded to Agnes, CT 1:135–36, no. 74, "ut pro Dei amore et suo, donum quod servi monasterio fecerant et ipsi concederent." Other cases: 1:162, no. 89, "propter Agnetis comitissae amorem"; 1:207, no. 111, "mediante comitissa Agnete"; 1:180, no. 98, "compellente comitissa Agnete. . . ."

11. CT 1:38, no. 18, records the purchase of an alod; pp. 153–54, no. 83, recounts the purchase of four quarters of land; pp. 155–56, no. 85, is the purchase charter for the handy meadow. 1:42–44, no. 22, recounts Agnes' purchase of the churches of Saint-Jean and Saint-Bienheuré; 1:117–19, nos. 62 and 63, both tell of her purchase of half the church of Pins; 1:127–29, no. 69, records the purchase of a half share of the church of Villerable. The manuscript is no. 120 in the municipal library of Vendôme, 1:169–70, no. 93.

12. CT 1:24, no. 9, and 1:135, no. 74, "Agnes, que monasterium fundaverat. . . ."

13. King, *Peterborough Abbey*, pp. 6–8.

14. CT 1:34–37, nos. 16–7, Walter settled a murder charge by forfeiture of a fief. 1:121–22, no. 65, lands in Ville-Junier and near Selommes were given as ransom. There were numerous other forfeitures: 1:20, no. 7; 1:45, no. 24; 1:123–25, nos. 66–7; 1:176, no. 96; 1:95–97, no. 44. See 1:163, no. 90, and 1:163, no. 91, for gifts of tax exemption.

15. "Annales de Vendôme," pp. 61 and 107. Also see "Chronicae Sancti Albini Andegavensis," *Chroniques des églises d'Anjou*, p. 23.

16. Alfred Richard, *Histoire des comtes de Poitou*, 2 vols. (Paris, 1903), 1:220. William the Great's first wife, Aumode, was the mother of William the Fat, and his second wife, Brisque, was the mother of Odo. Since Agnes was William's third wife, her sons' claims were weak unless bolstered by Geoffrey Martel's military strength.

17. Ibid., pp. 228–29. Also see the evidence of the charters in *Chartes et documents pour servir à l'histoire de l'abbaye de Saint-Maixent*, 2 vols., ed. Alfred Richard, Archives historiques du Poitou, 16 (Poitiers, 1887), 1:113–14, nos. 92 and 93.

18. Agnes' dynastic pretensions had encouraged her first husband, William of Aquitaine, to consider the offer of the Italian crown in 1025 for his eldest son. William had traveled to Lombardy to confer with the Italian barons, but the scheme never went any further. Richard, *Histoire des comtes de Poitou*, 1:181–85.

19. Guillot, *Le Comte d'Anjou*, 1:192.

20. Jean-François Lemarignier, "Aspects politiques des fondations de collégiales dans le royaume de France au XIᵉ siècle," *La vita comune del clero nei secoli XI e XII*, 2 vols., Miscellanea del Centro di Studi Medioevali 3 (Milan, 1959), 1:19–40. The author investigates the tendency of foundations to heighten the importance of their founders. Jacques Boussard makes this point even more emphatically. He argues that the possession of a great abbey was one of three ways a family could gain comital ascendency. "L'Origine des familles seigneuriales dans la région de la Loire moyenne," *Cahiers de civilization médiévale* 5 (1962), 308.

21. "Chronicon Sancti Sergii Andegavensis," p. 135, and "Chronicae Sancti Albini Andegavensis," p. 23, *Chroniques des églises d'Anjou*. Geoffrey and Agnes were related within the forbidden degrees of consanguinity.

22. Southern, *The Making of the Middle Ages*, p. 161. CT 1:56, no. 35, "ad communem multorum utilitatem. . . ."

23. On siting see Romain Plandé, "Géographie et monachisme. Sites et importance géographique de quelques abbayes de la région de l'Aude," *Mélanges Albert Dufourcq* (Paris, 1932), 21–35. For the following discussion, see Seymour, *Notre-Dame of Noyon*, p. 4; Hockey, *Beaulieu*, p. 19; Searle, *Battle Abbey*, pp. 21–22; Penelope D. Johnson, "Pious Legends and Historical Realities: The Foundations of the Trinité, Vendôme, Bonport, and Holyrood," forthcoming in *Revue bénédictine* 91 (1981).

24. Gabriel Plat, *L'Eglise de la Trinité de Vendôme* (Paris, 1934), p. 10, footnote 1.

25. Compain, *Etude sur Geoffroi de Vendôme*, p. 77.

26. CT 1:185, no. 100. In this charter dated 1054, Salomon of Lavardin complains of flooding from canals built by Geoffrey and Agnes to fortify the monastery. Cf. Dubois, *Saint-Fiacre-en-Brie*, p. 147. Knowles, *Christian Monasticism*, pp. 102–3, mentions the important work of this sort done by monks.

27. Compare the list of donations cited in no. 35 (CT 1:55–60) with the more modest endowments of Fulk's houses. For Beaulieu-lès-Loches see Louis Halphen, *Le Comté d'Anjou au XIᵉ siècle* (Paris, 1906), pp. 351–52. Also see Guillot, *Le Comte d'Anjou*, 2:59–60. For Saint-Nicholas in Angers see Laurent Le Pelletier, *Breviculum fundationis et series abbatum S. Nicolai Andegavensis* (Angers, 1616), p. 7, and further discussion in Halphen, *Comté d'Anjou*, pp. 86–87, and Guillot, *Le Comte d'Anjou*, 2:39–40. For the nunnery of Ronceray in Angers see *Cartulaire de l'abbaye du Ronceray d'Angers*, pp. 1–5, no. 1; discussion by Halphen, *Comté d'Anjou*, p. 87, and Guillot, *Le Comte d'Anjou*, 2:44–45. None of these endowments can match the lavishness of Geoffrey and Agnes to la Trinité at the time of its dedication.

28. Raoul Glaber recounts Fulk's search for the most powerful saints to whom to dedicate his new house. Fulk's wife suggested the "celestium virtutem," or Paraclete, but Fulk preferred the Trinity. The designation of the Trinity as patron for an eleventh-century monastery was rare, but not as unusual as that of the Holy Spirit. Fulk died after his last crusade and was interred at Beaulieu as he had requested. See Raoul Glaber, *Les Cinq livres de ses histoires,* ed. Maurice Prou (Paris, 1886), p. 23, for the naming and pp. 113–14 for Fulk's burial.

29. CT 1:56, no. 35, "pro remedio animarum nostrarum, necnon pro salute parentum nostrorum tam vivorum quam etiam defunctorum." Recent scholarship has tended to consider quite seriously the pious motives expressed by founders. See, for example, Hunt, *Cluny under St. Hugh,* p. 132, and Gaussin, *La Chaise-Dieu,* pp. 659–60.

30. CT 1:22, no. 8, "ad construendum edificandumque locum in honore Sancte-Trinitatis fundatum, qui situs fore noscitur in suburbio Vindocini, trans flumen Ledi."

31. CT 1:58–59, no. 35, "ego Agnes . . . concedo ecclesiam de Poio-Rebelli . . . meam quoque partem ecclesiae de Ponte Sanctonico."

32. Geoffrey received a large ransom for the release of William the Fat in 1036 that may have included property in Saintonge. Richard, *Histoire des comtes de Poitou,* pp. 231–32.

33. The date 1037 is recorded for no. 14 in B.N. MS nouv. acq. lat. 1939, fol. 9, and B.N. MS Collection Touraine 2, fol. 108; two manuscripts: B.N. MS Baluze 47, fol. 246, and B.N. MS nouv. acq. français 7433, fol. 124, have 1039 instead. This later date is more plausible, since the bishop and count were at war in 1037, making it highly unlikely that one was endowing the other's foundation in that year.

34. CT 1:57, no. 35, "in alodiis de Viveris omnia ea quae jam comparavimus vel comparabimus de futuro et quae jam villani dederunt, vel deinceps dabunt. . . ."

35. Garaud, *L'Abbaye Sainte-Croix,* pp. 9–10.

36. CT 1:57–58, no. 35, "apud Villam Episcopi . . . cum . . . exemplationibus quae postmodum ibi factae sunt"; and "cum exemplationibus de Monte-Hadelingis"; also, "sylvam de Hulsedo totam ad extirpandum et colendum. . . ."

37. Guillaume Mollat, "La Restitution des églises privées au patrimonie ecclésiastique en France du IXᵉ au XIᵉ siècle," *Revue historique de droit français et étranger,* 4th series 27 (1949), 399. Madeleine Dillay, "Le Régime de l'église privée au XIᵉ au XIIIᵉ siècle dans l'Anjou, le Maine, la Touraine," ibid., 4th series 4 (1925), 256–61."

38. "[M]ultosque alios quos nominare non est necesse. . . ."

39. See Guillot, *Le Comte d'Anjou,* 1:407–9.

40. CT 1:93, no. 41; 1:94, nos. 42 and 43; 1:95, no. 43². Incipits are found in B.N. MS nouv. acq. lat. 1935 dated pre-1070 by Henri Omont, *Catalogue des manuscrits latins et français de la collection Phillips acquis en 1908 par la Bibliothèque Nationale* (Paris, 1909), p. 69.

41. CT 1:59, no. 35. Compare the foundation document for Notre-Dame, *Cartulaire de Notre-Dame de Saintes,* pp. 4–5. Notre-Dame was also founded by Agnes and Geoffrey but in 1047, seven years after la Trinité. Its foundation charter uses formulaic wording in the protocol and *sanctio* that closely parallels that in la Trinité's foundation document.

42. Battle Abbey's total endowment has been estimated at around 200 pounds (Searle, *Battle Abbey,* p. 23); Agnes' outlay for purchases alone, out of all of la Trinité's endowment, exceeded 385 pounds.

43. *Libellus de diversis ordinibus et professionibus qui sunt in aecclesia,* ed. Giles Constable and B. Smith (Oxford, 1972), pp. 40–41.

44. "Annales de Vendôme," p. 61; "Annales de Saint-Aubin," p. 46; "Annales de Saint-Serge," p. 107. *Monasterium* is found in eleventh-century Cluniac manuscripts to be used for the church building itself. See Hunt, *Cluny under St. Hugh,* p. 109.

45. René Crozet, "Le Voyage d'Urbain II en France (1095–6) et son importance au point de vue archéologique," *Annales du Midi* 49 (1937), 54. "Annales de Vendôme," p. 67, state that Urban consecrated a cross on his visit to the abbey, while the necrology

commemorates the consecration of an altar to the Holy Cross and to St. Eutropus, CT 4:379. The annals were probably written at l'Evière in Angers, while the necrology (Vendôme B.M. MS 115) would have been produced in Vendôme, making it a more reliable source on this small detail. For further evidence see M. A. Dupré, "Bribes historiques sur le Vendômois," *Bull. Vend.* 9 (1870), 68–70.

46. Plat, *L'Eglise de la Trinité*, pp. 16–18 for the following discussion.

47. Plat, *L'Art de batir en France des Romains à l'an 1100 d'après les monuments anciens de la Touraine, de l'Anjou et du Vendômois* (Paris, 1939), p. 47, for the floor, p. 186 for the piers.

48. René Crozet, "Le Clocher de la Trinité de Vendôme," *Bulletin Monumental* 119 (1961), 139–48.

49. Plat, *L'Eglise de la Trinité*, p. 48, and *L'Art de batir*, pp. 123 and 181. Crozet, "Le Clocher de la Trinité de Vendôme," p. 146.

50. CT 1:24, no. 9, part one. Although burials took place in some monastic galilees, they also occurred in the area outside the porch: cf. "Nam inter istam mansionem et sacristiam atque ecclesiam, nec non et Galilaeam sit cimiterium ubi laici sepeliantur." *Chroniques des églises d'Anjou*, p. 312. Also note the evidence of the *Liber tramitis* (Farfa Customary) *Consuetudines Monasticae*, 5 vols., ed Bruno Albers (Stuttgart/Vienna, 1900–1912), 1:138.

51. CT 2:474, no. 600, which Métais has attributed to c. 1190.

52. CT 2:429, no. 565, and 2:516, no. 636, both describe burials in the cloister; 2:488, no. 612, relates that Lancelin of Vendôme was interred in the chapel dedicated to Mary Magdalen.

53. CT 1:136, no. 74, "in galileia Vindocinensis cenobii. . . ." CT 2:365, no. 526.

54. André Mussat, *L'Architecture gothique dans l'ouest de la France aux douzième et treizième siècles* (Paris, 1963), p. 315.

55. "[P]ropter pauperes et familiam monasterii Sancte-Trinitatis, in cujus et cimeterio sita est. . . ." CT 1:356, no. 222.

56. Ibid., "a fundamentis aedificata per manum fratris cujusdam Alberti. . . ." Plat dates the chapel to c. 1035. *L'Art de batir*, p. 33.

57. It was usual for an eleventh-century abbey to have had a lady chapel separate from the church as did Cluny, but unusual to have had a primitive church built for use while the major structure was being constructed.

58. The discovery of early twelfth-century frescoes on the south wall of the chapter house establishes that this wall is at least as old as the frescoes that Taralon dates stylistically c. 1100. Jean Taralon, "Découverte de peintures murales romanes dans la salle capitulaire de l'ancienne abbaye de la Trinité de Vendôme," *Bulletin de la société nationale des Antiquaires de France*, 9th series 8 (1973), 34.

59. Knowles, *Christian Monasticism*, p. 103.

60. CT 4:359 and 364 include evidence for the dormitory and refectory in the abbey's customary.

61. Plat, *L'Art de batir*, pp. 86 and 96.

62. CT 1:431, no. 278, "in auditorio, quod est de foris ad ostium claustri," and CT 1:386, no. 244, "in auditorio exteriori. . . ."

63. CT 1:451, no. 295, and 1:444, no. 289. The reason for this exclusion is not clear. The husband was allowed into the chapter house, but his wife had to make her donation in the *auditorium*. Was some general taboo functioning like the barring of women from the sanctuary on Old Testament authority (see Dubois, *Saint-Fiacre-en-Brie*, p. 151, where women were excluded from the tomb of the saint), or was this a personal rejection?

64. Knowles, *Christian Monasticism*, p. 99.

65. Kenneth J. Conant, "Medieval Academy Excavations at Cluny," *Speculum* 29 (1954), plate 7, is the plan for 1043 and plate 9 for 1085.

CHAPTER TWO

The Monastic Organism

T HE COMMUNITY of la Trinité was a living organism, shaped by its progenitors and nurturers to function within the social ecology of the Vendômois; its conventual buildings formed a body within which the monks acted as the animating force, assisted by their family of servants. Monastic officers directed activity both at la Trinité and throughout the network of dispersed priories, while nourishment to support the organism came from the priory system, the monastic exercise of lordship, domanial farming, and rents and mortgages. La Trinité's origins and anatomy have been discussed; its inner workings remain to be examined: personnel, priory structure, and income from lordship and exploitation.

Personnel

Today many medieval French abbeys are destroyed, or they survive only as ruins, museums, or rebuilt public buildings. We visit and are struck by the site, the buildings, and often by their crumbling beauty. Yet the stones and mortar are only a small part of the story of a monastery. It was the men—servants, visitors, pensioners, the sick, the dying, but particularly the monks—who shaped the monastic experience and whose lives invested the abbey with sanctity or scandal.

At what age did monks enter the abbey, and were they required to offer a dowry? Who were they, and what were their origins? Although it is imperative not to outline neat distinctions where none existed, the evidence in the case of la Trinité suggests

36

a tripartite organizing system of: choir monks (adult and child oblates); lay monks or *conversi;* and monks *ad succurrendum* (men who took the habit in illness or old age), although many subtle variations must have confused their tidy division.

The first choir monks at la Trinité were directed by Rainald, who had been intended as the second abbot of Fulk Nerra's abbey of Saint-Nicolas in Angers.[1] Rainald lasted only a short time in Angers, fleeing to Vendôme even before his consecration at Saint-Nicolas. Rainald probably arrived at la Trinité in 1039, and he may be the "Prior Rainald" in charter no. 47, an undated record of a donation to la Trinité "noviter constructo."[2] Since Rainald is not mentioned as abbot in any charters from the pre-1040 construction years, he may have been consecrated at the time the abbey was dedicated. After Rainald became abbot, Fulk, another Marmoutier monk, became prior in his stead.[3] Except for Rainald and Fulk, it is not possible to determine exactly the provenance of the earliest monks of la Trinité, although the tradition reported by Métais maintains that about forty of them came from Gondré near Montoire (CT 1:109, footnote 1). There is evidence that in la Trinité's earliest days:

> When the monastery was still young and disorganized [rude] and needed professed monks, monks lived in it brought together from whatever parts for their personal advantage more than for the profit of the abbey.[4]

After the abbey was built, according to Abbé Simon, most of the religious were sent away, and only novices and those men professed at la Trinité were kept, augmented by twenty-five monks from Marmoutier.[5] Probably the abbey had attracted runaway monks in its first six or seven years before it had an abbot at its head. It would have been reasonable for Rainald as the new abbot to have made such monks return to their original houses, and as a monk himself professed at Marmoutier, to have solicited a colony from his mother abbey to form the core of the new community. Evidence for such a plantation from Marmoutier to la Trinité is found in a chronicle written at Tours in the thirteenth century, which records that the count founded the abbey and "established monks from Marmoutier there."[6] Important members of the original colony were Vital, Guy, Raimbald, and Fromond, of whom Vital seems to have been a leading spirit. He appears most frequently in the charters, was hosteler (or hospitaler) in 1077, and is last mentioned in 1079. His service at la Trinité stretched over some forty years.

The new abbey attracted recruits from the neighborhood. Three of these earliest entrants typify the pattern that became common at la Trinité of recruiting from local knightly families. Ingelger was one of three sons who inherited an alod in Courtozé, a small village about nine kilometers northwest of Vendôme. (See Map 3.) The three brothers agreed to donate their inheritance to the abbey, although one brother retained his third for lifetime usufruct; the gifts were made so that Ingelger would be received by the abbey (CT 1:112, no. 57). He joined the community between 1040 and 1044 (Rainald's abbacy), and it is probable that he came from a knightly family.[7] Another monk of this early period was Ansald, brother of the powerful local knight, Burchard Caresmot.[8] Ansald was already in priestly orders when he entered the monastery, bringing with him as his monastic dowry a mill and the chapel of Chapelle Enchèrie, situated fourteen kilometers east of Vendôme. A third early entrant was the knight, Patrick, son of Engelbald, who was touched by divine inspiration to give up his worldly life and become a monk (CT 1:409, no. 260). His entry present to the abbey was alodial land in the parish of Broch in the easternmost tip of Anjou.

In the early years, the evidence suggests that all new postulants entered the monastery as adults. This is rather startling and difficult to account for. Certainly, the Rule (RB: 59) allowed boys to enter the monastic life, and normal practice for Benedictine houses in the eleventh century included receiving child oblates as was done, for example, at la Chaise-Dieu.[9] The evidence of la Trinité's charters may be misleading, since the age of an entrant is never noted in the charters; however, the designation of an individual as an adult is assumed for those who exercised adult functions. For instance, of the three examples cited, Ingelger alone might have been a younger entrant. There is no suggestion, however, that he was a child being offered by his guardians, but that he and his brothers worked out a donation of their property through sibling cooperation. One possible explanation for la Trinité's lack of youthful oblates could be that the first four abbots were exercising a reformist policy at a surprisingly early date.[10] Indeed, the first clear-cut evidence that child oblation contributed to the ranks of la Trinité's choir monks comes from the very end of the eleventh century, one year after Geoffrey of Vendôme's election to the abbacy. Perhaps Geoffrey abolished the previous practice; at any rate, in 1094 a monk of la Trinité who had been born in Normandy, returned to his home to bring back his son and offered him as a monk (*monachum obtulit*) (CT 2:90, no. 352). The use of the Latin *offere* strongly suggests that the charter records the oblation of a child. Another charter containing an unequivocal child oblation is dated 1097 when a knight, Gaudin Malicorne, gave his firstborn son to the lord abbot and the monastery "so that he become a monk" (*ut monachus fieret*) (CT 2:101, no. 357).

The second group of monks that can be identified is that of lay monks who at la Trinité were called both *monachi conversi* and *monachi laici*. The position of the *conversi* at la Trinité has been difficult to establish. At the outset, it must be distinguished from that of the lay brothers first introduced into reformed monasteries of the eleventh and twelfth centuries; the latter were illiterate manual laborers belonging to the community but clearly separated from and inferior to the choir monks.[11] These Cistercian, Vallombrosan, and Camaldolese brothers must, in turn, not be confused with the *conversi* of Cluniac houses, who were "fully monastic," although they "had entered the monastic life as adults and were illiterate and in no degree of clerical orders."[12] The key to the position of the Cluniac *conversi* was that the group was not closed; *conversi* could pass through the stage as they acquired the ability to read and thereby participate in the liturgy. Probably partly as a response to the new type of Cistercian lay brother, the position of Cluniac *conversi* experienced a gradual, negative shift during the twelfth century as they came to be increasingly subordinate to and distinguished from choir monks.[13] These two types of *conversi,* the reformed and the Cluniac, represented the two common patterns for medieval lay brothers of either subordinate or equal monastic position to that of choir monks.

A *conversus* at la Trinité belonged to the type represented by the Cluniac practice—he was fully monastic. To enter la Trinité, a layman had to experience the dramatic shift of his life away from worldly affairs to become a *conversus,* a convert "united by divine inspiration" who "in the time of his conversion" reordered his life to serve God as a monk and thereby purify his soul.[14] The *conversus* shared full membership in the monastic community with the choir monk. The key phraseology for *conversi* in the charters—"cum monacus Vindocinensis efficeretur"— is identical to that used for choir monks and monks *ad succurrendum* (CT 1:409, no. 260). Nevertheless, the choir and lay monk were distinguished one from the other at la Trinité. This was not the distinction identified by Knowles in Norman monastic practice between *monachi nutriti* (child oblates) and *conversi,* since there were no child oblates at la Trinité in its first five decades. Even when child oblation did occur at la Trinité, no division is discernible on the basis of age. The distinction between the two groups seems to have rested on literacy in Latin, which enabled the entrant to participate fully in the liturgy.[15] For instance, clerics who chose to enter la Trinité are never referred to as lay monks or *conversi;* the inference from silence is that since they were literate and already converted to *religio* they became choir monks. An illiterate layman, on the other hand, had to become a lay monk. But since *conversi* at la Trinité occupied an open group—as at Cluny—when they learned Latin, they might participate in the liturgy. Thus, for example, the customs of la Trinité for Christmas Eve note that *conversi* sang the O *magnum, Post partum,* and *Deus qui salutis* (CT 4:360–61).

A *conversus,* even unlettered, could hold an important position within the monastic structure. The castellan, Robert of Moncontour, became a lay monk in the last decade of the eleventh century and seems to have been prior of the domain of Coulommiers, which he had given la Trinité.[16] The monk *conversus,* Thibald, is another example of a lay monk who occupied a position of responsibility as obedientiary of Ville-Arvent where he carried on an aggressive program to augment the property of the abbey.[17] It was, indeed, eminently practical to appoint men like these to positions of authority and responsibility, since their secular lives had given them invaluable administrative experience. An unlettered *conversus* at la Trinité could also share in the liturgy—by carrying the new fire at none on Maundy Thursday and the censer and candles later at the collation (CT 4:348 and 352). In the Good Friday liturgy, lay monks also took part and one of their number received new vestments along with the other monks who served at none; some *conversi* again carried the censer and candles (CT 4:353 and 355).

In the eleventh century two castellans, Robert of Montcontour and Odo Dublell, had felt no compunction about assuming the habit as *conversi*.[18] But during the twelfth century no castellans entered the community, which may have been a response to a loss of importance in the status of *conversi* at la Trinité (as happened at Cluny), so that this position appeared demeaning to a great lord.

The third group of monks of the community of la Trinité were monks *ad succurrendum*. These were men facing old age or illness who desired to end their lives as professed monks, cared for within the abbey by their brothers and insured salvation by the monastic habit. Recognizing his failing health and imminent death, Frodo—a knight from a suburb of Vendôme—sent a message to the abbot, "praying that he might succor him and allow him quickly [to take] the monastic habit."[19] The standard wording of charters for men entering the abbey as monks *ad succurrendum*—"quando factus est monachus," "monachus . . . factus esset," "noster fieri monachus,"—is interchangeable with that of choir and lay monks except when specifying that they are to be cared for "monachalem habitum ad succurrendum induit. . . ."[20]

People were usually reluctant to be professed when ill and often waited until the last moment to take this momentous step, as did Hubert, who was professed one day and died the next.[21] The sick person's relatives might also display resistance to profession *ad succurrendum,* since they dreaded losing property. This was the case for Adelaide, who owned the villa of Boisseau jointly with her son, Archembald (CT 2:137–38, no. 386). When the young man fell gravely ill, he promised the monks his share of the villa together with his mother's part after her death. But

Adelaide refused to let him become a monk because she feared to be left destitute. As his condition worsened, Archembald again called the monks to him and succeeded in convincing them and his mother that he should be given the monastic habit. Similarly, when Abbot Geoffrey of Vendôme tried to persuade his cousin Rainald, lord of Craon, to take monastic vows, Rainald resisted, fearing to lose control of his lands or jeopardize his followers' tenures.[22]

Since monastic profession was often left to a man's last moments, arrangements had to be made in advance to make hurried inductions possible. One way was to allow any monk to stand in for the abbot and hear a sick man's profession.[23] Archembald was clothed in the habit by the monks whom Adelaide had hurriedly called to her home. The young man died shortly after while being carried to the abbey. In another case, a castellan allowed his wounded prisoner to be made a monk in the prison gatehouse by two of the religious of la Trinité, who lived in the nearby priory of Villedieu (CT 2:142, no. 391). Some considered it prudent to plan ahead against the possibility of sudden death or unconsciousness before death. Hervé Messor gave la Trinité half the tithes of a church in order to insure his acceptance as a monk if he should desire entrance at some future date as well as to endow his eventual burial within the monastic graveyard (CT 1:233, no. 131).

A study of la Trinité's charters of adult monastic profession leads to the conclusion that the three groups of choir, lay, and monks *ad succurrendum* were all fully professed monastics of equal status but varying functions. Common sense, however, suggests that these charters had particular audiences and purposes that dilute the former conclusion. The monastery protected itself against its rapacious neighbors by drawing up charters to affirm its right to properties received. Since relatives and lords of postulants were often tempted to challenge the abbey's right to entry gifts, the charters emphasized the full monastic status of the entrant so as to substantiate the legitimacy of the abbey's claim to its new member's gift. To the outside world, the three categories of monks were to seem to have the same institutional status; within the abbey it was probably otherwise. For example, the reception of aged and infirm men by la Trinité to be monks *ad succurrendum* involved accepting the burden of caring for those who were no longer contributing members of society—hardly comparable to the entrance of a healthy young man for a lifetime of service as a monk. The case of one monk *ad succurrendum* illustrates the possible complexity of the situation. When Hamelin Escherpell was apparently dying, he was made a monk; he recovered, "rejected leaving the monastery, and lived piously as a monk among the other monks."[24] His profession *ad succurrendum* actually made him a monk, such that he could continue in the monastic life. This he chose to do instead of leaving la Trinité—also a possible option despite his profession—suggesting that *stabilitas* was hard to enforce for those who recovered their health following a profession *ad succurrendum*.

The number of monks at la Trinité during its first century and a half tended to reflect general demographic trends in the population at large. The monastic community grew rapidly in its early years, and by 1088 there were one hundred monks present at an important chapter.[25] In 1100 a solemn gathering witnessed an accord between the count of Vendôme and the abbey at which sixty-one monks were present (CT 2:155, no. 400). The latter figure is low, since attendance would not have been obligatory in 1100 as it would have been for the chapter of 1088. By adding the number of monks who probably had remained in distant obediences and priories, an estimate of ninety-four monks can be obtained for 1100.[26] If la Trinité experienced the same pattern common to other houses, it probably had its largest population in the twelfth century and began to decline in the early thirteenth century. Indeed, by 1328, la Trinité had only fifty-three monks, and the number dropped to twenty-six in 1383 as a result of the demographic disasters of the mid-fourteenth century.[27]

Almost all of the monks about whom there is data came from knightly local families. The geographical range from which a monastery might draw its recruits varied for different houses. Dom Hockey estimates that at Quarr Abbey, two thirds of the monks came from beyond the immediate area.[28] In contrast, only a few men professed at la Trinité were definitely "foreigners" (Normans and Bretons); the social range also was constricted since only one can be described as bourgeois—Hugo Calvus, who had become famous through his philanthropy to the needy.[29] There were no comital entrants either from the founder's family, the counts of Anjou, or from the local counts of Vendôme. The next social level, that of the castellans, was represented by Robert of Moncontour, Odo Dublell, and Fulcher of Turre.[30]

All the postulants to la Trinité whose entries are noted in surviving records brought gifts to the abbey. This practice was acceptable according to the letter of the Benedictine Rule (*RB:*58) but was never supposed to become obligatory (and hence, simoniacal). Joseph Lynch, in his work on simony and monastic profession, indicates that the practice had developed without comment throughout Europe up to the very last years of the eleventh century, when criticism was first formally expressed at councils in 1089 and 1099; during the mid-twelfth century, attacks on entry gifts as simoniacal became common.[31] Geoffrey of Vendôme voiced concern about such gifts as possibly being "filthy gain," and when the hermit Hervé recruited likely candidates of modest means for monastic profession, the abbot assured him that these prospective oblates would be welcomed if they were of good character despite their lack of dowry.[32]

Most entry gifts to the abbey comprised property located in the Vendômois; only a few were situated in neighboring counties. These gifts could be particularly valuable for the abbey, since they sometimes rounded out partial holdings or settled tedious claims that had been annoying the monks.[33] Such fringe benefits enhanced the value of new property, making the custom of monastic dowry singularly attractive for the abbey and encouraging its perpetuation. In actual practice, a gift was almost always necessary for entrance into the congregation of la Trinité.

Recruitment of monks from the knightly class of the immediate vicinity tied the abbey securely to this vital landed group. Members of the local knightly families had reason to feel a strong rapport with an institution that housed relatives and might some day prove a receptive home for some of them. The abbey became indispensable to the noble families of the Vendômois as rapidly as their wealth and manpower became crucial to it. This interdependency of the monastery and surrounding families provided considerable support for the abbey as long as this one group on whom it relied remained numerous and wealthy. If the knightly class were to falter, la Trinité would feel the impact and suffer.

Beside the monks and usually under their direction, worked the abbey's servitors. They were needed to attend to daily necessities so as to free the monks for their primary spiritual obligation of the daily liturgy. Consideration of the workers raises a problem of definition. They are called *famuli, laici, villati, servientes*, or are included in the earlier witness lists without any specific designation.[34] They were both free and unfree, literate and unlettered. At la Trinité, the common denominator for such people serving the monks was that all were dependent on the abbey. They comprised the monastic *familia:* those who lived under the monastery's ban and ate the monastery's food (CT 2:129, no. 382). The members of the *familia* were generally servants but understood broadly also to include clerics in minor orders, pensioners, administrators with considerable responsibilities, body servants, and unfree colliberts and serfs.[35]

The members of la Trinité's *familia* can be grouped roughly in four categories. There were free men and women who could be commended to the abbey for training. This happened to the little boy, Magnelin, after the death of his father. His mother commended her son to the abbey to be received in the *familia* and trained in household management.[36] By this arrangement Magnelin was to retain full free status, but as a fatherless child, he was insured an education, a protector, and a livelihood. A second type of person in the *familia* was one who gave the abbey land in return for a pension of food and clothes (a corrody)—a practice that became common only late in the twelfth century when clerical pensions in particular became so burdensome that Innocent III allowed the abbot of Vendôme to renege on some (CT 2:489, no. 613; 4:13, no. 863).

The third and most common category comprised those who commended themselves and their possessions to the monastery, accepting servile status in exchange for support as members of the *familia*. In a few instances, such a commendation took place

in fulfillment of a debt: Girard of Boisseau commended himself
in reparation for damages he had inflicted on the abbey, and Ingelbald gave himself in fulfillment of a vow made when mortally
ill.[37] Most of the records of servile commendations fail to specify
any motive for the act but emphasize the ceremonial acceptance
of servile status in which the person commending himself first
placed four deniers on his head and then wrapped the bellcord
around his neck. All the servile commendations fall within the
abbacy of the second abbot, Oderic, who may have encouraged
the practice during a period of acute peasant need or enhanced
commendation through his personal charisma.[38]

Voluntary forfeiture of freedom may be foreign to a modern
perspective, yet it occurred quite frequently at la Trinité in the
third quarter of the eleventh century. Inflation—"times became
more expensive"—was a major problem often compounded by
natural disasters; local famines were recorded for 1042, 1043, and
1044; and warfare disrupted the countryside repeatedly in the
1050s and 1060s.[39] In one instance, a whole village commended
itself to the abbey, perhaps in the aftermath of a famine or flood,
since the abbey offered economic stability.[40] The abbey could be
relied on for subsistence; when Gautier commended himself and
his family to la Trinité, he received as his stipend two solidi, four
sesters of wheat, and three of rye.[41]

Another explanation for the practice of commendation is that
it was for some actually an improvement in status to become
serfs of la Trinité. Rainald, who had been reared and cared for
by the monks, decided when grown to give up his freedom and
commend himself to the abbey; but he added the disclaimer
that no one should believe that he was motivated by fear or greed
to acquire worldly riches.[42] A member of the *familia* might have
his own servants and could amass and hold property in his own
name (CT 2:413, no. 555). Richard Roillegot, a servant of the
monks, sold to the abbey land, rents, and rights to collect tithes
before apportionment in the village of Thoré (CT 2:366, no.
527). He received two pounds and a new hood in payment.
Some of the *familia* served as provosts and prefects—administer-
ing justice, collecting revenues, and overseeing monastic affairs
in outlying obediences.[43] A member of the *familia* could become

prosperous and powerful; he could be respected for his knowledge and skills as was Mainard, a forester, called in as an expert on the customary law when a dispute arose over the right to charge a toll (CT 1:146, no. 77). Despite evidence of the secure and advantageous position of many monastic *famuli,* the yearning for freedom persisted in some individuals. The serf Constantine, for example, humbly petitioned Abbot Oderic to emancipate him (CT 2:14–15, no. 308). An agreement was reached that seems to have been entirely to the abbey's advantage: to win his freedom, Constantine had to promise to stay at the abbey permanently, keeping all his property intact and willing all his worldly goods to la Trinité (save the customary allowance for his widow and children). In some parts of France, peasants could become dependents of a monastery, like Sainte-Croix of Talmond in Poitou, while still retaining free status; but in Anjou, servile dependence was such that a serf had no rights and even could be swapped for an animal.[44]

The fourth category of people in the *familia* was that of salaried servants. Hubert Mango made his home in the churchyard of la Trinité and was responsible for an unlikely combination of jobs: repairing three-legged stools and wooden dishes, and bleeding the monks (CT 1:341, no. 209). He was paid a yearly wage of five solidi and received a daily ration of one pound of wheat bread. Salaried servants had the greatest mobility of any group in the *familia,* probably due to a combination of their skills and capital in the form of tools. The smith, Remigius, counted as a member of the monastic *familia* before 1057 (CT 1:202, no. 109). A few years later, he was no longer listed as one of the monastery's *famuli* but was included in a witness list with a knight, a butcher, and the brother of one of the monks.[45] The demand for his particular skills may have tempted him to go into business on his own, for in this period the smith had tremendous opportunities as a man of local economic importance.[46]

Evidence suggests that the familial relationship of servant to abbey was heritable, but it is not clear whether this was only true for unfree members of the *familia* or developed as a general rule. Alcher, the baker, was a servant of la Trinité who witnessed a document in 1057 and was followed twenty-two years later by

his son Hervé both as baker and as witness.[47] Moreover, there
were whole lineages who belonged to the abbey's *familia;* uncles
and nephews are named among the abbey's dependents.[48] Heritable status for the *familia* would seem to have been to the abbey's
advantage, for it insured la Trinité a pool of trained craftsmen in
every generation. But the danger inherent in the hereditary principle was that a servant of the monastery might claim powers by
right of inheritance instead of exercising them only by appoint-
ment. This happened in the mid-twelfth century when William
was appointed provost of Villedieu after the death of his father,
Walter, who had held the same office.[49] William not only denied
his oath to respect the customs but also wielded his powers for
his own profit; adding insult to injury, he married without the
abbot's consent. There followed a period of alternating punish-
ments and reconciliations, during which time, however, William
was never replaced by another man. Despite his arrogance and
venality, the abbey had no candidate as well trained for the pro-
vostship as was William, who had grown up with the job.

The members of the monastic family practiced many and varied skills. The building trade was well represented by a glazier,
stonecutter, masons, and carpenters. Others worked in the necessary daily services as baker, miller, and cobbler and in the
crafts of saddlery and peltworking. Some outdoor laborers functioned as ass drivers, carters, gardeners, and foresters. Smiths
were numbered among the *familia,* which also included leeches
and a crossbowman. Starting in the second decade of the twelfth
century and increasingly as the century wore on, some of the
servants for the abbey began to be designated as cellarer, chamberlain, sacristan, marshall, and hosteler.[50] Since these men were
listed among the *familia,* they presumably did not usurp a monk's
office in defiance of the Rule (*RB:*31) but rather served as each
officeholder's right-hand man. The danger of lay servants usurp-
ing control over areas of monastic life was a real one. It could
become such a problem that at Battle Abbey, for instance, the
monks concocted forgeries to protect themselves from the en-
croachment.[51] This, however, did not become an issue at la
Trinité.

Although no formal credit is given to the *famuli* for their contribution to la Trinité, when one reads between the lines, it be-comes apparent that their talents and energies were crucial for the abbey's survival and growth. In the chapter house as in the workshop, the abbey made use of people's talents and resources to further its development. This utilization was one aspect of the constant interplay between the abbey and its social matrix—an interplay that usually proved mutually beneficial for la Trinité and for the families from which it drew its manpower.

During its first 150 years a change occurred in the integration of personnel into the abbey's structure—a change that embodied a more general growing tendency to categorize and formalize. For instance, early charters from la Trinité's first twenty years tend to lump together witnesses without regard for their varying status. In contrast, during the last quarter of the eleventh century and even more in the twelfth century, the tendency grew to list witnesses in groups according to status, using separate headings for monks, knights, townspeople, and servants.[52] At the same time, the size of the *familia* increased, reflecting the growth in the numbers of monks. Tighter systematization combined with the expansion of the monastic population contributed to a sense of growing impersonality in the abbey's life. The disappearance by the second decade of the twelfth century of the strongly emotive word *familia* may reflect this change.[53] During the mid–eleventh century, the little boy Magnelin had been accepted by the monks to be educated within the community, "in familia nostra," which was contrasted with the biological family "sua familia" he might want to establish some day (CT 1:55, no. 34). In the twelfth century the terms *famuli, laici,* and *servientes* were still employed, but the warm allusion to kinship faded out of la Trinité's vocab-ulary.

During the eleventh and twelfth centuries, the abbey's person-nel, locally recruited from diverse social levels to be monks and servitors, forged a human link between the monastery and its environment. The directing and ordering of these men and of materiel reinforced ties between la Trinité and the surrounding world that integrated the organism more tightly into its ecolog-ical system.

Organization

The abbey's manpower was organized in a hierarchy of officials who formulated and transmitted commands within the
monastery itself and to its numerous priories. Both choir and lay
monks held various administrative offices. The abbot, who
united in his person the roles of the representative of Christ in
the monastery and the executive corporation head, directed the
organization. During its first century and a half, nine abbots held
office at la Trinité for an average of 15.3 years. (See Appendix
II). Three had exceptionally lengthy abbacies: thirty-seven years
for Oderic, thirty-nine for Geoffrey of Vendôme, and twenty-
five for Girard. The abbots of Vendôme were elected, according
to the usual custom, in perpetuity.[54] Nevertheless, Abbot Berno
was retired when he grew too old and weak to carry out the
charge of his position (CT 2:84, no. 346), although all the other
abbots seem to have died in office. Three apparently came from
local families: the first abbot, Rainald, had a cousin in the Vendômois; Oderic's nephew was mentioned as a local witness; and
Geoffrey of Vendôme had at least two family connections among
the local nobility.[55] It is likely in light of the extent to which the
abbey was embedded in its milieu that other abbots may also
have come from regional families.

The image of the abbot passed through various permutations
during the Middle Ages. In the second chapter of the Benedictine
Rule, the abbot is spoken of in three symbolic forms, as the
Christ figure, master, and father. For the early Middle Ages, the
image of the abbot-father heading his monastic family struck the
most responsive chord and showed in the language of *pater,
fratres,* and *familia.* At la Trinité in its early years, Oderic reinforced the paternal image of the nurturing abbot-father in his
compassionate treatise on the vices and virtues.[56] Only a decade
later, the image of abbot was recast by Geoffrey of Vendôme,
who emphasized the abbot's role as vicar of Christ instituted by
God.[57] As the twelfth century unrolled, the abbots of Vendôme
acted in an increasingly lordly fashion, such that by 1150 it was
natural for a donation to be made to "the Lord Abbot Robert

sitting on his palfrey, Lancelin [brother of the castellan of Beau-gency], standing in front of him at his feet"—a picture of the abbot's power and importance (CT 2:365, no. 526). Outside the cloister, lay lordship manifested the growing dynastic spirit of the twelfth century that paralleled the contemporary monastic stress on the abbot's lordliness.[58] Noble families institutionalized the practice of knighting at the same time as they singled out their heirs through primogeniture. In the same vein, the monastic family emphasized and elevated its head, the abbot. This increased external show of power may also have been a response to the internal growth in importance of the corporate body of monks, the chapter. Increasingly in the late eleventh and early twelfth centuries, no major action could be taken by the abbot without the chapter's concurrence.[59] In this tendency the monastery was outstripping its local lay society, which was still quite innocent of corporate organization.

The abbots of la Trinité carried out the usual administrative functions, both internal and external. The internal duties involved life within the monastic organism where the abbot had to choose and oversee his officials, discipline monks, receive and dine with guests, write sermons, and lead the daily liturgical cycle.[60] External activities brought la Trinité's abbots into contact with their social environment through a continual exchange of letters with priories, other religious houses, bishops, barons, and Rome. Letters were often followed by visits, and if the number of trips taken by Abbot Geoffrey of Vendôme is any indication of other abbots' peregrinations, la Trinité's spiritual fathers were often away from Vendôme.[61] Abbots had to oversee and visit obediences and priories, arrange for provisioning of the abbey, attend councils, fight the abbey's legal battles, and preside over chapter meetings.[62] Each time a new abbot was elected, he had to take stock of the status quo by reviewing the appointments of officials. This might land him in a complicated and time-consuming inquiry, as it did Abbot Robert when he looked into benefices acquired before his abbacy.[63]

Chosen by him and sharing the abbot's delegated authority were the monastic officials, of whom the prior stood first in importance. The prior took charge of the monastery during the abbot's absence or illness, and a great part of the daily organization of the abbey devolved on him. The Rule (*RB:65*) specifies that abbots should appoint their own priors to avoid dissension within the abbey. In only one case at la Trinité was that rule perhaps not followed: Fulk, one of the original colony from Marmoutier and the abbey's second prior, served in that office under both the first and second abbots. (See Appendix II.) The tenure of priors was shorter than that of abbots at la Trinité; there were seventeen in the first 150 years. Of that number four—Rainald, Berno, Fromond, and Hubert—advanced from prior to abbot.

Ten other monastic officials regularly shared in the administration of the abbey: the cellarer, hosteler, doorkeeper, cantor, sacristan, almoner, treasurer, librarian, chamberlain, and infirmarian. Together with abbot and prior they add up to the apostolic number of twelve, which was probably intentional. As the abbey grew, two other executive administrators were needed; a subprior was active by 1105 and a third prior by 1144 (CT 2:175, no. 412; 2:356, no. 521). Knowles has calculated that in twelfth-century English Benedictine houses, about one half of the monks held office.[64] La Trinité came to exceed that rate as the number of monks holding office increased from 29 percent in the eleventh century to 61 percent during the twelfth century.[65] The rising proportion of officeholders reflects the proliferation of priories, each of which might have two or three resident monks, all serving as officials. This diversification of responsibility for internal affairs as well as for distant cells marked the beginning of la Trinité's monastic bureaucracy.

During the period under study, the practice evolved of decentralizing finances by subdividing revenues to be paid directly to various monastic offices. The first solid evidence of this system at la Trinité comes from the mid-twelfth century, although the custom may have originated earlier. These fiscal developments were part of a general monastic trend that can be discerned as early as the late eleventh century at Cluny, but generally were apparent by the second quarter of the twelfth century, as at Peterborough Abbey and la Trinité.[66] In 1147 Countess Richilde endowed the infirmarian of la Trinité with half her holdings in

Villiers to commemorate the anniversary of her death by providing a feast of game and fish for ailing monks (CT 2:346, no. 515). Such endowments to monastic officials proved destructive to the sense of community by fragmenting the chapter and setting officials in competition with one another. For instance, the cost of new manuscripts was borne by the cellarer and the treasurer at la Trinité, "but because contention developed between them about how much each one ought to pay, the management of the library was neglected. . . ."[67] Such could be the outcome of an increasingly decentralized, bureaucratic system.

The tendency to compartmentalize and decentralize was also evident in the development of the network of priories. (These were called deaneries in the Cluniac system and granges by the Cistercians.)[68] The need for a priory system had existed at la Trinité since the monastery's earliest days because of the distant location of some of the founders' original endowment and subsequent purchases. The purchase or gift of even a small property, no matter where it was located, often initiated a process of accumulation around it. After a sizeable amount of property in an area passed into la Trinité's hands, a monastic official was then appointed to oversee the new obedience and thereby tie it into the abbey's network.[69] Sometime between 1040 and 1060, Agnes of Burgundy had bought alodial land in Ville-Arvent (nineteen kilometers directly south of Vendôme near Gombergean) as a gift for the abbey (CT 1:38, no. 18). During 1060 and 1061, the monk Thibald bought twenty arpents, a mill, a meadow, and some plowland to add to the Ville-Arvent holdings, which were then designated an obedience. Ville-Arvent never became a priory in its own right, but by the early twelfth century it merged with one of the larger neighborhood priories (either Gombergean or Lancôme).[70]

A number of problems accompanied this process of growth: the separate cells could begin to act independently of the mother abbey; the monk in charge could fall ill far from any help; life in an isolated, small obedience could be marginal in some seasons if it relied on a single crop; the obedience could be threatened or seized by hostile neighbors; a small group of monks far from the home abbey could fall into a variety of errors.[71] The potential for trouble was great, but the geographically dispersed donations necessitated some sort of decentralized supervision. Gaussin identifies the same utilization of small priories as administrative centers by la Chaise-Dieu; but in the case of this house in the Auvergne, the little cells were seldom troublesome, rather, it was the large priories which caused problems.[72]

The need for various specialized products also encouraged the growth of the system. For instance, the priories on the coast of Saintonge and on the islands of Olonne and Oleron excelled in the production of two vital commodities, fish and salt. In addition to providing diverse foodstuffs, the priory system protected la Trinité against local disasters. If the Loir flooded the Vendômois destroying local stores, the granaries in Anjou and Maine could still be untouched; equally, a drought, famine, or crop failure in Saintonge or Poitou might destroy only part of the abbey's produce. Dom Dubois suggests that another advantage of the priory system was the potential it afforded individual monks to lead the eremetical life in an isolated cell.[73] Indeed, he suggests that there was more positive gain for monks in small obediences where a relatively autonomous spiritual life was led than there were drawbacks for the obedientiaries.

La Trinité also needed to diversify beyond Vendôme because of its unique political situation. The founding house of Anjou had been the local power in the Vendômois only for a few years. In 1056 Geoffrey Martel began to reassociate his nephew, Fulk Oison, with him as count of Vendôme; however, Fulk's hostile feelings for his uncle who had ousted him from Vendôme tended to spill over to include Geoffrey's protégés, the monks of la Trinité. Geoffrey and Agnes must have foreseen both the necessity of reinstating Fulk and the resultant problems for la Trinité. In 1049 they bought the church of Toussaint in Angers in order to provide a safe refuge for the monks and all their belongings in time of war, upheaval, storms, and floods.[74] The provision proved inadequate, and sometime soon after, they began to build a sister abbey in Angers to serve as a retreat for the monks of la Trinité. The site for the abbey of l'Evière had been purchased in 1047, and in 1056—the same year Fulk returned to Vendôme—Geoffrey and Agnes sought to protect both l'Evière and la Trinité from Fulk's probable hostility by placing them in the pope's care.[75] Even though the founders' marriage had been dissolved by 1052 at the latest, they were able to act together in 1056, overcoming any personal antagonisms for the sake of the safety of their joint foundation. L'Evière was dedicated to the Holy Trinity and sufficiently endowed to be a sister rather than a daughter to la Trinité. As a result, the monks thought of l'Evière as outside of the priory system, since it functioned as la Trinité's alter ego—an alter ego necessitated by the local political environment.

The economic success of the priory system during the eleventh and twelfth centuries is proof that its advantages outweighed any drawbacks, at least in terms of productivity. The income generated by the obediences and priories was of real importance to la Trinité, unlike Cluny's deaneries, which produced little or no surplus.[76] An eleventh-century list survives of ninety-six people who owed grain levies to la Trinité's priory of Cheviré in Anjou.[77] Individual dues could be as high as twenty bushels or as slight as one minat. The total was considerable; yet it represented only part of the income for one priory within the total priory system. One levy on the outlying cells yielded thirty-four sides of bacon at Christmastime (CT 2:192–93, no. 423), and funds could be raised from obediences and priories and earmarked for particular projects.[78] Furthermore, the system forged strong bonds with lay neighbors who tended to develop regional loyalties to the monks and priory within their midst. Such parochial sentiment often resulted in donations made directly to a priory or even at an obedientiary's urging.[79]

La Trinité's priory system flourished, so that by 1109 it encompassed twenty-four obediences and five priories, with the total rising to forty different establishments by 1157. By the early twelfth century, the bigger cells attained the status of priories as the system became increasingly decentralized. As long as recruitment of monks continued to grow, the priory system remained administratively vital, but when manpower began to drop during the thirteenth century, la Trinité found itself in growing difficulties. Moreover, the increase in their numbers reveals nothing of the spiritual health of the obedientiaries scattered in small groups around west-central France. The distance from the regulated monastic life in Vendôme may have negatively affected the monks who staffed the priories and obediences; on the other hand, in the quiet and privacy of an obedience, individual monks had the opportunity for spiritual growth in the eremetical tradition. An assessment, then, of the impact of la Trinité's priory system on monastic spiritual life is difficult; but it can be noted that the wealth from the exploitation of the priories and the unavoidable secular involvement of the obedientiaries were antipathetic to the monastic ideal of poverty and seclusion.

Income

A reconstruction of la Trinité's economic life is limited by the total absence of records of revenues, account rolls, estate surveys, or manorial documents. However, one can see at a superficial glance that the abbey grew wealthy, and although the historian is thwarted from making a detailed economic analysis of income, the general outlines can be discerned. Support for the monks derived from the abbey's network of relationships with people of all social levels in the environment through the exercise of lordship, the exploitation of land, and moneylending. The abbey's seigneurial rights were a complicated mixture of public powers and legal and economic rights (all valuable to varying degrees), here grouped into domestic, land, and banal lordship.[80] Domestic lordship encompassed the abbey's paternal role vis-à-vis serfs and servants. Unfree peasants, who had been acquired by gift and purchase, usually owed the abbey *taille* and sometimes *corvée* (CT 2:312, no. 492). Work service, however, seems to have been of negligible importance in the Vendômois, where rents and levies on produce were common during the period under study. The abbey's personal lordship over the unfree was absolute, including the right to free a serf without the count of Vendôme's assent.[81] On the other hand, the abbey had to remain vigilant that its serfs not quietly divest themselves of their servile status (which seems sometimes to have weighed heavily despite the economic security enjoyed by the abbey's *familia*).[82]

Landlordship involved jurisdiction over land held from the abbey by tenants, both noble and peasant. This lordship was always embodied in the person of the abbot, since only an individual could give and receive tenure from the hands of another individual. Indeed, the abbot was lord of numerous men, many of whom had sworn fealty at the time of the settling of claims or conflict, while occasionally la Trinité received a donation of land subinfeudated to knights who then became men of the abbot.[83]

The abbot of la Trinité was also lord of peasant tenants who paid *cens* or food levies for the lands they held and worked.[84] Sometimes peasants turned over alodial land to the monastery receiving it back to hold for *cens;* in other cases, when land was donated to the abbey, the tenants who had tenure were obliged to pay the *cens* to their new monastic landlord (CT 1:334, no. 200; 1:439, no. 282). The incidence of *cens* payments figured increasingly as monastic income during our period although the individual payments remained small. Comparing the three fifty-year intervals, the percentage of *cens*-paying property was 5 percent of the total number of charters in the first fifty years, 4 percent in the second interval, and rose to 17 percent in the last fifty years.[85]

The monks themselves were tenants of property in a variety of forms. Some property was held for *cens;* la Trinité paid the knight Ruspanon 5½ solidi annually for a piece of woodland (CT 2:223, no. 444). Sometimes the abbey was dependent on another lord for a piece of property. After Rainald of Craon and his wife endowed la Trinité with the war shields and deniers pledged by knights before battle, these were held as a fief by the abbey's chaplain at Craon (CT 1:416, no. 266).

The third type of lordship exercised by la Trinité was banal lordship. The ban was "the duty of maintaining law and order, the right to command and punish," and as such counted as by far the most valuable lordship during the eleventh and twelfth centuries. Banal lordship can be discussed under three categories: economic, juridical, and military.[86] Economic benefits accrued to the lord who held a burg—a banlieu—within which he could enforce observance of his custom; the immense value of the banlieu is shown by the sum paid by the abbey for the burg of Aimerica:

seventy-five pounds and a silver cup.[87] La Trinité's burg in Vendôme was occupied by its *familia* and bourgeois who fell under
the abbey's control and had to pay the abbot fines if they tres-
passed the monastery's banlieu (CT 1:45, no. 24). Each church
and priory held by la Trinité developed a burg around it, all net-
ting income from fees for the use of mills, ovens, and wine
presses as well as from sales taxes and monopolies.[88] Since bread
was the staple of existence, use of mills and ovens was continual
and lucrative. Banal juridical rights added to the lord's income
and could be bought by or were often donated to the abbey.[89]
The rights most often involved were *vicaria,* which could vary
tremendously, but generally included high justice: adjudication
of cases of rape, arson, and murder. The fines levied on malefac-
tors by the abbey's *vicarii* often proved substantial and constituted a major addition to monastic revenues.

Although at first glance it seems that la Trinité did not exercise
military lordship, it did enjoy a number of banal rights that represented fossilized remains of military lordship. The right to
requisition foodstuffs given la Trinité by Hugh of Amboise was
originally meant to support the feudal host, and tolls across rivers and on roads were remnants of the public authority's funding
for keeping the peace for the benefit of travelers.[90] The abbey
did not field an actual fighting force, but it did try to enforce the
provision that only its officials could summon la Trinité's men
when the secular lord needed to gather men to defend Vendôme
(CT 2:198, no. 427). Some abbeys, like Sainte-Croix of Talmond, for instance, went even further and defended themselves
with more extensive exemptions from military service.[91] La
Trinité, in contrast, accepted its military obligation but tried to
protect its men's exemption from paying castle-guard to a secular
lord, as well as its own authority to muster its men.[92]

La Trinité's economic base extended beyond the various perquisites of lordship to include its domanial farming, but no evidence survives concerning the abbey's exploitation of its demesne. The striking paucity of information on monastic demesne
farming can be partially explained by the abbey's penchant for
parceling out land to tenants and encouraging *hospites* (newcomers to the area) to clear and settle new lands. Some scholars warn

against a facile assumption that monastic efforts lay behind the *défrichement* of the central Middle Ages.[93] Nevertheless, studies of individual abbeys often turn up evidence that the monks were involved in opening woodlands, such as at Battle Abbey and at Sainte-Croix, and between 1032 and 1187 land was definitely being cleared and farmed in the Vendômois both by donors of land to la Trinité and by the abbey.[94] Countess Euphronia's gift to la Trinité in 1090 included cottars' dwellings around the church of Savigny in which the monks could settle *hospites;* her successor, Countess Matilda, endowed the monastery with dower land meant "for tenants to assart or newcomers to hold as tenants. . . ."[95] In the middle of the twelfth century the abbey settled differences with a knight over a joint tenure of land. In this case, the abbey wanted undivided tenure, since joint tenure had impeded plans to clear and exploit the land (CT 2:378, no. 533). If la Trinité was not the force behind assarting in the Vendômois, it definitely counted as part of a local effort.

Evidence of la Trinité's acquisition of property sharpens the picture of active monastic exploitation. The monastery consciously expanded and rounded out property by purchase, particularly in its early days. This was a common practice among medieval monasteries, since to rationalize landholdings made their administration simpler. However, it often proved difficult to consolidate property. King has demonstrated that Peterborough Abbey in the tenth century was involved in extensive land purchases aimed at consolidating estates, but by the eleventh century its property became more spread out, causing the monks a great deal of aggravation.[96] La Trinité generally managed to group its estates into substantial priories, but these remained scattered across the basins of the Loir and the Loire.

Not all of la Trinité's purchases, however, were intended to enlarge or regroup the monastic possessions; sometimes the monks were trying to remove an irritant, as when they bought out l'Evière's neighbor who had taken delight in harassing the monks and their men.[97] During the first fifty-year period, monastic purchases account for 13 percent of all charters, dropping in the second and third fifty-year intervals to 2 and 4 percent, respectively.[98] The initial big spurt reflects the abbey's early appetite for property, the amount of money at its disposal, and local desire or need to alienate land. From its founding until 1062 the monks spent 119 pounds (as well as payments of grain, gold, a horse, a shield, and spiritual benefits) to purchase property and economic and juridical privileges.[99]

La Trinité's outpouring of money for land slowed down dramatically at the end of Oderic's abbacy, which may have been felt in the Vendômois as an unfortunate decrease in the local circulation of money. Meanwhile, the abbey began to show a growing interest in using its money to extend credit to neighbors in need of cash. This development is often difficult to identify since, as Génestal points out, mortgage charters tend to disguise the payment of interest.[100] Nevertheless, most abbeys began to lend money by the twelfth century. The cleric Gisler, before leaving for Jerusalem, gave la Trinité two arpents of vines—the same property which his elder brother had already given the monastery upon his departure for the Holy Land.[101] This sounds suspiciously as if the elder brother had mortgaged land to the abbey and redeemed it on his return. A less enigmatic document relates that the abbey lent (*commodare*) twenty solidi to Ivolin, who had to pay a debt to another man (CT 2:123, no. 371). Despite the church's opposition, the monks continued to grant such mortgages, sometimes even using explicit language. In the agreement between la Trinité and the knight Ruspanon, two mills were pledged for sixty pounds and two gold marks to be redeemed (*disgagiare/diswadiare*) by Ruspanon in two years.[102] If he died in Jerusalem, no one else could redeem the pledge until the end of the two years, when his brother was to have first refusal at paying off the mortgage (*ingagiamentum/inwadiamentum*). The charter spells out the smallest details and all contingencies; it is attested by three pledges, four fidejussors, and sixty-seven witnesses.

Throughout our period, la Trinité took advantage of general trends to improve its economic base. In the second half of the eleventh century, the abbey benefited from the effects of inflation by buying property from peasants who were driven to sell their land to survive. Increased circulation of money led to monastic recognition of its seigneurial uses, and the abbey's *cens*-paying property grew by 13 percent during its first 150 years. Finally, the abbey began to develop some sophistication in handling money by extending credit to needy neighbors and taking mortgages on property.

Although the monastic organism was complete at its birth, its cells continued to grow and multiply. By the end of the eleventh century, child oblates jointed the adult monks, thereby introducing into the abbey new complications and responsibilities, and officials proliferated to handle the increased numbers of postulants and the rapidly growing priory system. Local disasters coupled with inflation worked to la Trinité's benefit, bringing the abbey commendations of men and women to swell the work force and allowing the monks to buy up property while the reception by the abbey of orphans, the ill, and dying helped reduce pressures on the lay people of the area. The abbey's growth in size and wealth helped effect a shift in the abbot's image from the paternal to a more lordly style at the same time as the abbey's servitors ceased to be called the *familia*. This expansion also escalated the tension between the primitive monastic ideal and the lay patrons' vision of the abbey and its mission.

The story of la Trinité's organization of property and personnel is a tale of increasing size, impersonality, and complexity; the early monastic familial pattern gave way to a bureaucratic organization run by a hierarchy of officials and funded by a subdivision of revenues by department. The mushrooming of the abbey's responsibilities tended to blur the line between monks and their lay helpers, so that by the mid-twelfth century the use of office designations such as "sacristan" had become common for lay assistants who were members of the monastic *familia*. Throughout the period, one parameter remained steady—the recruitment of monks continued to be dependent on postulants from knightly families of the immediate area. This had the effect of limiting la Trinité's chances to compete for monastic hegemony on a large scale with Marmoutier or Cluny. At the same time, the common local background of the monks formed the backbone of lay patronage for la Trinité. Without its lay benefactors, the monastic organism would have been weak, for lay patronage was crucial to monastic health.

Notes

1. B.N. MS Collection Touraine 2₁ no. 417. The dating of the charter recounting these events is probably faulty. It is given as the third year of the reign of Robert (1033), which does not fit with other internal evidence. Guillot, *Le Comte d'Anjou*, 2:65–66, suggests 1039, since the charter recounts in retrospect a long series of events, and Fulk's memory was hazy on the chronology. Dom Aubert wrote, "ie ne sc'ay pas pourquoy Renault quitta ainsy Foulques, si non qu'il pouvoit estre originaire de Vandosme. . . ." B.N. MS lat. 12700, fol. 174r and v.

2. CT 1:101, no. 47. Métais cites this phrase as evidence that the donation was made soon after 1040, although he ascribes no. 14 (1:31), which includes the similar phrase "nuper constructum est," to 1037. The phrase "noviter constructo" would be appropriate to describe conventual buildings erected in the years after the *donatio* but before the formal dedication of 1040.

3. CT 1:159, no. 87. "Fulco monacus Sancti-Martini professus, tunc prior monasterii Sancte-Trinitatis. . . ."

4. CT 1:109, no. 54, "quando monasterium adhuc rude erat et professis indigebat, habitabant in eo congregatitii undecumque monachi, propriis utilitatibus magis quam profectui loci vacantes. . . ."

5. Michel Simon, *Histoire de Vendôme et de ses environs* 3 vols. (Vendôme, 1834–35), 3:15 and 22. Simon cites no evidence for this rather startling assertion that monks were sent from the abbey.

6. *Recueil de chroniques de Touraine,* ed. André Salmon, Société archéologique de Touraine (Tours, 1854), p. 122, "comes . . . de Majori Monasterio monachos ibi posuit."

7. Ingelger is mentioned as having two brothers, Roger and Geoffrey, who all hold land in Courtozé. Another charter discusses three knightly brothers, Roger Piperata, Geoffrey, and Alcher, who also hold land in Courtozé. *Cartulaire de Marmoutier pour le Vendômois,* ed. M. de Trémault (Paris, 1893), pp. 112–13, no. 71; hereafter cited as CM. It is probable that we are dealing with the same three men but variant spellings of Ingelger/Alcher.

8. CT 1:129, no. 70. The entrance of Ansald, a priest, into the monastic life serves as a reminder of the strength of the monastic ideal in this period. Monastic profession was viewed by many as a superior, spiritual *ordo,* loftier than that of either canons or priests. This is further illustrated by 1:262, no. 150, and 2:406, no. 553.

9. Gaussin, *La Chaise-Dieu,* p. 122. The troublesome word "oblate" has not enjoyed a consistent scholarly usage. Pierre Riché uses *oblat* only for the literal rendering of the Latin *oblatus* (infants or children offered by their parents to monasteries for tonsuring as monks). "L'Enfant dans la société monastique au XIIᵉ siècle," *Pierre Abélard/Pierre le Vénérable* (Paris, 1975), p. 693. But Dom M. P. Deroux, "Les Origines de l'oblature bénédictine," *Revue Mabillon* 17 (1927), 102, first discusses child oblates as *oblats* and then uses the same term for lay brothers. Dom Ursmer Berlière compounds the confusion after having defined child oblates as *oblats* in "Les Ecoles claustrales au moyen âge, *"Académie royale de Belgique: Bulletin de la classe des lettres et des sciences morales et politiques* 5 S, 7 (1921), 550–72, he uses *oblat* for lay brothers as well as other people who commended themselves to a monastery (usually giving themselves bodily to the abbey): "Les Oblats de Saint-Benoît au moyen âge," *Messager des fidèles* 3 (1886/7), 55–61, 107–11, 156–60, 209–20, 249–55. Since la Trinité's charters from the eleventh and twelfth centuries do not use the word *oblatus* for any entrant to la Trinité, the word "oblate" will be used here only in reference to children.

10. Pierre Riché, "L'Enfant dans la société monastique," p. 693, argues that by the mid-eleventh century a move was growing to exclude children from the cloister.

11. This murky subject has an extensive bibliography, of which three short articles are particularly useful. For the origins of lay brothers: Kassius Hallinger, "Woher kommen

die Laienbrüder?" *Analecta sacri ordinis cisterciensis* 12 (1956), 3–104, and Knowles, "The Origin of the Lay Brothers," *The Monastic Order*, pp. 754–55. The best recent article with an extensive bibliography on the scholarly research into the subject is Giles Constable, " 'Famuli' and 'Conversi' at Cluny," *Revue bénédictine* 83 (1973), 326–50.

12. Knowles, *The Monastic Order*, p. 755, uses the words "fully monastic" to differentiate lay monks from the lay brothers who were primarily monastic workers. Constable, " 'Famuli' and 'Conversi,' " pp. 334–35.

13. Ibid., p. 338.

14. CT 1:409, no. 260, "divina inspiratione conjunctus," and 2:30, no. 322, "in ipso suae conversionis tempore. . . ."

15. Geoffrey of Vendôme wrote critically to the bishop of Angers, reporting that a lay monk of Saint-Nicolas had to speak in his mother tongue instead of in Latin in responding to an accusation of wrongdoing, *Ep.* 3:8 (PL 157:110). His disapproval is only comprehensible if, in his experience, lay monks learned Latin.

16. CT 2:104–5, no. 360, mentions that around 1098, "Robertus de Montecontorio monachus noster factus"; 2:89, no. 350, lists as a witness "Roberto monacho obedientiario de Columbariis," who is probably Robert of Moncontour. This would fit because a date between 1102 and 1105—the countess' regency for her minor son—is more likely for no. 350 than Métais' date of 1093. The only other Robert mentioned in this period is listed in a witness list (2:160, no. 405), which should be dated 1104 or 1105: cf. Geoffrey of Vendôme, *Ep.* 3:21 (PL 157:126). Since a descending social hierarchy of names in witness lists becomes the norm during the last quarter of the eleventh century, this is probably not Robert of Moncontour. For in no. 405, the monk Robert is fourth on the list, an unlikely position for a castellan, who was listed first (even before the countess) in no. 350. A monk exercising control of his donation was not unusual. For example, Geoffrey of Valeo and his son who was a priest both became monks, giving a house in Prunay as entry gift to the abbey. The house was specified as a dwelling for the donor and two other monks of whom, it is innocently remarked, the donor's son was to count as one. Geoffrey had comfortably established himself and his son in his own small obedience with one other monk (is he to do the dirty work?) to be supplied by la Trinité, CT 2:138–39, no. 387.

17. CT 1:244, no. 138; 1:244–45, no. 139; 1:247, no. 141; 1:248, no. 142; 1:260, no. 147.

18. CT 1:319, no. 184, of 1067 lists Odo as a witness: "Odo monacus, qui dicitur Dublellus."

19. CT 1:237, no. 134, "deprecans ut ei succurreret et habitum monachicum citius indulgeret."

20. CT 1:242, no. 137; 2:225, no. 444; 2:305, no. 487; 2:404, no. 551. An elderly knight, "qui quum seculi premebatur etate," sought reception at la Trinité as an old-age home, CT 1:29, no. 13.

21. CT 1:243, no. 137. From an early twelfth-century monk's point of view, taking the habit as a monk *ad succurrendum* expressed a person's penitence and was a thoroughly reasonable thing to do. See Latin text edited by Jean Leclercq, "La Vêture 'ad succurrendum' d'après le moine Raoul," *Analecta monastica* Studia Anselmiana, 3d series 37 (1955), 158–68.

22. Geoffrey of Vendôme, *Ep.* 5:27 (PL 157:209–10).

23. Cesáreo M. Figueras, "Acerca del rito de la profesión monástica medieval 'ad succurrendum,' " *Liturgica* 2 (1959), 381–82, states that a monk had to be delegated by the abbot to hear a profession *ad succurrendum*. This may have been the practice at la Trinité, although no evidence for it exists.

24. CT 1:382, no. 241, "egredi recusavit, et monachus inter monachos sanctissime vixit." Figueras, "Acerca del rito," pp. 395–97, reports that when a person survived after profession *ad succurrendum*, the original profession was considered still to constitute a true commitment, carrying the obligation of perseverance in the monastery until death. How-

ever, he or she was required to renew the promise—which indicates that some doubts existed in practice.

25. B.N. MS lat. 11819, 4:12.

26. There were twenty-four obediences in 1109, each of which housed at least two monks, and often three, CT 2:192–93, no. 423. There were also five priories (l'Evière has to be added to the four mentioned in no. 423). There were a dozen monks at Surgères in 1097 (Cartulaire Saintongeais de l'abbaye de la Trinité de Vendôme, ed. Ch. Métais (Paris, 1893), pp. 76–77, no. 42, hereafter cited as CS, which can serve as an average figure for the three other priories. Since some or all of these men were not present at the chapter house in 1100, the total census exceeded sixty-one. In consideration of the solemnity of the gathering, it is probable that most who could travel home were present. However, it may be assumed that the monks in the eight distant obediences (six in Saintonge and one each in Poitou and Normandy) may be presumed not to have made the trip. Figuring three monks per obedience and a dozen per priory, we might reasonably add thirty-three to the sixty-one for a total of ninety-four, a figure that certainly errs on the low side.

27. Ursmer Berlière, "Le Nombre des moines dans les anciens monastères," Revue bénédictine 41 (1929), 245; and 42 (1930), 33–38. The drop in numbers in the thirteenth century is clear at la Chaise-Dieu. See Gaussin, La Chaise-Dieu, p. 643.

28. Hockey, Quarr Abbey, p. 43.

29. There was one Norman monk and his son, CT 2:90, no. 352. Also, the hermit Hervé sent some Bretons as potential postulants to the abbey of la Trinité. See Geoffrey of Vendôme, Ep. 4:50 (PL 157:186–88). Hugo Calvus was "vir oppidi Vindocini," CT 2:66, no. 341, and was "solita miserationis compassione semper largus egenis, sibi pauper," 2:353, no. 519; CT 2:26, no. 319, names Hugo Calvus as acting in concert with a castellan and a knight at an important ceremonial occasion.

30. Robert of Moncontour was a Poitevin castellan (Yves Lepage, "Recherches sur le comté de Vendôme de la fin du Xe au milieu du XIIe siècle," Diss. Faculté des Lettres et Sciences Humaines de Tours, 1969–70, p. 57); Odo Dublell was lord of Montdoubleau (CT 1:99, no. 46); and Fulcher of Turre was probably lord of Lisle (first known for its castle as "Turre"). Fulcher is called "dominus" (CT 1:451, no. 295, and 2:26, no. 319), which in the eleventh century usually designated castellans in the Vendômois. The use of dominus for castellans was also customary in Berry. Guy Devailly, Le Berry: du Xe siècle au milieu du XIIIe, étude politique, réligieuse, sociale et économique (Paris, 1973), p. 176. Fulcher's son Jeremy (CT 2:103, no. 359) was known simultaneously as Jeremy of Turre (2:96, no. 355) and Jeremy of Lisle (2:336, no. 512), and Fulcher's grandson Rainald's possessions were described as being "in terra Rainaldi de Turre, ante ipsum castrum Insule sitam," CT 2:381, no. 536.

31. Joseph Lynch, Simoniacal Entry into Religious Life from 1000 to 1260 (Columbus, Ohio, 1976), pp. 69 and 71.

32. Geoffrey of Vendôme, Ep. 4:49 (PL 157:186).

33. CT 2:137–38, no. 386; 2:374–75, no. 531; 2:456–57, no. 586.

34. Ursmer Berlière, "La Familia dans les monastères bénédictins du moyen âge," Mémoires de l'académie royale de Belgique, 2d series 29 (Brussels, 1931), 1–123. The author tries unsuccessfully to bring order out of chaos but fails by attempting to deal with all western Europe throughout the Middle Ages.

35. CT 1:159, no. 87, Gislemar was both "clericus et famulus"; 1:342, no. 211, is an example of a pensioner; for servile administrators see 2:59, no. 338, and 2:374, no. 530; Gohar was body servant to the abbot, 2:59, no. 338; Hardimar Pinell was an unfree collibert de familia, 1:235, no. 132, and 1:234, no. 131. The colliberts in west-central France were the descendants of people coenfranchised in the tenth century who became burdened with servile dues and customs, so that by the eleventh century they had become dependent people. See the review of the literature and excellent new revision by C. van de Kieft, "Les 'colliberti' et l'évolution du servage dans la France centrale et occidentale X–XIIe siècles," Tijdschrift voor Rechtsgeschiedenis 32 (1964), 363–95. Also note review of

colliberts by Francis X. Hartigan, "The Colliberti of Poitou: A Rural Social Class in the Eleventh Century," *Proceedings of the Western Society for French History,* 1976 (Santa Barbara, 1977), 53–60.

36. CT 1:55, no. 34, "quatinus ipse puerulus in familia nostra susciperetur, et ut ingenuus et liber aliquo nostre servitutis instrueretur officio." Another case is recorded, 1:332–33, no. 198. The wording is somewhat ambiguous in the second case of a father giving his son to the abbey. I categorize this as a commendation, not a monastic oblation, as all the key words for oblation are missing. The boy is given "Christi servitio subditum," a phrase very similar to "sui Creatoris libere servituti" of 1:335, no. 201, a definite case of commendation.

37. CT 2:128–29, no. 380, and 1:449–50, no. 294. Also see 1:427, no. 275, in which only the bellcord was used as a symbol.

38. Oderic was in office from June 30, 1045, to October 4, 1082, and the servile commendations fall between 1047 and 1080. (CT 1:29, no. 13, seems to be a case of a reception *ad succurrendum* rather than a commendation.)

39. CT 1:365, no. 233, "tempora fieri cariora cepissent, ad tantam paupertatem devenerunt," of about 1072. Jean-Marc Bienvenu, "Pauvreté, misères et charité en Anjou aux XIᵉ et XIIᵉ siècles," *Moyen âge* 72 (1966), 391 and 402–3.

40. CT 1:328, no. 193, the men "de villa que ad Quartas dicitur, qui loco Sancte-Trinitatis se et sua tradiderunt. . . ."

41. CT 1:335, no. 201. Also see 1:343, no. 211, in which Constantine is to be fed and clothed like either an ox driver or swineherd of the abbey: "ut dum adviveret victus et vestitus largiretur ei de substantia monasterii, sicut uni de bubulcis atque subulcis. . . ."

42. CT 1:427, no. 275, and 1:426, no. 274. "Et ne quis putet timoris causa vel cupiditatis adquirendi aliquid transitorium me istud agere. . . ." The little boy Magnelin was intended to be raised by the monks in somewhat the same situation. He too may eventually have decided to give up his freedom to the monks.

43. CT 2:411, no. 555; 2:374, no. 530; 2:59, no. 338.

44. Garaud, *L'Abbaye Sainte-Croix,* pp. 78–79.

45. CT 1:294, no. 168. Remigius is listed as the *homo* of another man in 1059, 1:234, no. 131.

46. Robert Fossier, *La Terre et les hommes en Picardie jusqu'à la fin du XIIIᵉ siècle,* 2 vols. (Paris, 1968), 1:389. Fossier emphasizes the smith's growing importance to the economic upswing after 1050.

47. CT 1:210, no. 115, and 1:427, no. 275; also see 1:450, no. 294, for Bernard of Thoré and his son Geoffrey, and 2:60, no. 338, for Fulcher the toll collector and his son Burchard.

48. CT 2:403, no. 550. Also see two brothers listed in 1:234, no. 131.

49. CT 2:409–13, no. 555. Ernst Sackur, *Die Cluniacenser in ihrer kirchlichen und allgemeingeschichtlichen Wirksamkeit bis zur Mitte des elften Jahrhunderts,* 2 vols. (Halle, 1892–94), 2:418. Sackur discusses this process in the Cluniac obediences during the eleventh century.

50. CT 2:229, no. 444; 2:321, no. 500; 2:339, no. 513; 2:344, no. 514.

51. Searle, *Battle Abbey,* pp. 100–105.

52. For an early undifferentiated witness list see CT 1:162, no. 89; for a later more structured example see CT 2:370–71, no. 529.

53. The term *familia* crops up once more in 1151, CT 2:374, no. 530.

54. Pierre Salmon, *The Abbot in Monastic Tradition: A Contribution to the History of Perpetual Character of the Office of Religious Superiors in the West,* tr. Claire Lavoie (Washington, D.C., 1972), p. 44.

55. CT 1:109, no. 54, mentions that the knight Burchard Buccabona was a cousin of Rainald. Oderic's nephew was Savaric, 2:8, no. 302. Maurice of Craon and Adelard of Château-Gontier (2:172, no. 412, and 2:181, no. 417) were cousins of Geoffrey of Vendôme.

56. Vendôme B.M. MS 203, unedited.

57. Geoffrey of Vendôme, Op. 10 (PL 157:227–28), Ep. 4:22 (PL 157:165), "meminisse monachi debent, quoniam abbates Deus instituit. . . ."

58. Georges Duby, "Lignage, noblesse et chevalerie au XIIᵉ siècle dans la région mâconnaise," Annales E.S.C. 27 (1972), 803–27.

59. CT 2:186, no. 419. Also see 1:367, no. 234, and 1:373, no. 236.

60. Note Eadmer's account of Anselm's delegation of authority: Eadmer, The Life of St. Anselm, Archbishop of Canterbury, ed. Richard Southern (Oxford, 1962), p. 45. Geoffrey of Vendôme addressed admonitory letters to monks: Ep. 4:28 (PL 157:170); 4:41 (PL 157:177); 4:34 (PL 157:174). The collection of Geoffrey's sermons is indicative of the genre (PL 157:237–82).

61. Geoffrey of Vendôme, at the least, discussed making—or can actually be shown to have taken—twelve trips to Rome as well as innumerable visits to priories and trips to attend councils and elections.

62. Geoffrey of Vendôme, Ep. 4:31 (PL 157:172–73) and 4:30 (PL 157:172), for visiting priories; 4:35 (PL 157:174–75) and CT 2:192, no. 423, and 2:400, no. 549, for provisioning; B.N. MS lat. 12700, fol. 278r, for the calling of a chapter.

63. CT 2:361, no. 524. Also see 2:409–11, no. 555, for another review of a servant of the abbey.

64. Knowles, Monastic Order in England, p. 429.

65. The percentages are computed by comparing the total number of monks who can be specifically named and counted to those who are designated with an official office either in a priory or in the main abbey. The total number of monks known by name for the eleventh century is 95, of whom 28 (or 29 percent) held office. For the twelfth century, 106 monks can be named of whom 65 (or 61 percent) were officials.

66. Hunt, Cluny under Saint Hugh, p. 60; King, Peterborough Abbey, p. 89. Monastic officers were totally independent at la Chaise-Dieu by the mid-thirteenth century. Gaussin, La Chaise-Dieu, p. 558.

67. CT 2:400, no. 549, "sed quia inter eos contentio oriebatur, quantum quisque prebere deberet, librorum ordo negligebatur. . . ."

68. Colin Platt, The Monastic Grange in Medieval England (New York, 1969), p. 75.

69. CT 2:19–20, no. 314. Both the monastic property to be managed and the manorial administrative office were called obedientiae. By the end of the twelfth century, the bigger obedientiae were placed under the management of priors. See 2:192, no. 423, which carefully makes the differentiation between cells directed by priors and those under ordinary monks. This change in terminology was evidence of the growing independence of the larger cells.

70. CT 1:244, no. 138; 1:244–45, no. 139; 1:247, no. 141; 1:248, no. 142; 1:260, no. 147, are Thibald's acquisitions; in 2:192–93, no. 423, Ville-Arvent does not appear separately on a comprehensive list of dues from obediences.

71. Geoffrey of Vendôme, Ep. 4:45 (PL 157:179–80), 4:36 (PL 157:175), 2:32 (PL 157:104–6); CT 2:217–18, no. 439; Ep. 4:42 (PL 157:177–78) and 4:43 (PL 157:178). Cf. the positive summary of life in small cells by Jacques Dubois, "La Vie des moines dans les prieurés du moyen âge," Lettre de Ligugé no. 133 (1969), 10–33.

72. Gaussin, La Chaise-Dieu, pp. 643 and 338.

73. Jacques Dubois, "Les Moines dans la société du moyen âge," Revue d'histoire de l'église de France 60 (1974), 21.

74. CT 1:165–66, no. 92. "Metuentes enim operi nostro, insurgentibus undique bellorum ingentium turbinibus, ventorum concursiones vel aquarum intolerabilium inundationes . . . refugium tutum quesivimus."

75. CT 1:131–33, no. 72, describes the purchase of a site for building, 1:190–92, no. 105, is a diploma commending the new foundation to papal protection. Both Guillot, Le Comte d'Anjou, 2:121, and Hermann Meinert, "Die Fälschungen Gottsfrieds von Ven-

dôme," *Sonderabzug aus dem Archiv für Urkundenforschung*, 10 (Berlin, 1928), p. 324, designate no. 105 as wholly authentic. I suspect the second half to be a later interpolation, expanding and elaborating on the genuine commendation to Rome. See Appendix I.

76. Georges Duby, "Economie domaniale et économie monétaire. Le budget de l'abbaye de Cluny entre 1080 et 1155," *Annales E.S.C.* 7 (1952), 159.

77. Blois B.D. MS 21 H 144, no. 1 C (edited CT 2:60, no. 339); the list includes five women, two priests, and a doctor who owed grain to the abbey. Cheviré was an obedience by 1097 at the latest when its obedientiary appears in a witness list. Blois B.D. MS 21 H 144, no. 2 (edited CT 2:101, no. 357).

78. CT 2:400–401, no. 549. This amount was 2½ pounds and fourteen sesters of grain which was to be used for the library.

79. CT 1:316–19, no. 184. The Lady Matilda made her donation of half a church and its *vicaria* to la Trinité and its priory in Craon; 1:447–48, no. 293, records a castellan's gift of toll (*rotagium*), "sub monitione et precario Adelini monachi, qui tunc obedientiam Pruneti procurabat."

80. Jean-François Lemarignier, "La Dislocation du 'pagus' et le problème des 'consuetudines' (X–XIᵉ siècle)," *Mélanges Halphen* (Paris, 1951), pp. 402–8, uses this system (which admittedly is somewhat artificial) to describe seigneurial rights.

81. CT 2:232–33, no. 447. The count seems to have lost his temper when expected to give nominal approval to the emancipation of one of la Trinité's serfs.

82. CT 2:361, no. 524. Barbotin, after the death of both parents, tried to escape his servility by not honoring the customary dues. Also note the earlier discussion of motives for those who commended themselves to the abbey as serfs.

83. CT 1:296–98, no. 170; 2:58–60, no. 338; 2:63–66, no. 340; see 2:426–27, no. 563 for fealty at time of settlement, and 2:258–59, no. 468 for subinfeudation.

84. CT 1:111, no. 56; 1:327, no. 191; 1:408, no. 259. André Chédeville, *Chartres et ses campagnes XI–XIIIᵉ siècle* (Paris, 1973), pp. 238–42. The discussion of *cens* in the Chartrain shows it was typical of the situation in most of central France. *Cens* was a fixed amount, payable on some designated feast day and tending to become hereditary. It was like rent, except it could not be increased in each generation. For food levies see Blois B.D. MS 21 H 144, no. 1 C (edited CT 2:60, no. 339).

85. These figures are the result of comparing the number of cases mentioning property paying *cens* to la Trinité in the three fifty-year periods: 1032–81: 12, 1082–1131: 6, and 1132–87: 23, to the total number of charters in each interval: 304, 162, and 136. Cluny also experienced a general move toward the commutation of services to *cens* in this period. See Hunt, *Cluny under St. Hugh*, p. 70.

86. Georges Duby, *Guerriers et paysans VII–XIIᵉ siècle: Premier essor de l'économie européenne* (Paris, 1973), p. 73, tr. Howard Clarke as *The Early Growth of the European Economy* (Ithaca, N.Y., 1974), as well as Duby's *L'Economie rurale et la vie des campagnes dans l'occident médiévale*, 2 vols. (Paris, 1962), 2:452–55, tr. Cynthia Postan as *Rural Economy and Country Life in the Medieval West* (London, 1968). Also see general discussion off banal lordship by Guy Fourquin, *Seigneurie et féodalité au moyen âge* (Paris, 1970), pp. 93–94, tr. Iris and A. L. Sells as *Lordship and Feudalism in the Middle Ages* (New York, 1976). The differentiation between economic and juridical lordship is based on the different origins of the two and not on their outcome, which in both cases brought economic benefit to the lord. Economic lordship realized profits from monopolistic privileges, in contrast to juridical lordship, which derived income from the prerogative of hearing legal cases. The line is admittedly vague, since, for example, a fine for trespassing the lord's baking monopoly would be paid in the lord's court.

87. Robert Latouche, "Un Aspect de la vie rurale dans le Maine au XIᵉ et au XIIᵉ siècle: l'établissement des bourgs," *Moyen âge* 8 (1937), 44–64, vividly describes the development in Maine which is similar to the experience of the Vendômois. Also see André Chédeville, "Etude de la mise en valeur et du peuplement du Maine au XIᵉ siècle, d'après

les documents de l'abbaye de Saint-Vincent du Mans," *Annales de Bretagne* 67 (1960), 217–24. For Aimerica see CT 2:197–200, no. 427. This purchase was made by Geoffrey of Vendôme in 1112.

88. For examples of banal monopolies enjoyed by la Trinité: CT 1:281, no. 163; 2:9, no. 303; 2:32–35, no. 324; 2:145, no. 394; 2:263, no. 471; 2:454, no. 583.

89. CT 1:212, no. 117; 1:409, no. 260; 1:415, no. 265; 2:263, no. 471. The classic formulation on *vicaria* is: Ferdinand Lot, "La Vicaria et le vicarius," *Nouvelle revue de droit français et étranger* 17 (1893), 281–301.

90. CT 2:241, no. 454. Requisitioning is termed *captura*. For tolls see 1:160, no. 88, and 1:447, no. 293, in which case the men of la Trinité were partially exempt from the *rotagium*.

91. Garaud, *L'Abbaye de Sainte-Croix*, p. 13.

92. CT 1:202, no. 109, and 2:263, no. 471. But it could not be avoided when the custom was specified, CT 1:434, no. 279, or when a piece of property was already burdened by the fee, 1:359, no. 226.

93. Fossier, *La Terre et les hommes en Picardie*, 1:310. Chédeville, *Chartres*, p. 108, adds the caution not to speak of assarting at all, unless there is definite evidence for the practice.

94. CT 1:351, no. 218; 1:357, no. 224; 1:364, no. 232; 1:386, no. 244; 2:208, no. 433; 2:237, no. 450; 2:294, no. 481; 2:312, no. 492; 2:378, no. 533; 2:452–53, no. 582; 2:472, no. 598. Also note CS p. 55, no. 28, and p. 92, no. 54. The mention of *ruptura* and *agrerium* (both dues from newly cleared lands) suggests assarting. Other abbeys were involved in land reclamation: for instance, Searle, *Battle Abbey*, pp. 48 and 60; also see Garaud, *L'Abbaye Sainte-Croix*, p. 198. It is noteworthy that, however, the great abbey of Cluny showed no interest in assarting. Hunt, *Cluny under St. Hugh*, p. 68.

95. For Euphronia see CT 2:53, no. 334, "et hoc cum hospitalibus circa ecclesiam manentibus, in quibus hospites ad se convenientes monachus hospitari potuisset." For Matilda see CT 2:208, no. 433, "manentibus ad excolendum, vel hospitibus ad manendum. . . ." (Was there some reason that women might be particularly aware of the importance of settling *hospites*?)

96. King, *Peterborough Abbey*, pp. 8 and 19. Hockey also examines the consolidation of property in the twelfth century by *Quarr Abbey*, p. 67.

97. See, for examples of purchases, CT 1:211, no. 116; 1:212, no. 117; 1:225, no. 125; 1:269, no. 155. For land adjoining l'Evière, see CT 1:391, no. 246.

98. In the three intervals, 1032–81, 1082–1131, and 1132–87, there were, respectively, 39, 4, and 6 charters of purchases made by the abbey. The percentages are arrived at by comparing these figures with the total number of la Trinité's charters (excluding duplicates and incomplete documents) in each period: 304, 162, and 136.

99. See CT 1:183, no. 99, for grain; 1:212–13, no. 118, for three gold coins and a siege machine (*scrofa*); 1:218, no. 121, for one ounce of gold; 1:281, no. 163, for two ounces of gold; 1:234, no. 131, for a horse; CS p. 42, no. 14, for a shield; CT 1:236, no. 133, for spiritual benefits.

100. Robert Génestal, *Rôle des monastères comme établissements de crédit étudié en Normandie du XIᵉ à la fin du XIIIᵉ siècle* (Paris, 1901), pp. 3–5.

101. CT 1:354, no. 221. "Gislerius . . . donavit monachis . . . duos arpennos . . . quos illis jampridem ante dederat frater suus Hubertus. . . ." This was not a confirmation of the elder brother's gift but a gift made by Gisler.

102. Blois B.D. MS 21 H 54, no. 2 (edited CT 2:223–29, no. 444).

CHAPTER THREE

Relations with the Laity

T HE FLOW of offerings and the enormous richness of the result [between 1050 and 1150] reflect the fact that there was
an intimacy between the secular society of the day and the monastic order of a degree unique in the Middle Ages."[1] What were
the characteristics of this intimacy for la Trinité and its supporters? Did the founders' support differ in nature from that of other
patrons? Was there reciprocity between the abbey and its benefactors? What interchange took place between la Trinité and the
local power, the counts of Vendôme? Did the attitudes of patrons
change over time? To address these questions we turn first to an
examination of the relationship between la Trinité and the counts
of Anjou, who continued as benefactors of the abbey throughout
the period, although becoming increasingly impersonal in the
twelfth century as their arena of political involvement expanded
rapidly.

Counts of Anjou: Patrons and Protectors

Geoffrey Martel and Agnes had generously endowed their
foundation of la Trinité; but soon after its founding, a combination of events—the installation of Agnes' sons in Saintonge and
Poitou, Geoffrey's inheritance of Anjou, his separation from
Agnes, and his continuous wars—might have been expected to
draw the founders' attention away from the Vendômois. Yet neither Geoffrey or Agnes lost interest in their foundation; in fact,
for Geoffrey in particular, the house proved supportive in diffi-

cult times, and he showed his appreciation with grants and protection.

Geoffrey was constantly embroiled in conflicts with his neighbors, ranging from localized brush warfare to pitched battles. In
such times of stress, he sometimes turned to la Trinité and helped
himself to its property. In so doing, was the count abusing his
privileged position? The first of these incidents occurred in 1038
when Geoffrey was forced at a severe disadvantage—since he was
immobilized with a broken hip—to conclude the opening round
of hostilities with Bishop Gervais of le Mans (CT 1:125, no. 68).
The count's injury gave Gervais the upper hand, which he played
to coerce Geoffrey into giving him several fiefs belonging to the
count's men. Nihard (probably the castellan of Montoire) was
one of the Angevin men whose lands were transferred to the
bishop in this settlement. In 1047, when conflict broke out again
between bishop and count, Geoffrey acted cautiously demanding
an oath of fealty from his followers. Nihard, whom the monks'
charter described as "a deceitful man" (fallax), bewailed his loss,
and

> the count, aware of the deceitfulness and suspected faithlessness of
> that man [Nihard], again was forced to give to him an exchange
> for the land which he had been driven by necessity to acquire [to
> give Gervais in 1038] when he had been distressed; he arranged to
> give to [Nihard] that [exchange] from the assarts in the land of
> the Gâtines Forest, which previously he had given to la Trinité,
> for which he had accepted 150 pounds from his wife, Countess
> Agnes.[2]

By their depiction of Nihard as the villain of the episode the
monks showed that their loyalties lay securely with Geoffrey. La
Trinité took the side of its founder, despite the loss of its own
valuable property.

A few years later part of the settlement of post-battle claims
between Geoffrey and Count Thibald of Blois was Thibald's assurance that he would not prevent the men of la Trinité from
repossessing their oxen seized by his forces during the conflict.
This seizure had not been the impious act it might seem, since
the monastery's oxen had, at the time of the battle, been in the
use of Blois' enemy, Count Geoffrey.[3] Again the abbey had

acted to furnish support for its founder, and its loyalty was repaid. During this period Geoffrey accorded the abbey the right of first refusal on all property sold in the Vendômois, a right of preemption conceded specifically in order to circumvent Marmoutier's efforts to buy the church of Gombergean.[4] The preemption award may have been granted after la Trinité's crisis support against Thibald (1043–44) but probably before August 21, 1044, when Geoffrey became overlord of Tours and thereby nominal protector of Marmoutier.[5] It is probable that the document of preemption recognizes and rewards la Trinité's supportive role during the recent conflict.

Although Geoffrey had never ceased acting as the abbey's watchdog, he was not formally recognized by the papacy as the abbey's "defender and helper" until 1056/7.[6] Ironically, the monks only fully appreciated his value as la Trinité's founder and protector after his death—though in a negative way. The abbey "held [Gâtines assarts] without any counter claims as long as [Geoffrey] lived. But after he died, whoever desired and was able to, make claims on the monks and seized [property]. . . ."[7] As this was not an isolated incident, it fell to Agnes, after Geoffrey's death, to attempt to protect the monastery. The monks were driven to write to the countess with a list of abuses and atrocities, begging her sympathy and aid (CT 1:301, no. 173). But since Agnes had left the area after her marriage was dissolved, she was no longer readily available to help la Trinité in the Vendômois. Instead, she shifted her efforts to manipulating her two sons into confirming previous holdings and making new grants to la Trinité's priories in the Saintonge and Poitou.[8] After her death in 1068, her son Guy Geoffrey continued to function as patron; his younger brother, William, who succeeded him, also carried on the family tradition of patronage, albeit to a lesser extent.

The difficulties experienced by la Trinité after the count's death point to an interesting dichotomy. The absence of a strong lord and patron could leave a house open to attacks from the outside. This happened to many abbeys that, like Battle Abbey in the late twelfth century, found its property "in danger of becoming the spoils of those meant to stand between it and the world."[9] On the other hand (and perhaps more commonly), a

monastery could benefit from the failure of an overlord to establish control in an area. It was in such lacunae that Cluny and la
Chaise-Dieu grew and expanded rapidly in the tenth and eleventh centuries, respectively.[10] In La Trinité's case, its worst trou-
bles developed when Angevin control faltered.

Since Geoffrey Martel had no children, he designated his elder
nephew, Geoffrey Barbu, as his successor. At the same time, he
gave his younger nephew, Fulk Rechin, control of Saintonge and
the castle of Vihiers. (See Appendix III.) Geoffrey Barbu was a
poor ruler who managed to mishandle affairs so badly that the
pope eventually stepped in and awarded the comital title to his
younger brother in 1066/7.[11] During his short period in power,
Geoffrey Barbu's interaction with la Trinité was limited to ap-
proving two verbal donations which the monks claimed Geoffrey Martel had made just before his death (CT 1:271, no. 157;
1:273, no. 158). Fulk Rechin began to act as count in 1067, and
when he imprisoned his older brother on April 9, 1068, he became the count of Anjou in fact as well as in name. The first few
years of Fulk's rule were chaotic, for the "repulsive" Fulk, as
David Douglas called him, had to work to terminate the anarchy
he had created in the preceding eight years.[12]

During his first six years as count, Fulk did not exhibit the
same affection for la Trinité as had his uncle. He perpetrated such
atrocious injustices against the abbey that la Trinité was driven
to the extreme of acting out symbolically the pain being suffered
by the monastery. In this rite the monks laid the crucifix on a
bed of thorns on the church floor and prostrated themselves at
its foot while keeping up a stream of prayers and psalms. This
desperate monastic response signaled the despair felt by the
monks when their key patron turned against them—for it was
Fulk "who ought to obtain justice for them, [but] consorted
with their oppressors. . . ."[13] Despite this doleful picture, la
Trinité completely excused Fulk's behavior on the grounds of his
extreme youth, the guidance of bad men, and the exigencies of
war. The abbey's indulgent attitude toward the young count
seems naive, yet was subsequently justified. Later, when Fulk
found himself in a grim military situation while fighting the
count of Poitou, he begged God for divine aid, vowing in return
to right all the wrongs he had done to la Trinité. After his vic-

tory, Fulk fulfilled his vow and left la Trinité in peace. He made a donation to the abbey just before he died in 1109 and was buried (as he had requested) at l'Evière in Angers.[14]

The next two counts of Anjou, Fulk the Younger and Geoffrey le Bel, carried on the Angevin tradition of caring for la Trinité. Fulk the Younger made four donations to the abbey and often received appeals from Abbot Geoffrey of Vendôme for help against the abbey's enemies.[15] Geoffrey le Bel made no donations to the abbey but did manipulate the son of the count of Vendôme into renouncing the right to *gîte,* which the young man had been extracting from la Trinité's obedientiaries.[16] Geoffrey also later confirmed the count of Vendôme's concessions to the abbey. In 1146 Abbot Robert appealed to Geoffrey to enforce payment of tithes owed to la Trinité. The count responded by sending his steward to hold a court, which decided in favor of the abbey.

The last Angevin count during the period of this study was Henry II, count of Anjou, duke of Normandy, and king of England. Although the monastery dedicated to the Holy Trinity in Vendôme constituted only one trifling concern in the total Angevin holdings, Henry still felt a sense of responsibility toward the abbey. In an undated document, he issued a general confirmation of all la Trinité's property in Anjou, Poitou, and Saintonge, together with instructions to his officials to protect these properties.[17] In 1180 he intervened by urging John of Salisbury, bishop of Chartres, to receive the count of Vendôme, who, after one false start and only under considerable Angevin pressure, finally did penance before the bishop for his mistreatment of la Trinité, and was accordingly released from a three-year ban of excommunication. Henry had to force the count to make satisfaction; since

> the Lord King of the English grieved that [the count] had lain under excommunication for such a long time, he added his royal hand compelling him . . . to be absolved from the sentence of excommunication.[18]

Although the bishop's charter recounting this event stresses the king's concern for the count without mentioning any similar anxiety for the abbey, the act of reconciliation served to restore harmony to the Vendômois and thereby to la Trinité. Henry's third act relating to la Trinité, dated 1185, outlines the abbey's customs (CT 2:445, no. 578). This document represents an orderly effort to adjudicate with finality all the points of contention between the counts of Vendôme and the abbey of la Trinité.

Eleanor of Aquitaine also issued a number of charters for la Trinité. During her first marriage to King Louis VII of France, she had involved Louis in the abolition of unfair customary taxes as well as in confirming all the abbey's property in Poitou and Saintonge.[19] Barely eight weeks after her separation from Louis in 1152, she married Henry II of England and continued her support for la Trinité to whose priories in the Saintonge she gave the right of procuration, and, together with her son Richard, endowed the priory of Saint-Aignan with a marsh and saltpan.[20] Also, she confirmed the immunity of all la Trinité's priories from any customs. Finally, in 1199 she issued two charters reconfirming all the property held by the priory of Puyravault. Eleanor had previously made a gift to a man who later apparently claimed that it included some of Puyravault's customs. It was therefore necessary for the queen to specify that nothing granted him was to detract from the priory's rights and privileges. The notorious separation of Eleanor and Louis and the subsequent decades of resulting friction between the Angevins and Capetians were to have varied consequences for religious houses. Some suffered directly, as did la Chaise-Dieu when fighting broke out in the 1160s in the Auvergne and every local power had to chose to support one side or the other.[21] However, despite the extended hostilities, la Trinité fared well and never seemed hurt by its location in Angevin territory.

The Angevin counts throughout the eleventh and twelfth centuries played the role of la Trinité's chief patrons initiated by Geoffrey Martel and Agnes. The rapid expansion of their interests and influence tended, however, to diminish their ability to give close attention to la Trinité, so that their role altered somewhat over the years. Among all the subsequent Angevin overlords, Geoffrey Martell's two nephews adhered most closely to the founders' pattern of solicitude for the abbey, despite Fulk Rechin's abuse of the abbey in the first years of his rule. Fulk the

Younger restricted his relationship with la Trinité to that of small-scale donor and sometime protector. It was in the early twelfth century that the new style of Angevin comital patronage developed, as the overseeing of the monastery's well-being together with keeping the peace became more important to the counts than making donations of property. Geoffrey le Bel coerced cooperation from the count of Vendôme, confirmed acts, and instituted legal proceedings in recognition of which services the abbey identified him as "the protector of this church, after God. . . ."[22] Henry II redefined the role further in that the comital patron gave way to the ruler-patron. Confirmation of the abbey's property and clarification of its customs were part of his peacemaking endeavors. Since Vendôme was of peripheral interest in the huge Angevin territories, other religious houses that directly served Plantagenet needs benefited more substantially from their patrons' generosity. Only Eleanor, in her capacity as countess of Poitou, continued the older relationship of patronage, marked by donations to la Trinité and small-scale interventions on its behalf.

Henry was ruler of a vast domain in which he sought to maintain his control peacefully. La Trinité's scattered priories all fell within his jurisdiction, so that his protection was infinitely more valuable for la Trinité than that of the previous counts of Anjou, who could not protect the abbey's property in Poitou or Saintonge. Henry dealt with the abbey no longer as proud patron and founding parent in the style of Agnes and Geoffrey Martel but in his capacity as ruler of Vendôme, keeper of the peace, and judge of his subjects.[23]

La Trinité supported and respected its Angevin patrons throughout the period. Even when Fulk Rechin wreaked havoc on the abbey, driving the desperate monks to allow the crucifix to suffer symbolically, the abbey was understanding of the reasons for his depredations and totally forgiving. By the late twelfth century, monastic support in brush wars was a thing of the past, and the abbey would never again achieve the distinction of burying one of its Angevin patrons. La Trinité could still benefit from measures like Henry II's articulation of the customs, which contributed much to the establishment of local harmony,

but the abbey had lost its personal and familial bonds with its
founding family.

Counts of Vendôme: Predators and Patrons

La Trinité's relationship with the house of Vendôme was the
most complex and contradictory of any it maintained in the period under study, due to the ambivalence felt for the abbey by
the counts of Vendôme. The comital family was generally hostile
to the monks except when acting as benefactors in hopes of as-
suaging monastic wrath and ecclesiastic sanctions. The uneasy
situation is graphically symbolized by Fulk Oison's uncomfortable position when Geoffrey Martel reinstated him as count of
Vendôme between 1056 and 1058.[24]

When Fulk returned to Vendôme, a strong, young monastery
had grown up in his absence. It was under the control of saintly
Abbot Oderic, and its ostensible purpose was pious and peaceful.
At the same time, its security was guaranteed by the powerful
Angevin whom Fulk could not fail but to see as a usurper, and
its endowment included extensive property, like the Gâtines,
which Fulk had considered to be under his own *dominium*. Under
these circumstances, it seems probable that respect and awe bat-
tled with anger and envy within the young count. Geoffrey Martel and Agnes were aware of the potential danger Fulk might
pose as a neighbor of their foundation. They tried to protect the
abbey by providing it with a refuge for its monks in Angers and
extracting from Fulk an oath to respect the monastery's possessions.[25] Since the issue of protecting the abbey from Fulk was
temporarily uppermost in their plans, they obtained a special
privilege from Pope Victor II (April 16, 1055–July 28, 1057).
Victor reasserted that the count of Anjou was to be the defender
and supporter of la Trinité and that no dispute could be forced
on the abbey without papal consent.[26]

After Geoffrey's death Fulk seemed inclined to live up to his
oath. He came to la Trinité's chapter house "of his own free
will" and placed a voluntary charter on the altar confirming his
oath.[27] This act was performed with great publicity in the sight

of "all the saints" and before the monks and others gathered as witnesses. Fulk's good intentions were short-lived, for he soon began to perpetrate various abuses on the abbey. The monks sought help from Countess Agnes, sending her a detailed letter complaining of Fulk's depredations.[28] Most of the offenses had been committed by the count's men and were more in the nature of insults than severe injuries. Property was stolen: land, a mule, a horse, and the possessions of a monastic *famulus,* while some of the abbey's colliberts were forced illegally to do work service for the count. The monks recounted that when one of their number reported the attempted theft of a horse to Fulk, the count became violently agitated and stabbed the perpetrator (his own man) in the belly, despite the monk's efforts to calm Fulk. At one point the thievery became so bold that the monks felt compelled to secrete their most valuable treasures in safe places. At last, in 1064, Fulk was persuaded to behave properly—"driven by the fear of the Lord"—and not only swore his good faith but also promised to leave the abbey's property in peace.

Despite this reconciliation, a number of potential irritants remained which could renew local hostilities. One source of trouble was the enduring rivalry between the abbeys of la Trinité and Marmoutier, which often found themselves at odds over property rights. At one time in the mid-eleventh century, the pannage paid by the peasants in Sentier was at issue (CM p. 128, no. 82). Marmoutier gave Count Fulk and his wife Petronilla 2½ pounds and a family of pigs to confirm its right to the pannage. (The familial model is reflected in the gift of the boar to Fulk and the sow and piglets to Petronilla.) Such favoritism only acted as an invitation to continued bad feelings.

Differences over legal procedure constituted an even more dangerous source of friction. When a certain Hubert claimed some priory land belonging to la Trinité, Count Fulk preempted the right to try the case and adjudicated it on the spot (CT 1:308, no. 178). This behavior put the assembled monks in a difficult position. They sent one of their knights to explain to the count that they could not assent to his findings in the abbot's absence. Fulk postponed the finalization, giving the abbot until the octave of St. Michael to settle the issue with him. The outcome of this case is not known, but the broad question of legal priority continued to make trouble.

Fulk Oison died on November 21, 1066, leaving a minor son, Burchard the Young, in the care of his uncle, Guy of Nevers, who served as regent with the help of Fulk's widow, Petronilla. (See Appendix III.) The regency lasted until 1075 and helped temporarily to modify the family's behavior toward la Trinité, since whatever Petronilla's and Guy's personal feelings for the abbey, they initiated a brief period of friendly relations with the monks.[29] When Burchard attained his majority and assumed control of the honor in January, 1075, he granted a full confirmation of all the abbey's possessions to la Trinité (CT 1:392, no. 247). A few months later, he acquiesed in the abbey's requests to buy the customs of a servile shoemaker who was a member of the monastic *familia,* as well as acceding to the monks' right to hold a fair (CT 1:393, no. 249).

After his mother's death in 1078, Burchard the Young began to display the same ambivalence toward la Trinité as had his father. He respected the abbey as a spiritual power but disliked its challenge to his lordship. One day two years after his mother's death when he went to the abbey to pray, the prior, Hildrad, took him aside and raised a question of juridical precedence: at issue was the locus where a fine should be paid to the count by two men of the abbey who had offended against his banlieu (CT 1:450, no. 295). Arguing the authority of custom, the prior urged Burchard to send his *vicarius* to the abbot's court to collect the fines. This suggestion angered the count, who left the abbey with the worried prior following close behind him. When Hildrad reached the castle, he had to content himself with arguing the abbey's position before one of Burchard's barons, Fulcher of Turre. Hildrad stressed that Geoffrey Martel had given la Trinité the privilege—subsequently ratified by Fulk Oison—for the abbot to call his court in any case of the distraint of his men. The charter ends enigmatically, and although there is no indication that Count Burchard actually assented to the abbey's claim, this is the presumption of the document. The obscurity of the charter reflects the partial or temporary nature of the settlement, since the issue was not yet fully laid to rest.

A scuffle between the count's squires and some of the abbey's *famuli* over the harvest in the meadow of St. Beatus brought about a further confrontation in October, 1084 (CT 2:25, no. 319). This time the abbey succeeded in persuading Burchard to come to the chapter house and there, in the presence of all his barons, to give the abbey a charter guaranteeing its juridical claims. To make the occasion even more solemn, the document was placed on the altar by three local notables: Fulcher of Turre (a castellan), Hugo Passapictavinus (a knight), and Hugo Calvus (a bourgeois). Then the count openly admitted his error, asked for forgiveness, and promised to observe the customary legal practice as long as he should live. Burchard's antagonism was evidently quite strong and extended beyond clashes over legal rights even to confrontations over relatively insignificant issues like the ownership of a house (CT 2:29, no. 321). An uproar ensued when the count sent his men to seize a building, and a court date was set; but cooler minds prevailed, and a confrontation was avoided. Burchard eventually backed down and recognized the monastery's legal claim to the house.

When Burchard died without heirs, his sister Euphronia's husband, Geoffrey Preuilly (also called Geoffrey Jordan in recognition of his status as a pilgrim), succeeded to the honor of Vendôme. Geoffrey's assumption of control ushered in a period of good relations with la Trinité. Burchard's death on February 28, 1085, had been followed by that of Abbot David on August 6, 1085. Since the new abbot, Berno, did not succeed until April 23, 1086, Geoffrey Preuilly and Euphronia were able to establish themselves in the eight-month interval without having to contend immediately with the abbey's leadership. Even when Berno was installed, he posed little threat to comital pretensions since he was old and feeble. The new count proceeded to perform the expected gesture by granting the abbey confirmation of all its holdings (CT 2:42, no. 328). Geoffrey's initial friendliness evaporated when one of his barons, Bertran of Moncontour, enlisted his support in a case against la Trinité. However, the count abandoned Bertran and switched back to the abbey's side when he needed la Trinité's help after he had been imprisoned by Lancelin, lord of Beaugency.[30] At that time Geoffrey sent word to

his wife to give to la Trinité the church of Savigny for the re-
demption of their souls and those of their parents, and children,
"as well as for the freedom of his body. . . ." Euphronia was
quick to follow his command, which she was able to implement,
since the church in question was part of her dower. After being
freed, Geoffrey went with Euphronia to the church of Savigny
to finalize the donation. Had the monks pressured or paid Lancelin to secure Geoffrey's release? We will return to this question.
The goodwill between count and monks did not end directly,
since in 1093 Geoffrey endowed the abbey with a forest in Villedieu (CT 2:88, no. 349).

The unusually long and mutually satisfactory period of good
relations came to a close within a few years after the election
(1093) of Geoffrey of Vendôme as the new abbot. The first stage
of the renewed hostilities concerned three unrelated issues whose
resolution necessitated the calling of Bishop Ivo of Chartres to
Vendôme to act as judge.[31] Count Geoffrey was pressing three
claims. He argued that when he required la Trinité's men and
some failed to report, he was the injured party. He also maintained that men who lived in the abbey's burg and in any territory under la Trinité's ban should compensate him (this probably
referred to legal fines). Finally, he argued that the men of the
priory of Villedieu had no right to take bark from trees in the
Gâtines Forest. Abbot Geoffrey responded with a spirited defense, pointing out that Geoffrey Martel's original gifts of forest
and burg had been given free of any rightful claim by subsequent
counts of Vendôme. The abbot produced the charters of privileges and won Ivo to his side.

The abbot's victory may well have seemed hollow a few years
later when tensions reached such a level that the count physically
attacked the abbey. The situation so frightened the abbot that he
fled to Tours, from which haven he convinced Bishop Ivo to lay
an interdict on the county of Vendôme (CT 2:153, no. 400).
When he heard of the discord between the two Geoffreys, a dis-
sident monk of la Trinité named Daniel, who had left his priory,
lost no time in bringing to the count a number of damaging tales
about the abbot.[32] Fueled by this propaganda, Count Geoffrey
led his men into the chapter house and seized it. Eventually, after

the uproar had subsided, the count became aware of the serious-
ness of his actions and sent his wife, Countess Euphronia, to
Tours to negotiate a reconciliation. She swore fealty before the
bishop and named seven barons as hostages for her husband's
good behavior. The final and humiliating act for the count was
played out on the abbey's turf before a large crowd of monks
and lay people. Count Geoffrey had to come bound and barefoot
(*constrictus, nudis pedibus*) into the chapter house and prostrate
himself before the altar at the abbot's feet, where he swore to
renounce all claims against la Trinité and never again do it harm.
He then placed four deniers on his head and a knife on the altar.[33]
These symbols of penance and servility made this a scene of un-
forgettable repentance.

Count Geoffrey Preuilly died in Jerusalem a few years later in
1102. When the news reached his widow, she swiftly reclaimed
the church of Savigny, which she had given to la Trinité to ex-
pedite her husband's release from imprisonment (CT 2:159, no.
405). Euphronia may have needed the income from her former
dower property or, more likely, may have acted out of personal
bitterness toward the abbot, her husband's antagonist. Indeed,
she probably also was aware of the extreme dislike Abbot Geoffrey felt for her and had vividly expressed in several scathing
letters addressed to Bishop Hildebert of le Mans.[34] Her seizure
of the church incurred excommunication, a sentence finally lifted
by the bishop of le Mans, who restored the church to la Trinité.

Geoffrey Grisegonelle—the son of Geoffrey Preuilly and Euphronia—became count in 1102 and with his wife, Matilda of
Châteaudun, continued the hostilities initiated by his parents.
When the abbey's men violated the castle's immunity, Abbot
Geoffrey of Vendôme offered the new count compensation "in
the court of la Trinité just as in the past Count Geoffrey [Mar-
tel], the founder of the church, had ordained for all time.
. . ."[35] Thus, the subject of juridical precedence again became
an issue, to be aggravated by the barons of the Vendômois, who
encouraged Count Geoffrey to seize the abbey's burg. Like his
father's, Geoffrey Grisegonelle's impulsive violence was punished by an interdict, pronounced by Ivo of Chartres at the abbot's insistence.[36] Later, regretting his actions, Count Geoffrey

made his submission at la Trinité, placing a knife on the altar and vowing that he would protect the abbey in the future. Such incidents convinced the monks of their need for protection to guarantee them legal precedence over the house of Vendôme. A number of spurious charters of privileges accordingly appeared, articulating the principle advanced by the monks, that "the judgment should be given not in the court of the count, nor in any other secular court, but in the court of the abbot"; the count was also denied the right to receive the customary half of the fines.[37]

The son Geoffrey repeated the father Geoffrey's behavior in many ways. Geoffrey Grisegonelle was imprisoned by his enemy, Count Thibald of Blois, but managed to ransom himself.[38] After his release, he came to the abbey and humbly begged "aid" (*auxilium*), by which he must have meant the feudal subsidy paid by a vassal for his lord's ransom. Because the charter is truncated by an unfortunate ellipsis, it is unclear whether Abbot Geoffrey was sufficiently impressed by the count's humble entreaty so that he paid the *auxilium;* at the least, he admitted the count to the monks' spiritual brotherhood. When Geoffrey Preuilly had been imprisoned in 1090, la Trinité had exercised some form of pressure to gain his release, although it is unclear whether the abbey actually paid a ransom. Certainly it would have been futile for the countess to endow the monks with the rich church property of Savigny without expectation of their willingness to help her imprisoned husband. The abbey's exact responsibilities vis-à-vis an imprisoned count of Vendôme, however, had not yet been clarified, and would be fully articulated only later in the century.

Countess Matilda had a series of run-ins with la Trinité's men over the taking of bark from the Gâtines (a right previously disputed between the monks and her father-in-law), the seasons when monastic animals could be grazed in the woods, and her right to order the felling of the abbey's wheat sheaves.[39] When she fell seriously ill in 1119, her past actions troubled her to such an extent that she conceded the forest rights to la Trinité and received a thousand masses for her soul.

It seemed that the two powers in Vendôme, spiritual and secular, could not leave each other in peace for long. When the abbot freed a serf, the count made a scene by knocking the charter of liberty off the man's head, because he thought emancipation required his consent (CT 2:232, no. 447). Following their parents' example, the count's sons, John and Geoffrey, troubled the abbey with claims to woodlands and the right to gîte.[40] At one time, John's youthful misbehavior occasioned a fierce response from Abbot Geoffrey of Vendôme, who accused John and his cronies of having actually tormented men of Marmoutier and Saint-Laumer, making "a prison of captives from a cloister for monks."[41] Geoffrey Grisegonelle had one final passage of arms with la Trinité in 1134 over payments of pannage (CT 2:260, no. 470).

By the time John succeeded to the county in 1145, he seemed to have outgrown his early propensity for harassing the monks. With his wife, Richilde of Lavardin, he instituted a policy of peaceful coexistence with la Trinité. The passing of the old abbatial order before John became count may have made this possible, since Abbot Geoffrey of Vendôme had died in 1132 and his protégé, Fromond, who became the next abbot, died in 1139. In the following years, John and Richilde experienced benign encounters with la Trinité, marked by their periodic small gifts to the monks.[42] The lack of friction between count and abbey was in part a peripheral benefit of John's position as a loyal Angevin baron, often absent from Vendôme in attendance at the peripatetic royal court.[43] John concerned himself generally with the larger issues of the Angevins instead of battling the petty annoyances generated by friction with la Trinité.[44] Only in 1180 near the end of his forty-year rule, when his age may have kept him mostly at home, did he clash with the abbey. John remained excommunicate for three years, a situation that was eventually resolved, primarily through Henry II's efforts.[45]

The last trouble in the period under study between a count of Vendôme and la Trinité occurred in 1185, the first year of Count Burchard IV's rule. This conflict concerned the much-disputed customs and was resolved, as has been noted, by Henry II's clear outline of both parties' privileges (CT 2:445, no. 578). The customs were articulated in such a way that the count was to have no right to food provisions or taille from the abbey but was to receive relief of 150 pounds when his eldest daughter married, when he undertook his first trip to Jerusalem, and when he found himself in need of ransom. The count received the assurance of fifteen days of annual service from la Trinité's men for work on defensive ditches and for the defense of the town against attack. The abbey's forest rights in the Gâtines were carefully outlined, as well as the procedure for settling conflicts over units of measure for grain and wine. Finally and most critically, the juridical rights of both parties were detailed: the *duellum* (the fine paid in place of trial by battle) went to the abbot when two men of the burg were involved and to the count when one of his men was in litigation with a man of the abbey; the count had jurisdiction over la Trinité's men in cases calling for a sentence of death or mutilation, but the abbot heard all other cases involving his men. The abbey was free of all customs except those owed the count in his juridical authority.

To summarize the relationship between the house of Vendôme and la Trinité, all the counts began their rule with a goodwill gesture to the abbey—except for Geoffrey Grisegonelle, who succeeded to the honor in 1102 at the height of the conflict with Abbot Geoffrey of Vendôme. However, pleasant relations were usually only short-lived, and except for the regency of Guy of Nevers, all periods of rule were marred by flareups of hostilities with the abbey. Each of the four counts—Fulk Oison, Burchard the Young, Geoffrey Preuilly, and Geoffrey Grisegonelle—pushed his episode of the conflict to such extremes that an act of submission was necessary for a peaceful resolution. Only John and Burchard IV, the last count in the period under consideration, who were as much courtiers of the Angevins as they were counts of Vendôme, saw differences settled by their overlord's decision rather than by ritual penance. The hostilities peaked between 1097 and 1134, closely paralleling the abbacy of Geoffrey of Vendôme (1093–1132). During these years, the two counts, their wives, and their children all molested the abbey and twice even used armed force to seize monastic property in Vendôme. The inescapable conclusion is that Abbot Geoffrey's claims to powers and privileges were in excess of what had been customarily claimed by la Trinité and thus generated extreme friction with the local lords.

Particularly at issue were the proper court at which payment of fines to the count by the monastery's men should be made (three cases), and overlordship of the Gâtines woodland with its various forest rights (six cases). Both of these problems were resolved in Henry II's charter of customs drawn up in 1185. This document also specified the abbey's obligation to pay ransom for the count—a responsibility inadequately articulated in the past. In the abbey's pursuit of autonomy from secular control, it had been in the monks' best interests to leave relationships undefined, and thereby unbinding. This led inevitably to contradictory claims and conflicts. Henry's settlement worked effectively, so that the next two counts lived peacefully as neighbors of the abbey, but this harmony was achieved at the expense of monastic immunity from lay ties. By agreeing to pay feudal aids, the monks accepted the responsibilities of vassalage to the house of Vendôme. Other sources of irritation would emerge in the thirteenth century, but never again with the violence that characterized the eleventh and early twelfth centuries when the vagueness of territorial boundaries and of juridical jurisdictions led inevitably to conflict.

Patrons from the Loire Basin

The local supporters of la Trinité in its early days came from a wide range of social and economic groups eager to share in the prestige and spiritual benefits of the abbey. During the latter part of the eleventh century, the abbey's supporting group shifted to become almost exclusively noble—the knights and castellans of the Loire basin, whose interactions both positive and negative with the monks occupied a central position in the abbey's life.

In la Trinité's first five decades, it was not uncommon to find a smith or a carpenter alongside a noble in the ranks of the monastery's patrons, or to discover that men at the extremes of the ecclesiastic scale were among its benefactors. In the summer of 1061, the monastery recorded donations of three arpents of meadow from a smith's son in the same month that it received a fully armed destrier from a dying knight; similarly in these early days, a parish priest donated a house to the monks and an abbot gave them real estate.[46] This juxtaposition, although common within the abbey's first fifty years, would have been unlikely after 1082, since the proportions of patrons from various groups altered significantly. Peasants and craftsmen ceased to be patrons of la Trinité at the same time that clerical endowments fell off dramatically. Comital gifts also declined, although the abbey still derived legal support and protection from the counts of Anjou. The decrease in endowments from these three groups was only partly offset by small increases in gifts from castellans and more significantly increased donations from knightly families. Overall, during the first 150 years of the abbey's existence, the yearly number of la Trinité's patrons declined, and they became more homogeneous so that by the third quarter of the eleventh century, la Trinité received the bulk of its gifts from the knightly families of the Vendômois. (See Figure 3.)

The geographic area from which the abbey drew its greatest support was an elongated rectangle enclosing the two parallel valleys of the Loire and its smaller northern tributary, the Loir. (See Map 1.) The castles of Fréteval, Lisle, Lavardin, Montoire, and la Chartre, lying along the Loir as it runs southwest, all housed patrons of the abbey, as did those of Montdoubleau and Château-la-Vallière on tributaries of the Loir. Along the Loire and its tributary the Brenne were the seats of the lords of Beaugency, Blois, Amboise, and Château-Renault; the three castellans of Craon, Rancon, and Château-Gontier joined the barons of these castles as patrons of somewhat lesser degree.

A discussion of the patronage of the castellans of Montdoubleau is instructive for identifying some of the characteristics of seigneurial support. (See genealogy in Appendix III.) First, patronage tended to become a family tradition: the abbey received donations from Hugo, the first lord of Montdoubleau, and later from his son Odo Dublell and his grandson Hugo, together with wives and daughters in the family.[47] The support of noble families tended to be positive, although at the same time, it could have problematic results when relatives challenged the abbey's right to property granted by a family member, as did Nivelon Pagan, who disputed his father's gift of pannage.[48]

Figure 3. Donors to la Trinité.

	1032–1081		1082–1131		1132–1187		% of Overall Increase or Decrease
Number of donations	142		41		40		
Total documents★	304		162		136		
	Donors	% of Total† Documents	Donors	% of Total Documents	Donors	% of Total Documents	
Counts	29	20	7	17	4	9	−11
Castellans	13	9	8	20	7	16	+7
Knights	41	28	15	37	18	40	+12
Clerics	17	12	1	2	2	4	−8
Commoners	12	8					−8
Unknown	35	24	10	24	14	31	

Note: Some of the donations were given by multiple donors. Figures include gifts made for future reception as a monk and *ad succurrendum* reception. Excluded are gifts for commendation and oblation, as in these two cases the donor is acting less as a patron than as a supplant.

Percentages of each group's donations of the total donations, 1032–1187.

counts 18%
castellans 13%
knights 33%
clerics 9%
commoners 6%

★ *Total documents*: The heading, "Total Documents" represents the charters remaining within each fifty-year interval after discounting all forgeries, duplications, and incomplete texts.

† *% of Total documents*: As the body of documents available for the first period is almost twice as great as that applicable for the other two intervals, percentages are recorded of specific donors to number of donations in each fifty-year period. This provides a basis for comparison between the three intervals.

Second, women were crucial to the continuity of family patronage in two ways. Successive marriages for women were
common and could unite two families, as did the unions of Placentia and also those of Adele, while in the event of attrition of
male members, women could transmit inherited property and
lordship to their husbands.[49] In the process of these feudal transfers, the daughters of a house also passed on to their husbands
and children their own enthusiasm for the abbey to which their
natal family had close ties. For instance, la Trinité's major monastic competition as beneficiary of local gifts was Marmoutier,
with which the family of Fulcher the Rich of Vendôme was
closely associated. After Adele—daughter of Fulcher—married
Hugo Dublell of Montdoubleau, she introduced her concerns
into her new family, and patronage of Marmoutier became a
subsidiary theme in Montdoubleau's gift giving.[50] Nevertheless,
the family of Montdoubleau concentrated on endowments to la
Trinité, which was geographically and became emotionally
closer to the family than was Marmoutier.

A third characteristic of family patronage was that the bond
between patron and abbey could be strengthened by the entrance
of a family member into the monastery. Odo Dublell, the second
lord of Montdoubleau, became a monk of la Trinité by 1067 at
the latest.[51] Not only did his profession encourage the family to
take a personal interest in the abbey's well-being but also monastic suffrages must have seemed more particular and therefore
more efficacious.

Finally, family patronage drew members of a lineage to la
Trinité in times of spiritual and emotional crisis. For example,
when Hamelin and Helvisa's seven-year-old son, Walter, died in
1085, the monks buried him and gave his mother the comfort of
membership in their prayer fellowship (CT 2:37, no. 326). The
parents endowed the abbey with a tithe from pannage as well as
cens of four deniers per arpent from vineyards, fields, and woods
to pay for candles to illuminate the altar of the cross.

Patrons from knightly families, like castellans, tended to establish a tradition of support for the abbey. Again, this commitment
was highly localized, since most knightly donations came from
within the two river valleys, with the exception of a sprinkling

of gifts given by families from their lands in the Saintonge. Of all the knightly benefactors, the most notable patrons included members of the family of the provost of Vendôme, together with the lineages of Ingelbald Brito, Joscelin Bodell, Burchard Caresmot, and Odo Rufus.

Ingelbald Brito serves as a good example of the support the abbey realized from this social group. He was a knight in the Vendômois who had probably immigrated from Brittany to further his career as an official serving Geoffrey Martel.[52] He married Hildegarde—who may have been a daughter of Fulcher the Rich—when she was such a young bride that her consent was deemed unnecessary for one of Ingelbald's donations.[53] (See genealogy in Appendix III.) Whatever her parentage, she seems to have been wealthy in her own right, and together they established a notable knightly family in the Vendômois. In 1067 they donated land near Selommes (southeast of Vendôme) to la Trinité, and three years later they acted with three of their sons to give woodland in Anjou to the monastery.[54] They were all received into the monastic prayer fellowship, written into the abbey's martyrology, and their anniversaries were to be celebrated by the monks. Often they were present when the abbey needed support for its affairs and witnesses for its documents. Over the years they continued to make various donations of land and income, the last of which Hildegarde initiated in memory of her husband together with her son, Vulgrin (CT 2:93, no. 354).

The pattern of strong patronage set by Ingelbald and Hildegarde was to be followed by their descendants. Their son, Geoffrey Pagan, and their grandson, Bartholomew, continued the pious tradition of gifts to the abbey.[55] But the charitable sentiments of the lineage's founders finally began to erode in the mid-twelfth century when Adelaide (Ingelbald and Hildegarde's great-granddaughter) and her husband sold property to la Trinité for fifteen pounds in lieu of donating it as their predecessors would have done (CT 2:361, no. 524). Furthermore, although Ingelbald had made only one gift to Marmoutier in recompense for damage he had done the monks, his sons and grandsons showed less particular loyalty to la Trinité, and made substantial donations to Marmoutier.[56] Since the lineage of Ingelbald Brito is well documented, it serves as an example of the impact knightly patronage could have on la Trinité. In the case of Ingelbald's family as well as that of the castellans of Montdoubleau, patterns of patronage were linked to feudal dependencies, such that the patrons' staunch support rested on their early identification with the interests and patronage of their lord, Geoffrey Martel.

The abbey's benefactors received concrete returns from the monks; one of these benefits was the reception of family members into the order as monks *ad succurrendum*. There were other secondary benefits, including hospitality for a patron and even sometimes the promise of help in times of crisis beyond anything customarily owed. Thus, for example, in settling the salt monopoly with Duke Guy Geoffrey of Aquitaine, the monks agreed that if the duke were to be badly pressed by wartime exigencies or other crises, they would support him financially above and beyond any customary dues.[57]

Other benefits granted by la Trinité included spiritual privileges which could be extensive. Hugo and Richilde of Alluyes received the monks' *beneficium* and prayers for themselves and their parents.[58] Specifically, a daily mass was to be said for them, a psalm sung after the Gospel, and their names included in the canon of the mass. Also, the monks would feed a pauper daily in their memory. When each donor died, thirty masses would be said and his or her name included in the martyrology. An additional honor would be the celebration annually of the anniversary with a commemorative feast and a pealing of bells. If Hugo died while still a layman, he was to be buried in the church he had given to la Trinité. In contrast, spiritual benefits for some patrons could be limited to inclusion in the abbey's prayer brotherhood (*beneficium orationum*) or to the right of monastic burial.

Monastic spiritual privileges were considered valuable by lay patrons as aids to salvation, and donors often acknowledged that gifts were made to insure salvation:

> This, however, I do first for the love of our Lord and God, second for the salvation of the souls of my father and mother, third for the safety of my sons. . . .[59]

Although, as Marc Bloch cautioned, "the reasons that a man gives, publicly, for his acts are not always those he obeys in his innermost heart—far from it," still the monks' prayers were commonly regarded as an important aid to salvation and, in this particular case, as a shield for the donor's young sons.[60] Association with a monastery gave the patron a sense of greater spiritual security and, at the same time, increased his or her own sense of importance. The richer and more powerful the monastic foundation, the more glory it reflected on its supporters; medieval men and women "would have thought it a poor reward for their munificence if they had found marks of poverty in the buildings, dress and equipment of the monks."[61]

Some of the more intangible aspects of this mutually profitable relationship between patron and monastery are evident in a donation made to la Trinité in 1124 by Count Fulk the Younger of Anjou and his wife (CT 2:235, no. 449). In return for the gift of a fishing monopoly on the Mayenne River, the abbey was to celebrate the donors' anniversaries as it would those of its own monks with the added benefit of a commemorative feast for the entire chapter paid for out of the fishing fees. Such a return for patrons would have been meaningless if they had not believed in the efficacy of monastic prayers and ceremonies. Fulk and his wife made a second demand on la Trinité in exchange for their gift: the monks were to adorn the tomb of Count Fulk Rechin in l'Evière so that it would outshine the monument to Count Helias of le Mans at Couture. Thus, la Trinité not only helped its patrons along the difficult road to salvation but also enhanced its benefactors' family prestige in this world.

Aside from the bitterness displayed toward la Trinité by the counts of Vendôme, the picture painted here has been one of positive contributions to the abbey by lay supporters. But time and time again after a donation was made to the monastery, trouble developed between the monks and the family or lord of the donor. (See Figures 4A and 4B.) Conflict usually grew out of overlapping claims to property, since a donor's generosity to the monastery diminished his family's estate. If a donor bequeathed the lion's share of his goods to la Trinité, his family could be

Figure 4A. Claims and Litigation against la Trinité.

	1032–1081		1082–1131		1132–1187	
Number of Claims	37		33		47	
Total Documents*	304		162		136	
	Number of Claimants	% of Total Documents†	Number of Claimants	% of Total Documents	Number of Claimants	% of Total Documents
Counts	1	.3	9	6	5	4
Castellans	8	3	12	7	5	4
Knights	14	5	5	3	16	12
Clerics	4	1	6	4	9	7
Unknown	12	4	2	1	10	7

*Total documents: The heading, "Total Documents" represents the charters remaining within each fifty-year interval after discounting all forgeries, duplications, and incomplete texts.

† % of Total documents: As the body of documents available for the first period is almost twice as great as that applicable for the other two intervals, percentages are recorded of specific donors to number of donations in each fifty-year period. This provides a basis for comparison between the three intervals.

Figure 4B. Increases in Litigation.

By Claimant

Counts	3.7%
Castellans	1 %
Knights	9 %
Clerics	6 %

By Period

1032–1081	12%
1082–1131	20%
1132–1187	35%

23% increase overall

Means of Settlement

	1032–1081			1082–1131			1132–1187		
	Number of Settlements	% of Total Documents	% of Total Settlements	Number of Settlements	% of Total Documents	% of Total Settlements	Number of Settlements	% of Total Documents	% of Total Settlements
Court	16	5	43	8	5	24	7	5	15
Compromise	21	7	57	25	15	76	40	29	85

totally disinherited.[62] When a family member felt misused, his or her anger and anxiety could lead to diffuse claims, litigation, and even sometimes armed attempts to regain property. Of the twelve major noble donors to la Trinité from the ranks of knights and castellans, nine harassed the monks with claims or seizures at some time. Only three of these key families managed to avoid any clash with the monastery: those of Odo Rufus, Ingelbald Brito, and Joscelin Bodell—notably all men who came to power first as officials of Geoffrey Martel. Ingelbald Brito and Odo Rufus were not, however, above fighting with monks, for they had their differences with Marmoutier at various times yet maintained an unswerving loyalty to la Trinité.

It is not possible to evaluate the validity of claims against la Trinité, but the increase in litigation in the period under study is noteworthy. From 1032 to 1187 the incidence of claims brought against la Trinité increased by 23 percent.[63] (See Figure 4B.) At the same time that litigation was on the upswing in the Vendômois, the tendency grew for the monks to work out compromise settlements with claimants. Although formal legal settlements remained a feature of the abbey's handling of disputes, they were overshadowed by the use of compromise settlements in the eleventh and twelfth centuries. In 1063, when Nivelon Pagan claimed his father-in-law's gift to the monks of the forest of Varennes, he invaded and seized the woodlands.[64] "After the exchange of a great many superfluous arguments," some meetings occurred, and, through the diplomatic intervention of friends and officials Nivelon was convinced to respect la Trinité's claim. Such negotiated settlements accounted for 57 percent of all settlements in the first fifty-year interval, rising to 76 percent and 86 percent in the last two periods, respectively.

Stephen White has investigated the handling of claims in west-central France during the eleventh century and has found that compromise was generally a more important method of settling disputes than judicial proceedings.[65] He argues that the popularity of the method of compromise lay in its unique ability to reconcile conflicting and often equally valid claims, leading to a stronger bond between litigants after the dispute. This thesis does not work for the most persistent litigants against la Trinité;

on the contrary, disputes often continued despite previously negotiated settlements. For example, the castellans of Fréteval had
claims which overlapped with those of la Trinité to property in
the village of Boisseau. In 1087 a compromise settlement was
reached between Nivelon of Fréteval and la Trinité and sealed
with the gift of seven pounds Dunois to Nivelon (CT 2:46, no.
330). Nevertheless, the former conflict over the priory of Boisseau flared up again in Nivelon's old age, and the castellan was
excommunicated (CT 2:217, no. 439). This time, Nivelon and
his son renounced (guirpire) all rights, and the dispute was finally
laid to rest.

When affairs got badly out of hand, the monks sometimes requested episcopal mediation (CT 2:434, no. 569), and, of course,
a small proportion of claims was settled in court. There is some
evidence to suggest that the monastery preferred informal means
of negotiation because it proved less difficult to achieve a compromise settlement with a noble litigant than to bring him to
court. In the second half of the eleventh century, a conflict with
the count of Vendôme was settled out of court when "wiser
counsel prevailed," and the claim of Lord Bertran of Moncontour was negotiated, since "he feared to lose everything by a
judgment of the court. . . ."[66] Was there, perhaps, the feeling
among nobles that a weak claim was best settled informally if
the claimant was to realize any return? By negotiating in 1092,
Bertran managed to secure one third of the disputed property of
Coulommiers. Once again, however, an informal solution failed
to satisfy the litigant. Bertran's claims were renewed and finally
settled for just under 100 pounds in 1098 when he needed to
finance his journey to Jerusalem.[67]

The longevity of a claim (despite various compromise settlements and gifts to the litigants) could be impressive. A knight
from the Vendômois, Fromund Turpin, sold the church of Villemardy to la Trinité for thirty pounds and a good horse in
1086.[68] Fromund's brothers all received money from the monks
for their consent to the sale, but later one of the brothers, Guy,
claimed that he still retained rights to the church. The monks
paid him three times: six solidi at the time of the sale, four
pounds around 1100, and twelve pounds in 1110 when Guy fi-

nally made peace with the monks because he wanted to go to Jerusalem. At this time, he also endowed la Trinité with Villemardy's tithes, which in their turn then became subject to claims by Guy's sons in the mid-twelfth century. In the same period, William Turpin—another of Fromund's brothers—also brought claims, which he eventually dropped, against the monastery for the land of Taillator. To hold on to the church of Villemardy and its appurtenances was a tedious and expensive process for the abbey. The important point here is that la Trinité finally won in . this controversy, as in almost all contests with lay men and women, for the abbey was a wealthy corporate community that could keep alive and defend its claims beyond the temporal and financial limits possible for most families.

La Trinité had other methods of defending its property besides negotiating settlements and going to court. One popular method of coping with claimants was to resort to feudal controls. For example, the troublemaker's overlord could be encouraged to pressure his follower into submission, as did the counts of Blois, Anjou, and Poitou.[69] On the other hand, it was sometimes useful to convert a troublesome claimant into a fiefholder or protector of the abbey. A nuisance like Guy of Gastineau agreed to give up his claim to a piece of la Trinité's property, accepting instead two *bordaria* to hold in fief from the abbot (CT 2:427, no. 563). A cheaper means of dealing with a claimant when the abbot did not want to invest him with property was to exact a promise of protection from such an opponent, strengthening it by his oath taken on relics.[70]

Gifts were given by the monks to litigants in one third of the cases of claims brought against la Trinité, although the practice was far from assuring the monks that no further claims would develop.[71] In some instances it proved useful to allow the claimant to retain usufruct (four cases), as did Bertran of Moncontour. More commonly, la Trinité gave money (twenty-six cases), spiritual privileges (ten cases), or a horse (four cases) to settle the dispute. Once only did la Trinité actually give away capital property in a settlement when Geoffrey of Vendôme did so for the benefit of his cousin, the lord of Château-Gontier (CT 2:182, no. 417). A characteristic payment to settle claims was one made to

the castellan of Lavardin. He had complained that the monks had
failed to solicit his consent for a millsite sold them by his son;
that they had unlawfully taken some of his land and his bees
from the woods; and that his property had sustained water damage from the abbey's moats. "For all these claims and complaints
he accepted forty solidi from us with membership in the prayer
brotherhood of our congregation. . . ."[72]

The fourth method by which the monks might manage difficult claimants was by wielding the weapon of spiritual sanctions.
Excommunication and interdict were sometimes used as threats
to force a settlement.[73] At other times sanctions were actually
enforced, as in 1105 when the lord of Craon was coerced into re-
storing property to la Trinité after enduring the disruption of
interdict on his lands (CT 2:175, no. 412). Once he had sworn to
return what belonged to the abbey, he was absolved by his
bishop.

Beyond judicial procedures, feudal controls, various types of
gifts, and formal ecclesiastical bans lay the diffuse and potent
spiritual power that carried the greatest weight of all the tactics
available to the monks in the eleventh and twelfth centuries. Because monastic prayers were considered as highly effective to attain salvation, when death approached or sudden disaster occurred, litigants tended to drop their disputes and seek the benefit
and comfort of the abbey's spiritual privileges. Terminal illness
drove Rothon of Lavardin to give up his claim to the church of
Villévêque, and anxiety about a forthcoming battle induced the
knight Maurice to confirm the abbey in its holdings in Pezou.[74]
Both men feared the long journey ahead of them and wanted
monastic prayers to help them on the way. The shock of sudden
death in a family (especially that of a child) was a powerful in-
ducement for a litigant to drop a dispute. When in the mid-
twelfth century Juliana of Pray's little daughter died unexpect-
edly, she feared it was a divine judgment on her for the bitter
controversy she had carried on with the monks and for which
she had been excommunicated.[75] She came weeping bitterly to
the chapter house accompanied by her son and there gave up all
her claims. For Juliana, excommunication had been an ineffectual
punishment, but the anguish she felt for her daughter's immortal

soul was a potent stimulus to be reconciled with the spiritual power she feared and respected—the monks of la Trinité.

In conclusion, the intricate intimacy between la Trinité and its lay patrons continued to evolve for the great lords but stayed relatively constant between the abbey and its lesser supporters. The comital family of Anjou increasingly divested itself of the founders' close involvement with the monks to become by the late twelfth century impersonal peacemakers and judges. Whatever the Angevins did in the period—including the violent attacks perpetrated by Fulk Rechin—was viewed tolerantly by the monks, who prudently refused to find fault with their prime patrons. Somewhat the same decrease in feelings (although of negative emotions in this case) was experienced by the counts of Vendôme, whose personal and immediate hostility subsided during the mid-twelfth century when they followed their Angevin overlords onto a larger political stage. The counts of Vendôme, however, never ceased to view la Trinité as a foreign body unfairly feeding on usurped family property, and when la Trinité was ruled by an aggressive abbot with extreme claims—like Geoffrey of Vendôme—conflict was inevitable.

Knightly families and castellans in the area supported the monastery by exchanging property for spiritual reassurance. During the course of a century and a half, a shift took place so that donations became smaller and more often took the form of *cens* instead of land, while litigation became more common. Interchanges tended to remain personal, although they often became strident when donors or their relatives contested property rights with the monks. The great irony was that attacks and claims on the abbey were seldom random violence or usurpations perpetrated by total strangers; most of the people who made trouble for la Trinité were its own patrons or their relatives who regretted previous familial generosity. Nevertheless, la Trinité gained more from its lay patrons than it lost to their claims because payments to litigants were made from income, rather than capital property, and the monastery's institutional continuity allowed it to outlast and usually overcome individuals in disputes over property.

A geographic unity that cut across feudal frontiers and loyalties existed among monastic supporters. Men and women who lived in the abbey's sphere of influence along the two rivers might turn to la Trinité for spiritual strength regardless of whether they were within the orbit of power of Vendôme, Blois, Tours, Anjou, or Beaugency. There was also a social uniformity evident by the late twelfth century, since the abbey's patrons came to be drawn almost entirely from the area's knightly families. La Trinité's strength was also its potential weakness; patronage for the abbey had shrunk to a narrow base, tying the monastery to the economic well-being of one group in a limited geographic area. La Trinité had lost the early general support evident in the enthusiasm of the eleventh-century endowments from peasants as well as lords. But this is just half of the picture of la Trinité's external relationships, since the abbey interacted not only with lay people but also with ecclesiastics. La Trinité's contacts with religious bodies and individuals was a second facet of the abbey's involvement with the world outside the cloister and often proved to be intermeshed with its secular interchanges.

Notes

1. Christopher Brooke, *The Monastic World* (New York, 1974), p. 95.

2. CT 1:126, no. 68. "Intelligens comes fraudulentiam viri et suspitiosam habens perfidiam, rursus compulsus est dare ei comcambium pro ipsa terra, de quo inveniendo cum esset anxius, necessitate urgente, statuit ei dare illud de examplis, que antea donaverat Sancte-Trinitati, in terra foreste Guastine, pro quibus etiam acceperat ab uxore sua comitissa A. tria milia solidorum."

3. CT 1:202, no. 109. "Si boves illorum ad opus Gaufredi comitis fuerint deprehensi, et homines nostri eos rapuerint, non respondebimus illis. Si homines illorum contra nos venerint, et eos ceperint, nichil ad nos pertinebit."

4. CT 1:265–67, no. 153. Guillot, *Le Comte d'Anjou,* 2:135–36, lists this charter among authentic documents while mentioning his suspicions of such a sweeping right of preemption, dating it only between July 20, 1031, and November 14, 1060. The charter names Geoffrey "Count of Vendôme," a title he ceased to use after 1056. Since the war with Thibald took place in 1043–44, this document may be dated more closely to between 1043 and 1056, at the very latest.

5. Ibid., 1:63, describes the conflict as lasting at least a year. Geoffrey's new interest in Marmoutier is evident in CM p. 104, no. 65, and p. 183, no. 117.

6. CT 1:193, no. 106, "defensor et adjutor. . . ."

7. CT 1:20, no. 7, "quod sine calumnia tenuit donec ipse vixit. Postquam vero obiit, quicumque voluit et potuit calumniatus est monachis, et invasit. . . ." For other examples of seizures of la Trinité's property effected after Geoffrey's death, see CT 1:249, no. 143; 1:297, no. 170; 1:346, no. 216; 1:419, no. 268.

8. CS p. 41, no. 14; p. 44, no. 16; p. 53, no. 25; p. 55, no. 28. Guy Geoffrey's patron-

age is evident in CS p. 56, no. 29, and p. 58, no. 33; and William's is recorded in p. 65, nos. 36–37, and p. 93, no. 55. Geoffrey of Vendôme wrote William asking his help, *Ep.* 5:19 (PL 157:201–2).

9. Searle, *Battle Abbey,* p. 91.

10. Hunt, *Cluny under St. Hugh,* p. 25, and Gaussin, *La Chaise-Dieu,* p. 89.

11. Guillot, *Le Comte d'Anjou,* 1:109.

12. David Douglas, *William the Conqueror* (Berkeley, 1967), p. 228.

13. CT 1:387, no. 245, "is qui justitiam illis acquirere debebat, raptoribus consentiret. . . ." Patrick Geary mentions this as traditional monastic practice with a saint's relics when monks needed an effective symbolic weapon to use against a wrongdoer: *Furta Sacra: Thefts of Relics in the Central Middle Ages* (Princeton, 1978), p. 23. La Trinité chose this action, "non quidem dedecoris, sive opprobrii causa adversus Dominicum signum, sed ut tali facto malefactores deterriti ab ecclesiae injusta invasione et rerum ablatione cessarent."

14. CT 2:190–91, no. 422, was Fulk's gift of customs to the abbey just before his death. See "Annales de Vendôme," p. 69, for his burial.

15. Fulk Rechin's successor should have been his oldest son, Geoffrey Martel IV, but Geoffrey died in 1106 before his father. The year before his death, Geoffrey supported la Trinité's claim that Maurice, lord of Craon, was unjustly holding its goods. The case was heard by Fulk Rechin, and the court decided for la Trinité. CT 2:171–76, no. 412. For charters of donations and confirmations issued by Fulk the Younger see CT 2:193–94, no. 424; 2:197–200, no. 427; 2:208–9, no. 434; 2:235–37, no. 449. Geoffrey of Vendôme saw Count Fulk as a potential protector: *Ep.* 1:8 (PL 157:46–48) and 1:27 (PL 157:67–68). In 1119 Fulk helped the abbey to regain property 1:26 (PL 157:66–67).

16. CT 2:318–19, no. 499; 2:342–45, no. 514; 2:349–51, no. 517, are Geoffrey le Bel's charters for la Trinité. *Gîte* was the right to hospitality and lodging.

17. *Recueil des actes de Henri II,* ed. Léopold Delisle, 3 vols. (Paris, 1920), 2:171–72.

18. CT 2:440, no. 573, "dominus rex Anglorum doleret illum tandiu excommunicationi subjacere, regiam adjecit manum, eumdem compellens . . . a sententia excommunicationis, qua tenebatur, faceret absolvi."

19. See Louis' charters, CS nos. 58 and 60, pp. 96–102, and Eleanor's charter no. 59, pp. 98–100.

20. For Eleanor's activities vis-à-vis la Trinité after her Angevin marriage, see CS p. 103, no. 62. Procuration (*procuratio*) was a right to collect a compulsory food levy from an area's inhabitants. Blois B.D. MS 21 H 163, no. 4 (edited, CS p. 115, no. 70); p. 105, no. 65; p. 117, no. 72; p. 118, no. 73.

21. Gaussin, *La Chaise-Dieu,* p. 170.

22. CT 2:318, no. 499, "hujus ecclesiae defensore post Deum. . . ."

23. W. L. Warren, *Henry II* (London, 1973), p. 629. Henry II "overcame the old disintegrating force of baronial separation, and resisted the newer ones of municipal independence and clerical exclusiveness, not in order to destroy—for Henry II was fundamentally conservative—but in order to bring all into balance under royal control."

24. CM p. 188, no. 117; p. 195, no. 118; p. 197–99, no. 119; also see Guillot, *Le Comte d'Anjou,* 1:93.

25. It is patently unlikely that Geoffrey drafted CT 1:171–75, no. 95, in 1050. This is a forgery (see Appendix I). It was, however, suggested to the forger by the real circumstances of Fulk's oath given at Geoffrey's insistence and reported in CT 1:305, no. 175. Something of Fulk's difficult personality may be adduced from his nickname, "Anserulus" (2:29, no. 321). It could derive from *anser, anseris,* a gander, or from the obscene poet, Anser, who was a friend of Mark Antony. Neither seems complimentary.

26. CT 1:193, no. 106. Meinert asserts that this is a genuine diploma. "Die Fälschungen," p. 324.

27. CT 1:305, no. 175. This was done "sub attestatione sanctorum omnium. . . ."

28. The tale of Fulk's depredations is contained in CT 1:302, no. 173, and his attack is

described: "comes hominem suum minis pluribus et conviciis gravibus valde insectaretur, quod monacho res ad modicum contradicenti, statim in viscera cultellum immerserit." Also see CT 1:303, no. 174, and 1:306, no. 175, when Fulk reforms "tandem timore Domini cumpunctus. . . ."

29. Guy of Nevers is recorded as having held one court apparently without any challenge from the abbey: CT 1:324–25, no. 188, which suggests amicable working relations. As she was dying, Petronilla bequeathed three arpents of vines to the abbey. This extremely modest gift might be evidence that she owned little in her own right from which to endow the monks, or perhaps it was an indication of the lack of warmth she felt for la Trinité, CT 1:421, no. 270.

30. CT 2:52–54, no. 334, and Blois B.D. MS 21 H 69, no. 3 (edited CT 2:63–66, no. 340), records the count's efforts to win his freedom, "nec non pro sui corporis liberatione. . . ."

31. CT 2:98–100, no. 356. Also see CT 2:94–97, no. 355, which is Bishop Ivo's charter of the settlement of the episode.

32. Also Geoffrey of Vendôme, Ep. 2:3 (PL 157:72–73), and Ivo of Chartres, Ep. 82 (PL 162:103–4).

33. The "Annales de Vendôme," p. 68, recount Geoffrey's penance. Pierre Petot discusses the servile symbolism of the count's submission: "Sur une charte-notice Vendômoise," Mélanges Halphen (Paris, 1951), p. 586.

34. Geoffrey of Vendôme, Ep. 3:15 (PL 157:121–22); 3:16 (PL 157:122–24); 1:3 (PL 157:37–38); 3:19 (PL 157:125–26); 3:21 (PL 157: 126), contains Geoffrey's famous warning: "Usitatus est valde ad decipiendum sexus femineus." Ep. 4:24 (PL 157:167–68) also provides evidence of his extreme misogyny.

35. CT 2:188, no. 420, "in curia ista Sancte-Trinitatis, sicut antea Goffridus comes, qui hanc ecclesiam a novo fundavit, firmiter instituerat. . . ."

36. Geoffrey of Vendôme, Ep. 2:16 (PL 157:83–85). In this case, I believe Wilmart's dating (c. 1110) is too late. This should be dated 1108, the year of charter no. 420, which recounts the same incident.

37. CT 1:289, no. 164, "non in curia comitis, nec in qualibet curia saeculari judicium fiat, sed in curia abbatis, pro dignitate loci. . . ."

38. CT 2:189–90, no. 421. "Goffridus Grisagonella, comes Vindocinensis, venit in capitulum Vindocinensis monasterii, cum plerisque baronum suorum, quando se de comite Theobaldo redemit, . . . et cum abbas Goffridus vidisset ejus humilitatem . . . [ellipsis in text] et inde societatem sumpsit."

39. CT 2:207, no. 433. Matilda incurred the wrath of Geoffrey of Vendôme in her efforts to recover the bark: Ep. 2:21 (PL 157:88–89).

40. CT 2:237–38, no. 450, reports that John claimed assarts in the Gâtines; 2:251–53, no. 463, deals with Geoffrey's attempts to obtain the woods near Villedieu. CT 2:318–19, no. 499, recounts John's claim of gîte settled in 1144 just before his father's death.

41. Geoffrey of Vendôme, Ep. 2:32 (PL 157:104–6), "monachorum claustra carcerem fecerunt captivorum."

42. CT 2:463, no. 592, deals with cens from a mill and from vines, and 2:345–47, no. 515, is the gift of half the crop of Villiers, both from Richilde. CT 2:347–49, no. 516, cites a donation by John located in the Gâtines and is confirmed by Geoffrey le Bel 2:349–51, no. 517.

43. John's loyalty to Henry was not always emulated, however, by his son Burchard. See Warren, Henry II, p. 132.

44. For example, Garnier mentions John's presence in England in 1163 and that he was known and respected by Thomas Becket. London British Library MS Harley 270, fol. 18v.

45. CT 2:439–40, no. 573. "Annales de Vendôme," p. 73, record for 1177, "in hoc anno exulavit conventus Vindocinensis Andegavi toto anno et mensibus II a facie furoris Johannis."

46. CT 1:260–61, no. 148, was the gift of meadow on June 10, 1061, followed on July 3 by the gift of a warhorse made by a brother in the name of his dying comatose sibling, 1:261–62, no. 149. CT 1:163, no. 91, was the gift of a house in la Chartre by the priest, Garnier; 1:300, no. 172, was a donation from the abbot of Maillezais.

47. CT 1:98–100, nos. 45–46; 1:395, no. 250; 1:44, no. 23; 2:38, no. 326.

48. CT 2:36, no. 325. The Nivelon in this charter is Nivelon Pagan, not (as is mistakenly indicated in Métais' summary) Nivelon of Fréteval.

49. Placentia was first married to Odo Dublell (see Appendix III), referred to as "f." (filius, mistakenly instead of gener, son-in-law) of Placentia's father, Nihard of Montoire (CT 1:363, no. 230) and later to Alberic (1:269, no. 155, and 1:230, no. 128). Adele was first married to Hugo Dublell, (CM p. 96, no. 59) and then to Roger of Turre (CM p. 50, no 31). After Hugo Dublell died (CT 1:396, no. 250), the honor of Montdoubleau first passed into the hands of his sister Helvisa and her husband, Hamelin of Langeais; then instead of going to Helvisa and Hamelin's children, it reverted to the son of Hugo's other sister, Fredescinde, and her husband, Nivelon Pagan, CT 2:36–37, no. 325.

50. Adele made a gift of her extensive alods in Bezay to Marmoutier (CM p. 96, no. 59), probably c. 1050, since she was married to Hugo Dublell before Roger of Turre. CM p. 99, no. 61, repeats the same information but mentions Adele's children by her second marriage. This charter must have been drafted c. 1070—after Adele's death—to solidify Marmoutier's claim to the property in Bezay. At the same time or soon after Adele's gift c. 1050 (cited in no. 59), her first husband, Hugo Dublell, also gave property in Bezay to Marmoutier, probably at his wife's instigation, CM p. 100, no. 62.

51. CT 1:319, no. 184. The sister of another monk also named Odo became a major patron of la Trinité in 1079, CT 1:438–39, no. 282.

52. Chédeville, Chartres, p. 101, refers to the presence of Breton emigrants usually bearing the name Brito. CT 1:20, no. 7, mentions Ingelbald as a forester of Geoffrey Martel.

53. Hildegarde was sometimes called Domitilla (CT 1:353, no. 219), which from the evidence of another woman—"Ennoguena, cognomine Domitilla"—seems to have been a nickname: see CT 1:416–17, no. 266. Even if Hildegarde belonged to the lineage of Fulcher the Rich, which supported Marmoutier, her marriage occurred when she was so young that she came fully to adopt her husband's interests.

54. CT 1:320, no. 185, and Blois B.D. MS 21 H 40, no. 1 (edited CT 1:351–52, no. 218). There is no telling which Ingelbalds and Hildegardes in the martyrology are which. (There are eleven Ingelbalds and eight Hildegardes.) However, the death of their son Geoffrey Pagan is commemorated on January 18. Vendôme B.M. MS 161, fol. 146r.

55. CT 2:360, no. 524; 2:315, no. 494; 2:410, no. 555.

56. CM p. 222, no. 129; p. 375, no. 61A: p. 382, no. 66A. Ingelbald's descendants may well have married women whose families supported Marmoutier.

57. CS p. 61, no. 34, and p. 52, no. 23, "ut si quando sese aut belli impetus urgeret, aut grandis alicujus necessitatis eventus compelleret . . . quid sibi fieri vel largiri de rebus monasterii vellet, modesta postulatione suggeret."

58. CT 1:383–84, no. 242. This nonfeudal use of beneficium, especially in a region well advanced in the establishment of dependent military relationships, is of particular interest.

59. CT 2:348, no. 516. "Hoc autem facio primo pro Dei et Domini nostri dilectione, secundo pro salute anime patris mei et matris mee, tercio pro filiorum meorum incolumitate. . . ."

60. Marc Bloch, Mélanges historiques (Paris, 1963), 1:272, tr. as Slavery and Serfdom, Selected Essays (Berkeley, 1975).

61. Southern, The Making of the Middle Ages, p. 161.

62. CT 1:294, no. 168, "coeperunt flentes conqueri uxor ejus et filii, dicentes se exhereditatos esse. . . ."

63. There were 37 claims (out of 304 total documents), or 12 percent between 1032 and 1081; 33 claims (out of 162), or 20 percent between 1082 and 1131; and 47 claims

(out of 136), or 35 percent between 1132 and 1187. The differential is an increase of 23 percent.

64. CT 1:293, no. 166, "post multa verba recitandi modo superflua. . . ."

65. Stephen White, "Pactum . . . Legem Vincit et Amor Judicium": The Settlement of Disputes by Compromise in Eleventh-Century Western France," American Journal of Legal History 22 (1978), 281–308.

66. CT 2:29, no. 321, "terminum placito posuit. Sed concilio meliore postea accepto, mandavit abbati et monachis se omnino de ea re cum eis non placiturum"; and Blois B.D. MS 21 H 69, no. 3 (edited CT 2:64, no. 340), "timens judicio curiae totum perdere. . . ."

67. Blois B.D. MS 21 H 69, no. 4 (edited, CT 2:105–7, no. 361). The monks paid ninety pounds to Bertran, five each to his wife and eldest son, and one solidus each to his two other sons.

68. For the litigation over the church of Villemardy and its appurtenances, see CT 2:40, no. 327; 2:196, no. 426, and 2:141, no. 390; 2:404–5, no. 552; 2:231, no. 446. The land of Taillator can not be located now but would probably have belonged to the ecclesiastical property of Villemardy.

69. CT 2:311, no. 491, and 1:387–90, no. 245; CS p. 56, no. 29.

70. CT 2:300, no. 485. "Robertus et Radulphus . . . sed pro posse suo contra omnes homines illam nobis expugnaturos." Also see 2:503, no. 624. This method was indeed popular and was used to reinforce la Trinité's purchases, CS p. 109, no. 66, and donations received, CT 2:403–5, nos. 550–52.

71. White, "Pactum . . . Legem," p. 296, states that informal settlements "always left both parties with something." This was not the case for la Trinité's compromises, for the acceptance of a settlement was not automatically assured after a litigant accepted a gift.

72. CT 1:185, no. 100. "Pro his omnibus calumniis et clamoribus quadraginta solidos a nobis accepit cum societate beneficii nostrae congregationis. . . ."

73. CT 2:255, no. 465, and Geoffrey of Vendôme, Ep. 5:25 (PL 157:207–8), deal with threatened sanctions.

74. CT 1:419, no. 268, and 1:445, no. 290. Maurice received membership in the abbey's societas for his confirmation. For other examples of submissions induced by illness, see CT 2:207, no. 433; 2:312, no. 492; 2:365, no. 526.

75. CT 2:376, no. 532. "Cujus mortem Juliana, non mediocriter admirans, illam esse mortuam potius ultione divina quam infirmitate corporea omnino credidit, atque gemens et flebilis, cum Petro filio suo et pluribus secum comitantibus, in capitulum Sancte-Trinitatis de Vindocino venit. . . ." Also see CT 2:396, no. 546.

CHAPTER FOUR

Relations with Other Ecclesiastics

THE ABBEY of la Trinité functioned within an environment that supported two different populations: the laity and those in religious orders. As in the case of la Trinité's relationships with lay men and women, its ties to other ecclesiastics were a mixture of both amicable and hostile interchanges, and the abbey both influenced and was influenced by other religious. Relations with clerics involved the abbey with individuals and corporate bodies, in matters relating to property as well as spiritual privileges, locally and far afield. An examination of la Trinité's interdependencies with other monks, the papacy, and area bishops will help to fill in the broad picture of the abbey's world.

Monasticae fraternitatis infestatio: Relationships with Other Monasteries

La Trinité's relations with other monasteries often tended to be antagonistic. Historians have found this to be the general case for interactions between medieval abbeys, and the recognition of the resultant litigiousness has proved an embarrassment to some scholars. If, however, we accept the widespread substitution of legal processes instead of the sword to defend and acquire property in the central Middle Ages, then the monasteries can be seen as part of an evolutionary process that involved all of society. In their clashes with other houses, the monks of la Trinité reflected the general syndrome of monastic rivalry that was fostered (often unknowingly) by lay patrons, supporting local abbeys as an ad-

junct to their own power so that often secular jealousies contributed to a competitive monastic climate.

Nevertheless, la Trinité could have a good working relationship with another house, as it did generally with the body of
religious nearest to it, the canons of Saint-Georges, who were
situated only a stone's throw away within the walls of the castle
of Vendôme. Countess Agnes had instituted these canons to
serve as daily celebrants for her family.[1] By and large, the interplay between canons and monks remained pleasant, involving at
different times a canon's gift of land to la Trinité, a compromise
over conflicting claims to a forest, and a canon's profession *ad
succurrendum* to the abbey.[2] The canons existed as a small and
humble community; they came into conflict with the monks only
when they lost the common bond of having the same patrons,
the counts of Anjou. After Fulk Oison's reinstatement in Vendôme, the canons became clients of the house of Vendôme. This
meant that canons and monks then adhered to rival camps—the
ramifications of which became apparent in 1108 at the time of
the crisis involving Count Geoffrey Grisegonelle and Abbot
Geoffrey of Vendôme. After the county had been laid under interdict at the abbot's behest to punish the count for his invasion
of the conventual buildings, the abbot angrily informed Bishop
Ivo of Chartres that the canons of Saint-Georges were defiantly
celebrating mass with the church doors open, "against your interdict. . . ."[3] Only such a cataclysmic local clash, however,
could embolden the canons to oppose their powerful monastic
neighbors in support of their count's position. For the most part,
the monks and canons coexisted peacefully.

Within the Vendômois proper there was only one other ecclesiastical foundation, also of canons, Saint-Georges du Bois, situated west of Lavardin. This foundation had two disputes with la
Trinité over contested property (CT 2:249, no. 460; 2:335, no.
512). The resolution of the second conflict is revealing of the part
secular supporters could play in monastic interchanges for this
disagreement was finally adjusted due to the efforts of the bishop
of Chartres and Lady Bertha of Lisle. To persuade the monks of
la Trinité to give up the parish fee of Lisle, Bertha endowed them
with land on which to build their own church and cemetery

where they could support a priest, an hereditary tenant farmer, and one monk. It required the pressure and the resources of a strong patron to bring harmony to the two houses.

But la Trinité also had relationships with religious foundations beyond the Vendômois. The abbey maintained communications with monasteries spread across a wide geographic area. Sometimes formal spiritual bonds existed between two abbots, like the *societas* and *confraternitas* shared by Abbot Geoffrey of Vendôme and Abbot Hugh of Cluny, or the *beneficium* shared equally by all the monks of la Trinité and the nuns of Fontevrault (CT 2:179, no. 416; 2:201, no. 428). The latter—initiated by Geoffrey of Vendôme and Robert Arbrissel—was not, however, proof against a later, acrimonious dispute between the two houses over fields near Villemardy (CT 2:432, no. 567). La Trinité also established spiritual bonds with the canons of the cathedral of Saint-Maurice in Angers (CT 1:276, no. 159). This pact was signed in 1062 and witnessed by Count Geoffrey Barbu, and also (surprisingly) by Countess Agnes, who made the journey to Angers in support of la Trinité, despite the meeting's location in the capital and stronghold of her late, estranged husband, Geoffrey Martel. The tie between la Trinité and the Angevin cathedral made it natural for the canons to request in 1101 that Abbot Geoffrey of Vendôme lend his "advice and help" in the election of a new bishop (CT 2:157, no. 401). The contested election that followed led to one of Geoffrey's most notorious battles, which will be reviewed later in the chapter.

Monasteries kept in touch across the face of Europe by means of messengers who traveled between religious houses carrying *rotuli mortuorum* (parchment rolls commemorating the death of an important religious). The monks of la Trinité learned of the deaths of men like Bertrand of Baux and Vital of Savigny when such messengers came to la Trinité, at which time one of their monks added suitable sentiments to the parchment before the messenger departed for the next religious house. Vital was commemorated by a monk of la Trinité, who recorded the pedestrian sentiment: "may his soul and the souls of all the faithful departed rest in peace," and when a messenger came to Vendôme with the *rotulus* for Bertrand, the abbey spokesman added the common supplication that all who read the roll should pray for the founders and abbots of la Trinité.[4]

The many undignified quarrels carried on by la Trinité with other monastic communities overshadowed its more high-minded relationships; disputes even occurred between members of the same religious family—in the case of la Trinité, with other Benedictine abbeys.[5] One certain trigger of controversy was the acceptance by a monastic foundation of a fugitive from another house, thus helping the runaway to break his vow of *stabilitas* and thereby undermining his abbot's authority. Two mitigating factors were seen to exist for *transitus:* a monk could usually transfer to another house if it enjoyed a general confraternity with his own house, and the vow of stability did not interfere with a move up the spiritual ladder to a more austere house, which during the eleventh century often meant Cluny.[6] However, when in 1111 a monk of la Trinité, Peter Joscelin, fled la Trinité for Cluny, neither the limited, personal confraternity of the two houses' abbots nor the old view of Cluny as a universal spiritual harbor of refuge kept Geoffrey of Vendôme from writing to Abbot Pons of Cluny that if the Cluniacs knew Peter to be a fugitive, they were acting as robbers rather than as spiritual shepherds in taking him in.[7] Geoffrey argued that monastic profession could neither be repeated nor broken, for St. Benedict, like St. Peter, bound a man with indissoluble force. If Cluny continued to harbor Peter, warned Geoffrey, the friendship established with Abbot Hugh would be destroyed.

Arguments over jurisdiction, like those over personnel, were sure to ruffle monastic sensibilities; ironically, the well-meaning actions of lay patrons often initiated the monks' hostilities. At the very end of the eleventh century, Lord Geoffrey Mayenne donated the three churches of la Chartre to the monks of la Trinité (CT 2:146, no. 395). La Chartre belonged to the parish of Marçon (CT 2:320, no. 500), which was under the lawful control of the monks of Saint-Julian of Tours—a situation probably unknown or unimportant to Geoffrey. The conflicting jurisdictions led to hostilities that eventually were adjudicated by Count Geoffrey le Bel. His settlement did not endure, and Henry II finally resolved the problem by granting la Trinité possession of the three churches, while forcing the two abbots to be reconciled and to swear mutual peace.[8]

Lack of enthusiasm to fulfill the monastic duty of hospitality counts as a third common cause of monastic conflicts. The considerable expense incurred in offering monastic hospitality and the subsequent establishment of costly precedents may have contributed to this reluctance. Two twelfth-century cases of this origin involved Abbot Geoffrey of Vendôme who was denied travelers' accommodations in priories. The first of these incidents is related in detail. Geoffrey was traveling to Saintes when he was caught in a fearful storm; he sought shelter at the priory of Pin, a cell of Saint-Florent, Saumur.[9] The cellarer, who was in charge in the prior's absence, was inexcusably rude, "showing no reverence for Geoffrey's station" and arguing that he barely had room for a dozen of Geoffrey's horses. The party from Vendôme eventually gained entrance, but the cellarer haughtily refused to eat with the travelers to whom he offered bread and wine (although he knew they carried such fare) but not forage for the animals (which the travelers lacked). The affair occasioned one of Geoffrey's blistering letters demanding of the abbot of Saint-Florent that the cellarer be punished.

In the second incident, the obedientiary of a cell of Saint-Aubin in Poitou actually went so far as to refuse hospitality to Geoffrey and his companions, driving the abbot into a fury and occasioning two acerbic letters to the abbot of Saint-Aubin.[10] Hostile behavior of this sort was hardly in keeping with Benedict's command to "let all guests that come be received like Christ" (RB: 53). Such interchanges seem to be evidence of a deep-seated competitive spirit among monasteries, and were extremely disrupting antisocial behavior. The fracas over hospitality in Poitou may have prompted Geoffrey to reopen an old quarrel with Saint-Aubin over the tenure of Saint-Clément of Craon. This affair is typical of the conflicts that were carried on by la Trinité with other religious houses and is particularly well documented; it serves to illuminate some facets of la Trinité's activities outside the cloister.

In the first half of the eleventh century, an Angevin kight, Suhard Vetul, gave the parish church of Saint-Clément in Craon to

Saint-Aubin. He stipulated that the church be enlarged and refurbished, which was done.[11] La Trinité would later argue that there had been a second requirement—"that an abbot be established in the church of Saint-Clément as soon as possible"—on which the monks of Saint-Aubin reneged. After Suhard's death, his two sons successively held the honor of Craon. When Suhard (the second son and father's namesake) died, Geoffrey Martel, acting as overlord according to la Trinité's version, declared the honor forfeit to him, since Suhard had treacherously supported the count of Brittany against his true Angevin overlord. Then in 1053, Geoffrey donated Saint-Clément to la Trinité, "driven by Countess Agnes," in the waspish words of the Saint-Aubin scribe.[12] Geoffrey's donation set the stage for lengthy, acrimonious and often transmontane litigation.

Saint-Aubin's appeal to Count Geoffrey in 1055 began the first round of the long battle (CT 1:231, no. 130; 1:374, no. 237). Geoffrey, with the bishop and other of his lords, heard the case and confirmed la Trinité's right to the church. This decision temporarily stopped the legal activities of the Angevin monks. They were renewed, however, after Count Geoffrey's death deprived la Trinité of his protective presence. The monks took their case to the new count, Geoffrey Barbu, but their plea was short-circuited in 1060/1 by Abbot Oderic of la Trinité, who claimed that only the pope had the right to adjudicate cases involving the monks of la Trinité (CT 1:250, no. 144). Both parties then set off for Rome where Pope Nicholas arranged a tribunal of seven bishops to judge the case. Oderic presented the documents affirming Geoffrey Martel's gift and the bishop of Angers' confirmation and with these documents convinced the court of the justice of his claim. A few years later in 1070, Abbot Oderic sought a confirmation of la Trinité's right to Saint-Clément from the new lord of Craon and his wife (CT 1:349, no. 217). The monks of la Trinité were willing to pay the large sum of fifty-seven pounds for the confirmation—an indication of their estimation of Saint-Clément's value.

Despite a local comital decision, episcopal confirmation, papal court verdict, and immediate overlord's confirmation of la Trinité's right to the church, the monks of Saint-Aubin still doggedly continued to appeal the case, turning in 1072 to the papal legate.[13] Both parties of monks trailed after the legate from Tours to Chartres to Paris—to no avail. The Angevin monks felt slighted at every turn and publicly shamed in Paris. They must, indeed, have been importunate, for the legate threw one of their number out of his house with his own hands. Both sides finally recognized the futility of pursuing the legate and repaired to Chartres where Bishop Arrald, a former monk of la Trinité, was prepared to hear their conflicting claims. Arrald arranged a *concordia* in which he tried to satisfy both sides: la Trinité retained the church but paid Saint-Aubin two hundred pounds in settlement of all Angevin claims. Each side had to obtain the agreement of its chapter, which, complained the Angevin monks, was accomplished at Saint-Aubin by waiting until an occasion when only a few young monks were present to be bullied into consenting to the compromise. Despite Arrald's help, the monks of la Trinité must have felt they needed more ammunition, since a forgery of a papal privilege to la Trinité appeared in the early 1070s, giving the abbey the right to excommunicate its enemies if the bishop of Chartres should fail to see justice done (CT 1:378, no. 238-JL 4699).

By this time the battle had dragged on for twenty years without either side losing interest, Saint-Aubin again launched an appeal to the new papal legate, and the case was set to be heard in Bordeaux (CT 1:376, no. 237). La Trinité presented the findings of the previous papal court, which the legate accepted contingent on a careful scrutiny. A decade later, the Angevin monks went to Rome once again to press their claim and managed to prevail on Pope Urban II to order his legate to reopen the case (CT 2:78, no. 345). Both sides sent delegations to Bordeaux, but the abbot of Saint-Aubin was refused passage across Poitou by the provost of the count of Poitou. The count of Poitou had been involved in extensive, open hostilities with Count Fulk Rechin of Anjou, and the monastic litigation presented an opportunity for him to harass Angevin monks and thereby irritate their overlord.[14] The provost of Poitou who turned back the abbot further humiliated the monks by searching their sleeves (apparently, handy hiding places for money). Arguments were to no avail, and an envoy sent to the count of Poitou brought back the clear message that the count did not want the Angevin monks to reach the court and perhaps wrest Saint-Clément from his client, la Trinité. Eventually four Angevin monks (but not their abbot) were allowed through to Bordeaux. At the hearing, the monks of la Trinité produced another forgery. Despite its denunciation as spurious by a servant of the Angevin monks, the court found in la Trinité's favor.

Once again the indefatigable Angevin religious set off to appeal to the pope and found Urban II in Calabria.[15] The case was presented yet again, and Urban, like Bishop Arrald before him, worked to establish a compromise: la Trinité was to keep Saint-Clément but, in return, to offer Saint-Aubin the choice of one of its three churches in Anjou; the Angevin monks acquiesced and chose Saint-Jean-sur-Loire. The tired issue was to be raised yet one more time when Abbot Geoffrey of Vendôme tried to retrieve this church.[16] Geoffrey may well have reopened the case because of his irritation at the inhospitable treatment he had been accorded by one of Saint-Aubin's cells.

The litigation over Saint-Clément lasted sixty-two years, and its cost to both sides must have been staggering. There were three trips to Italy, two to Bordeaux, one to Paris, and a great deal of local traveling, all costly in terms of time and resources. Money was expended on bribes, largesse, and a whole gamut of expenses incurred by travel. In addition to the unspecified sums, la Trinité spent 257 pounds and gave away a church property. Only wealthy, self-sustaining communities could have borne the burden of such protracted litigation. In disputes with laymen, la Trinité could usually outlast its opponents, but when two monasteries differed over a claim, an endurance trial of mammoth proportions could ensue.

In ecclesiastical litigation as in lay suits, compromise was no more guaranteed to succeed than were formal juridical procedures. Even when the monks of la Trinité made an appeal to Bishop Arrald, support was not considered thoroughly assured despite his status as a former confrere; as insurance the monks produced a forgery giving them powers to excommunicate enemies. When each side had a stubborn sense of the justice of its

own claim, only the passage of many years and major concessions on both sides could finally end monastic contentiousness.
Although each of the two abbeys turned to the ecclesiastical hierarchy for support, their lay patrons played a considerable role
in the drama as well. Geoffrey Martel's exercise of overlordship
originally removed the church of Saint-Clément from Saint-Aubin's control and bestowed it on his own choice. Count Geoffrey
served as the first court of appeal, and la Trinité was later careful
to solicit the new lord of Craon's assent to its tenure of the
church of Craon. Finally, the blatant favoritism of the count of
Poitou served la Trinité's cause.

In addition to Saint-Aubin and presenting even more of an immediate competitive problem for la Trinité, was the abbey of
Marmoutier in Tours, with which la Trinité had to contend for
lay support in the Vendômois. Marmoutier had held some property in the area since the ninth century, but during the second
half of the eleventh century it dramatically increased its holdings
in the Vendômois. This created a unique confrontation between
the two abbeys within the county and even in the town of Vendôme itself. Before la Trinité was even dedicated, Marmoutier
had acquired the church of Saint-Médard in Vendôme and was
accumulating property in the parish.[17] The obedience of Saint-
Médard soon encompassed a mill and land within the town walls
as well as property in the nearby towns of Villiers, Courtiras,
and Courtozé—towns in which la Trinité also held land.[18] In addition to the obedience of Saint-Médard, Marmoutier established
priories in Lavardin and Sentier, cells in Lancé and Bezay, while
acquiring a few scattered possessions in other parts of the Vendômois. Thus, by the third quarter of the eleventh century, the
two abbeys and their men were in almost constant contact.

Despite la Trinité's possible informal filiation from and proximity to Marmoutier, no evidence exists of any formal spiritual
bonds established between the two abbeys. Marmoutier did
grant *societas* to a certain Robert, who became a monk of la Trinité after being archdeacon of Chartres—in which office he had
always acted as a friend to Marmoutier (CT 2:167, no. 408). But
this was a private bond unlike confraternity between abbots or
chapters. There were, instead, a series of small conflicts between

the two houses that were never allowed to escalate to unmanage-
able levels, since accommodation rather than confrontation seems
to have been the goal of both sides. Confrontation is an uncomfortable stance when an opponent is omnipresent and almost
equally powerful. When the two abbeys disagreed over the pannage of Sentier, Marmoutier's provost cleverly managed to get
Count Fulk Oison to award the custom to his priory (CM p.
128, no. 82). Subsequent passages of arms involved tithes in areas
where both abbeys had priories and therefore conflicting
claims.[19] Tithes were again at issue in 1119 when Abbot Geoffrey of Vendôme sought help from the bishop of Chartres to
regain a tithe from the monks of Marmoutier, "who strike continually at us with the arrows of robbery and secular violence."[20]

Although litigation between the two abbeys was generally in-
consequential, the lay response to such monastic competition was
a polarization of patronage. Since the house of Anjou supported
la Trinité, the counts of Vendôme became patrons of Marmoutier. Fulk Oison and his son Burchard made donations to Marmoutier's priories in the Vendômois while at the same time harassing la Trinité's establishments.[21] When the two abbeys had
conflicting claims, Fulk Oison was apparently readily persuaded
to side with Marmoutier.

Like the counts of Vendôme, the castellans of Lavardin
counted as patrons of Marmoutier. It was Salomon and Adele of
Lavardin who gave Marmoutier the church of Saint-Médard in
Vendôme and also endowed Marmoutier with the church of
Saint-Gilderic in Lavardin and its extensive property.[22] Only in
one instance did a member of this castellan's family annoy the
monks of Marmoutier.[23] Lavardin's neighbor, the castellan of
Montoire, lived only 2.5 kilometers down the Loir, so that Montoire and Lavardin were closer than any other two castles in the
Vendômois. This proximity may have led to bad feeling and
competition, and since Lavardin supported Marmoutier, Montoire became a patron of la Trinité and lost no opportunity to
annoy the monks of Marmoutier.

Walter, the son of the castellan of Montoire, managed to sell
a church twice over to Marmoutier, despite which his father later
had the gall to raise doubts about the monks' rights to their own-

ership of this same church.[24] The castellan's brother, on another occasion, claimed land bought by Marmoutier, so that the monks had to pay him to drop the claim (CM p. 89, no. 55). In contrast, the castellans of Montoire frequently witnessed la Trinité's documents and supported its monks. Hamelin, the third castellan of Montoire, held some mills in fief from the abbot and in 1081 confirmed all that la Trinité held in Montoire (CT 2:215, no. 438; 2:7, no. 302). His son Peter also held of La Trinité's abbot as well as serving as the abbey's patron and supporter (CT 2:297, no. 483). On only two occasions did the lords of Montoire clash with la Trinité—both times with the contentious Abbot Geoffrey of Vendôme—but for neither episode did the claims escalate into a major confrontation (CT 2:147, no. 397; 2:183, no. 418). When the family experienced a personal crisis, such as the death of the heir, the parents turned to la Trinité for comfort and prayers (CT 2:37, no. 326). The family of Montoire tended to remain loyal to la Trinité as a result of the many personal ties it had established with the monks and as a statement of its opposition to Lavardin and thereby to Marmoutier, the client of the castellans of Lavardin. By the middle of the twelfth century, however, the evidence for noble families' loyalties to either la Trinité or Marmoutier becomes sparser. It seems probable that as the antagonism between la Trinité and the counts of Vendôme lessened, so too did the polarization of barons into these two camps.

Despite the evidence of mutual irritation between the two abbeys, la Trinité did recognize, even if obliquely, its filiation from Marmoutier. This is evident in the spurious papal bulls that enumerate la Trinité's privileges. Many of these documents specify that when seeking a candidate for the abbacy, the chapter should turn to Cluny or Marmoutier if it failed to find a good man among its own number.[25] Pride and the desire to see themselves numbered with the major abbeys of central France may also have motivated the monks of la Trinité to include this directive in their forgeries.

In conclusion, la Trinité's relationships with other monastic bodies were more often antagonistic, expensive, and tedious than they were fraternal, although they never reached the levels of virulence and violence that marked some interchanges with lay people.[26] The explanation for la Trinité's litigious behavior as well as that of other houses can be found, in part, in the inadequate systems available to medieval society for avoiding and resolving conflicts. However, immediately behind much of this unseemly monastic squabbling lay the acts of secular patrons. Powerful lay people used their patronage of monastic foundations to emphasize their alignments in lay society. Lay men and women were judges, mediators, and confirmers in monastic conflicts; but, of even greater importance, they were perpetrators of discord both by ill-considered gifts of unclear title (like Saint-Clément) and muddied jurisdiction (like the churches of la Chartre) as well as through the general secular insistence that monasteries fulfill worldly needs, often at the expense of monastic ideals. Donations of property in the Vendômois made by the lords of Lavardin to Marmoutier sought to gain the family's salvation but acted to heighten an ugly antagonism between Marmoutier and la Trinité. Thus, secular power and wealth not only affected the obvious relations of lay people to the abbey but also often underlay the relationships among monasteries.

Ad limina Sancti Petri: Relations with the Papacy

At the time of its dedication in 1040, la Trinité received a confirmation from Pope Benedict IX, of which only the title and incipit remain (CT 1:94, no. 42). It is, therefore, not possible to ascertain whether the abbey received any papal privileges at that time. Sixteen years later, the founders placed both la Trinité and l'Evière under papal protection (CT 1:190, no. 105). Such commendations to the papacy were becoming common during the eleventh century and can be identified by an abbey's commitment to pay *cens* to Rome.[27] The gift of la Trinité and l'Evière was made, in part, to insure that the monks would have a patron strong enough to deter the newly reinstated young count of Vendôme, Fulk Oison, from major depredations. The other probable

reasons for the founders' decision have been brilliantly reconstructed by Olivier Guillot.[28]

In 1054 a synod was held at Tours and presided over by the
legate, Hildebrand. Around this time it seems highly probable
that Count Geoffrey Martel and Hildebrand worked out a mutually beneficial agreement. Geoffrey needed ecclesiastical help to
disentangle himself from what was, for him, an insoluble problem. After his second falling out with Bishop Gervais of le Mans
in 1051 and 1052, he had categorically denied Gervais access to
the see of le Mans. This action left Geoffrey in the uncomfortable
position of being censured by the church for his behavior but
unable to renege without losing face. The resolution of his difficulties came on October 15, 1055, when Gervais was translated
to Reims—an advancement great enough to make it possible for
the bishop also to salve his pride while dropping his claim to the
see of le Mans. It seems likely that in exchange for this resolution
of his dilemma, Count Geoffrey acted to meet several ecclesiastical demands. Before two weeks were up, he was present at the
election of the abbot of Saint-Florent and was content to invest
the abbot with only the *temporalia*—investiture exactly as the reformers would have it. Three actions during the next year may
also have been part of Geoffrey's response to Hildebrandine pressure: he returned disputed lands to Marmoutier; he reassociated
Fulk Oison with him in the honor of Vendôme; and he gave la
Trinité and l'Evière to Rome. Pope Victor II recognized la Trinité's new relationship to the papacy by a confirmation in 1056 or
1057 of all its property and the first in a series of privileges: a
general excommunication was not to touch la Trinité and
l'Evière, nor were lawsuits against the abbey to be heard without
consulting Rome (CT 1:193, no. 106). Victor, one of the early
reforming popes, may have envisioned la Trinité as a possible
locus of pre–Gregorian Reform activity.

The next pontiff with whom the abbey had any interaction
was Pope Alexander II, who on May 8, 1063, issued a general
confirmation of la Trinité's property (CT 1:290, no. 165). The
monks were to be left in peace by all their neighbors, both lay
people and ecclesiastics, and despoilers of the abbey were to en-

dure horrible retribution. Three years later the pope confirmed an agreement reached by Abbot Oderic and Hildebrand, who was then archdeacon and treasurer of the monastery of Saint Paul's (CT 1:310, no. 180-JL 4594). Hildebrand gave the church of Santa Prisca on the Aventine in Rome to Oderic to use and hold with a cardinal's status (*dignitate cardinali*). The abbey was to try to maintain twelve monks at Santa Prisca but never to let the number fall below eight resident monks. The endowment enhanced la Trinité's prestige, but due to the problems of maintaining a monastic body at such a great distance from the mother house, it proved to be an expensive nuisance. The grant to Abbot Oderic of a cardinal's dignity raised him to number among the most powerful ecclesiastics of western Europe. The bestowal of such a high honor was a personal recognition of Oderic's value to the papacy and was not conceived of as a transferable dignity. Nevertheless, when forged privileges including the grant in perpetuity were shown to Innocent II in 1135, he mistakenly reconfirmed the honor such that it became a heritable privilege (CT 2:266, no. 472-JL 7694). The pope, however, recognizing the difficulties of maintenance for la Trinité, made the confirmation in name only and allowed the church of Santa Prisca to pass into other control.

Hildebrand was the motivating force in recruiting Oderic into the pre–Gregorian Reformers' camp. Not only was he present at Tours in 1054 when Count Geoffrey was probably persuaded to give la Trinité to the papacy, but also he worked to effect Oderic's creation as a cardinal priest in 1066. Along the way their relationship could have deepened when the abbot visited Rome in 1056 (CT 1:189, no. 104). By this time Hildebrand was functioning as the pope's "first minister," deeply committed to the reform program he would pursue as pope.[29] Other abbots held the cardinalate in the third quarter of the eleventh century; three abbots of Monte Cassino were made cardinal priests in 1057, 1058, and 1088, and Cardinal Richard became abbot of Saint-Victor, Marseille, in 1079.[30] The timing of these appointments by popes who were themselves reformers suggests that the papacy may have been trying to introduce men of like concerns into power circles at Rome. Despite the indications that Oderic was highly respected by the papal reforming party, almost no evidence exists to indicate that he ever became actively involved in church reform.[31]

With the end of the 1060s, la Trinité's intercourse with the papacy petered out until the last years of the eleventh century. The reawakening of papal interest in la Trinité followed an unusual episode in 1094 when the newly elected abbot, Geoffrey of Vendôme, braving many dangers and traveling incognito, went to Rome.[32] He found Urban II struggling to gain the upper hand in Rome over the antipope, Guibert of Ravenna. Urban was hiding in John Frangipani's house where Geoffrey sought him out and stayed with him through Lent. Two weeks before Easter it became known that the man appointed by Guibert to hold the Lateran Palace in his name was offering to turn it over to the highest bidder. Although Urban canvassed all his supporters for money, he was unable to collect funds sufficient for the bribe. At this crucial moment, the young abbot was touched by the sight of Urban weeping and resolved to do his part to help. Geoffrey therefore sold his pack animals and horses and gave the proceeds together with all the cash at his command to the pope. With this money Urban was able to buy back the Lateran, and Geoffrey was the first triumphantly to embrace his feet when the pontiff finally sat in the apostolic seat.

The only source for this episode is the account by its hero: Geoffrey of Vendôme, whose overweening pride and tendency to exaggerate make the reader a little suspicious of his inflated role. His arrogance does not, however, necessarily discredit the tale, and he may, indeed, have offered some service to the pope. Urban's visit to la Trinité in 1096 during his travels around France to promote the crusade gave evidence of his favor, as did the three general exemptions issued for the abbey in the next few years.[33] The personal tie between la Trinité and the papacy continued under Pope Pascal II who also visited the abbey in 1107, staying for eleven days; nevertheless, in 1111 Geoffrey repaid the pope's solicitude by a ferocious epistolary attack, castigating the investiture compromise Pascal had reached with the emperor,

Figure 5A. Papal Privileges.

Free Election of Abbot		Bishop of Chartres to Consecrate Abbot		Any Bishop to Consecrate Abbot	
authentic	spurious	authentic	spurious	authentic	spurious
no. 407—1103	no. 36—1040	no. 407—1103	no. 37—1040		no. 146—1061
	no. 76—1047		no. 76—1047		no. 164—1063
	no. 107—1056/7		no. 107—1056/7		no. 367—1098
	no. 146—1061				no. 472—1135
	no. 164—1063				
	no. 367—1098				
	no. 472—1135				

Figure 5B. Papal Privileges.

Exemption from Episcopal or Legatine Councils

authentic	spurious
	no. 36—1040
	no. 76—1047
	no. 107—1056/7
	no. 146—1061
	no. 164—1063
	no. 366—1099
	no. 472—1135
no. 436—1119	

Exemption from Episcopal Excommunication

authentic	spurious
no. 106—1056/7	no. 76—1047
	no. 107—1056/7
	no. 146—1061
	no. 164—1063
	no. 366—1099
	no. 367—1098
no. 407—1103	no. 472—1135

Exemption from Legatine Interference

authentic	spurious
	no. 36—1040
	no. 107—1056/7
	no. 146—1061
	no. 164—1063
	no. 366—1099
no. 436—1119	

Abbatial Right to Excommunicate

authentic	spurious
	no. 238—1070/3

Abbatial Court Precedence Superseding Comital Court

authentic	spurious
	no. 36—1040
	no. 76—1047
	no. 107—1056/7
	no. 146—1061
	no. 164—1063

Key for Figures 5A and 5B:

no. 76 = JL 4147   no. 146 = JL 4458   no. 472 = JL 7694   no. 366 = JL 5714
no. 107 = JL 4352   no. 164 = JL 4512   no. 407 = JL 5899   no. 238 = JL 4699

Henry V.[34] In 1119 Pope Calixtus II visited Tours where he was met by Abbot Geoffrey. Geoffrey was able to repeat his earlier success in a more modest fashion by giving the pope a gray fur coat after the pontiff had been stripped by thieves.[35] Calixtus responded with a charter of privileges reiterating rights found in earlier—both legitimate and spurious—papal documents (CT 2:211, no. 436-JL 6747).

During this period la Trinité had acquired various papal privileges, only a few of which were genuine at the outset. Others were articulated first in forgeries and then subsequently incorporated into genuine documents. (See Figures 5A and 5B.) Even with reiteration, however, some false privileges—like the precedence of the abbatial court over the comital court—were not reconfirmed in a genuine papal charter, and only one false attempt was made to promote the right of the abbot to excommunicate his enemies in the absence of action by the bishop of Chartres. Nonetheless, by the early 1060s la Trinité had amassed what amounted to almost full exemption, as it is defined by David Knowles.[36]

The relationship of la Trinité to the papacy was generally one-sided and quite distant. Despite Geoffrey of Vendôme's dramatic services to two Roman pontiffs, it was the abbey that was generally the recipient of rights, privileges, and promised protection from Rome. However, warm friendships could and did develop between an abbot and a pope, like that which grew up between Abbot Geoffrey and Calixtus (CT 2:219, no. 441-JL 7119). It may well be that during Oderic's abbacy, the reforming party in Rome solicited and received support from la Trinité in furthering its efforts. Nevertheless, what transpired between la Trinité and the papacy was muted by distance, a situation that must have suited the monks, since forged privileges usually stressed the impotence of papal legates vis-à-vis the abbey, such that legatine councils, excommunications, and interference were all forbidden by numerous charters. Since only the pope had any rights over the abbey and he was at a great distance, the abbey was virtually free of control. Papal protection amounted to de facto autonomy. However, although the pope was in theory the highest power in the church, it was the bishops who most affected la Trinité.

Paternitatis Episcopalis:
Ties to Episcopal Power

The bishops of Chartres, Angers, le Mans, and Tours exercised powers that made them important to the life of la Trinité. The participation of one of their number was, in fact, necessary for the consecration of an abbot, the dedication of church property, the acceptance of the monastery's vicars in its churches, and the imposition of excommunication and interdict on the abbey's enemies. Furthermore, a bishop could often serve as a convenient mediator or judge for the abbey when it became involved in litigation, although he could just as well be the focus for a battle when la Trinité felt its autonomy threatened by episcopal power.

An abbot's consecration required the authority of a bishop, who was traditionally the diocesan. Although it is not known who officiated at the consecrations of most of the abbots of la Trinité, when Berno retired, Geoffrey of Vendôme was elected by the chapter and was consecrated on September 24, 1093, by Ivo, bishop of Chartres ("Annales de Vendôme," 67). At his consecration, Geoffrey made a *professio* to Ivo, the extent of which is still undetermined and which went unremarked for several years.[37] One interpretation of this *professio* is that Geoffrey made a personal—not a corporate—submission to the bishop, being fully aware and protective of the abbey's privileges. However, when the abbot later defended his action, he based his argument on his ignorance and youth rather than on the grounds of having made a perfectly defensible personal act of fealty. Another commentator suggests that the *professio* was part of an arrangement Geoffrey made with Ivo to insure the abbacy for himself when Berno stepped down.[38] As Geoffrey was young and not yet in priestly orders, it is quite possible that recognizing his limitations as a candidate, he promised a more extensive submission to Ivo than was usual in order to win the bishop's backing; Ivo certainly expected that the *professio* committed Geoffrey to some particular kinds of behavior and angrily chastised the abbot for failing to live up to his promise.[39]

The *professio* was annulled by Pope Urban II a few years before the turn of the century, "because it was done against the author-ity of the Roman church. . . ."[40] Geoffrey had been in Rome immediately after his consecration, and as a result of his financial support of Urban, might then have successfully requested papal nullification of his former promise. As it was not until after the pope had visited the abbey in 1096 that the annulment was is-sued, the chapter may have been instrumental in bringing the complaint before Urban. If this was the case, the *professio* was surely not a personal submission—to which the other monks could not have objected—but rather was an act that involved the entire abbey in recognizing Ivo's authority. The issue was raised once again when Geoffrey's successor, Fromond, was elected by the chapter with four abbots assisting in the spring of 1132. When Bishop Geoffrey of Chartres was asked for his blessing, he tried to exact a *professio,* which Fromond firmly and successfully resisted.[41] The subject was then laid to rest, and future consecra-tions took place without incident.

As far as can be determined, only the bishops of Chartres ever consecrated la Trinité's abbots, a natural pattern, since la Trinité fell within the diocese of Chartres. Nevertheless, the monks were eager to establish their freedom to choose any bishop—a privi-lege that was articulated in four of the falsified charters. (See Fig-ure 5A.) Although in practice the monks called on Chartres to consecrate their abbots, in theory they wanted to exercise auton-omy in the choice of celebrant. In its desire for this freedom, la Trinité was acting out a common monastic scenario whose inter-changes could sometimes border on farce. For instance, when Battle Abbey received a demand from its bishop, the abbey re-fused compliance; however, when the bishop politely requested a response from the monks, they acquiesced.[42] Battle Abbey, like la Trinité and similar monasteries, jealously guarded its free-doms.

Episcopal intervention was also necessary to enact ecclesiastical sanctions against lay men and women. An abbot could excom-municate his own monks, and in the person of Geoffrey of Ven-dôme did so frequently; but when a lay person acted so as to merit excommunication, the abbot had to call on the bishop who had jurisdiction in the particular diocese to separate the wrong-

doer from the church.[43] Another function which could be exercised at la Trinité only by episcopal authority was the dedication
of a liturgical building or object. A bishop (probably of Chartres)
must have been present in 1040 for the dedication of the church.
Later, in 1070, Bishop Arrald of Chartres came to la Trinité,
where on December 5, he consecrated the lady chapel to the Virgin and five other saints (CT 1:355, no. 222). It was a rare honor
in 1096 for the monks to have had the consecration of a new
cross performed by no less than the bishop of Rome, Pope Urban II.[44] But no such happy event took place when Pascal II visited the abbey in 1107.

Episcopal authority was indispensable for the abbey in confirming its tenure of churches. When a secular owner gave a
church to la Trinité, the diocesan had to confirm the abbey's
ownership and collect relief from the abbey on the entry of each
new vicar; in the diocese of le Mans, for example, this amounted
to the considerable sum of five pounds.[45] Pope Urban II prohib-
ited this practice at the Council of Clermont, much to the disgust
of bishops, who considered these fees legitimate episcopal income. In response, some bishops attempted to institute an annual
tax on churches in their dioceses in place of the relief.[46] When
Bishop Ulger of Angers attempted to exact this tax from Geoffrey of Vendôme, the abbot resisted. The pope effected a compromise, so that the tax question was dropped and the bishop
received baptismal fees while the abbot retained fees from puri-
fications and weddings (CT 2:272, no. 473-JL 7753).

The bishops also performed mediatory, juridical, and advisory
functions for the monks. These were not required of them as
spiritual superiors but were expected as secular overlords. When
the tithes of Gombergean were at issue between la Trinité and
Marmoutier, Bishop Arrald of Chartres judged the case (CT
1:362, no. 230). Later, during the tumultuous years when the
abbey contended with Count Geoffrey Preuilly of Vendôme,
Bishop Ivo came to Vendôme to warn the count that la Trinité
enjoyed papal protection; also, on several occasions Ivo responded to queries about internal discipline with advice to and
support for the abbot.[47]

The monks of la Trinité also interacted with neighboring bish-

ops on planes other than that of abbatial needs met by episcopal
authority. The problem of a fugitive monk could create tension
between the abbey and a bishop, as it did between two monasteries. Geoffrey of Vendôme carried on an extensive, angry cor-
respondence with Bishop Hildebert of le Mans trying to recover
the monk John, who is referred to as *caementarius* and probably
worked as an architect.[48] Hildebert was rebuilding the cathedral
of Saint-Julien in le Mans and needed men of talent and training.
Geoffrey's frantic efforts to force John to return may have reflected the abbey's pressing need for John to direct a particular
building program at la Trinité (a subject that will be investigated
in Chapter Five). The dedication of the cathedral of le Mans took
place in 1120, but it is unclear if John then returned to Vendôme.
Perhaps, having been excommunicated by his abbot, he felt it
politic to remain at a distance from Geoffrey. It has been suggested that the church of Troo was rebuilt by John of Vendôme,
because of stylistic parallels between it and parts of the cathedral
of le Mans.[49] As Hildebert came from Lavardin and would have
passed through Troo often on his way from le Mans to Lavardin,
he may have been asked for advice and suggestions about enlarg-
ing and remodeling the church. If this was the case, he might
have recommended John for the job. Thus, by a circuitous route,
the abbey of la Trinité shared its talent as far as the periphery of
the Loire basin.

The monks also clashed with bishops over jurisdictional and
juridical problems.[50] When Abbot Geoffrey was trying to coerce
Countess Euphronia into returning the church of Savigny, he
nagged Hildebert to set a date for hearing the case and warned
him not to be taken in by Euphronia's wily arguments. In a letter
to Pope Pascal II, Geoffrey complained of various episcopal
shortcomings: that Hildebert was delaying Euphronia's trial and
refusing to return the monk John; that the bishop of Angers had
illegally allowed a church to be founded without la Trinité's
agreement; and that the bishop of Saintes was jeopardizing the
abbey's rights to property held for over thirty years. Misunder-
standings as well as willful opposition could generate bad feelings; when hostility escalated, it could be acted on by denying
hospitality to a bishop (an indignity probably perpetrated by la
Trinité against Ivo of Chartres).[51]

Interactions between la Trinité and its surrounding bishops involved not only episcopal services to the monks or hostile encounters but also complex relationships like that of Abbot Geoffrey of Vendôme to Bishop Rainald Martigné of Angers. The election of a new bishop of Angers was set for 1101, and Abbot Geoffrey was invited to assist and to lend his "counsel and aid" in the process.[52] He came, but the election degenerated into an emotional mass meeting at which an unruly crowd, led by a prostitute, proclaimed Rainald bishop. In the midst of the turmoil, Geoffrey was unable to make his negative vote heard. Geoffrey then tried to rally ecclesiastical opinion against Rainald to block the bishop elect's consecration by Raoul, the archbishop of Tours, but to no avail. The abbot based his criticism of the election on three points: Rainald was under the canonical age for admission to the episcopacy; he was not in higher orders; his investituture by a layman (the count of Anjou) was heretical and was, in fact, simony. Geoffrey argued that the lay person investing a bishop either extorted money from the prelate or forced the bishop to subject himself to lay power—both abominations that had been clearly labeled as simoniacal by Pope Gregory VII. Once Rainald was consecrated, however, Geoffrey almost totally dropped his opposition, accepted the *fait accompli,* and endeavored to make the best of the situation.

Over the next seventeen years, Geoffrey's letters provide evidence of this policy of cooperation.[53] That is not to say that he treated Rainald with understanding or affection but that the abbot dealt in a matter-of-fact manner with the bishop as a fellow ecclesiastical administrator. Geoffrey addressed several letters to the bishop advising and encouraging him to resist lay encroachments, and on other occasions, the abbot attempted to elicit Angevin episcopal support in cases of monastic administrative difficulties. In all these years, only one case of a concrete dispute arose between the two men, involving the tenure of the church of Toussaint in Angers.[54] The church was originally to have been la Trinité's refuge away from Vendôme, but after l'Evière was built, Toussaint became redundant and was returned to the bishop. Geoffrey reopened the question, arguing that the chapter of la Trinité had never confirmed Oderic's alienation of Toussaint and that the exchange was therefore illegal. The affair was settled reasonably in 1108 with the understanding that if Toussaint ever passed out of the canons' hands, it would go to la Trinité.

In spite of this cooperation, Geoffrey disliked and disapproved of Rainald as bishop. The abbot's attempts to work with Rainald, however, were probably neither hypocritical nor cowardly, since Geoffrey generally made a practice of showing no fear in rebuking the mighty. Geoffrey's real feelings surfaced in a letter written around 1110 to Abbot Berner of Bonneval, assuring his fellow abbot that Berner's efforts to fight Rainald as a simoniac were appreciated.[55] Sometime during the years 1116–18, Bishop Rainald precipitated an open expression of the abbot's feelings, so that Geoffrey wrote Rainald and unhesitatingly outlined all his objections to the bishop's election while emphasizing that he had come to a peaceful understanding with Rainald.[56]

Geoffrey functioned on four levels in his interaction with the bishop of Angers: he acted as a prince of the church, called upon to attend an election and to lend weight to a consecration; he related to Rainald as a fellow ecclesiastical executive, cooperating in administrative affairs; he responded on a personal level of active dislike that he subordinated to pragmatic needs after Rainald's consecration; and he tried unsuccessfully as a reformer to rally the ecclesiastical community to act on the ideals of the Gregorian Reform. Such multifaceted relationships probably commonly existed between other abbots—for whom we have less information—and their neighboring bishops.

In concluding this review of la Trinité's interactions with the powers of the church, it is important to underscore that outside events and forces were constantly affecting these interchanges. The great movement of reform in its earliest days involved Oderic as a cardinal priest and potential ally of Rome, while years later, Geoffrey of Vendôme advocated a strong anti-lay-investiture reformist position. The activity of an antipope in Rome provided an opportunity for la Trinité to win papal friendship and subsequent privileges. The preaching of the crusade that brought Urban to France gave the abbey an opening to have an unfortunate *professio* of submission revoked. The feud between Anjou and Poitou helped the monks of la Trinité against those of Saint-

Aubin. Thus, the political and social context affected the relations of religious confreres, since even the holiest of men had to function within a worldly environment.

The bishops emerge as the ecclesiastics whose constant interaction with the monks over questions of property and discipline both inside and outside the abbey was of greatest importance to la Trinité. Relations with other monks were more often contentious than fraternal but had little lasting impact on la Trinité. Papal actions affected the monks even less. The papacy might bestow a major privilege on la Trinité's abbot—a cardinalate—but it had little practical consequence beyond increasing the monastery's sense of importance. Papal privileges and exemptions accumulated over the years (generally as imitations of forged documents). However, the monks of la Trinité seem to have felt a certain ambivalence between their desire for autonomy and their need for protection and other episcopal services. Thus, for example, they falsified charters incorporating freedom from the obligation to attend episcopal councils but continued to solicit local bishops' help. At the same time, even extensive exemptions on parchment did not release the monks from the necessity of remaining continually alert to defend their rights against incursions.

Warm and supportive relationships occurred within the body of the church: confraternity with other monasteries, the ties of caring generated by the circulation of *rotuli,* friendships between individual abbots and other prelates. These added a personal dimension to other business-related interchanges. But nowhere in la Trinité's dealings with other ecclesiastics is there the depth of concern that the abbey showed for its lay patrons—vividly symbolized in the extraordinary forgiveness expressed for Fulk Rechin in spite of his flagrant mistreatment of the abbey. La Trinité's real dependency was on lay men and women, and it was for them that the monks expressed their strongest emotions—both positive and negative. Fellow monks, the Roman pontiff, and bishops of the surrounding dioceses made up the system—the church—within which the abbey was defined, but did not have the same immediacy for the abbey as its surrounding secular environment.

Notes

1. *Chroniques des comtes d'Anjou et des seigneurs d'Amboise,* p. 62. "Uxor vero ejus [Agnes] edificavit in supercilio montis ecclesiam Sancti Georgii canonicosque posuit et capellam consulis vocari precepit."

2. CT 1:330, no. 195; 1:171, no. 94; 1:242, no. 137.

3. Geoffrey of Vendôme, *Ep.* 2:17 (PL 157:85), "contra interdictum vestrum. . . ."

4. *Rouleaux des morts du IXe au XVe siècle,* ed. Léopold Delisle (Paris, 1864), pp. 323 and 386.

5. Hockey, *Beaulieu,* p. 78. "Disputes between religious houses are frequent enough, but are not to be expected within the same religious family." But, he observes, such interfamilial quarrels did occur.

6. Gaussin, *La Chaise-Dieu,* p. 384, comments that confraternity allowed abbots to send a monk to a brother house for a rest or a change. Douglas Roby, "Philip of Harvengt's Contribution to the Question of Passage from one Religious Order to Another," *Analecta Praemonstratensia* 49 (1973), 70, discusses the acceptance of a monk's "going up higher" to a more elevated spiritual life.

7. Geoffrey of Vendôme, *Ep.* 4:2 (PL 157:149). Another fugitive, who took refuge at Beaulieu in Angers, was ordered back to la Trinité by Pope Honorius II, CT 2:249, no. 461.

8. CT 2:413–16, no. 556. Edited in *Recueil des actes de Henri II,* 1:234–36.

9. Geoffrey of Vendôme, *Ep.* 4:7 (PL 157:151–52), "nullam ordini reverentiam exhibens. . . ."

10. Ibid., 4:10–11 (PL 157:156–57).

11. These two charters are, respectively, the Vendômois (CT 1:175, no. 96), and the Angevin versions of the story, 1:179–82, no. 98: "ad augmentandum in ea rerum possessionem et divini servitii honestatem . . . ut in ecclesia Sancti-Clementis abbas constitueretur mox. . . ." A third version is CT 1:178, no. 97, which is a charter of the bishop of Angers, who confirmed la Trinité in its ownership at Geoffrey Martel's request.

12. CT 1:180, no. 98, "compellente comitissa Agneti," although Geoffrey Martel was married to Countess Grecia at the time of the gift, 1:176, no. 96.

13. CT 1:366–68, no. 234, and 1:370–73, no. 236, which latter is a letter written by the monks of Saint-Aubin to a nephew of the pope complaining of their mistreatment and recounting the ignominious treatment of one of their group: "Quam inhoneste Frotmundum bene vobis notum, ex hospitio suo ipse pulsando manibus suis expulit?" This letter also records the unorthodox acquisition of consent to the bishop's settlement: "Noster igitur abbas, priore suo absente, nec vocatis decanis, nec viris majoris intelligentiae et aetatis, minorem partem, quae praesens inerat in capitulo suo, sensu vel aetate puerilem conventioni annuere coegit. . . ."

14. Guillot, *Le Comte d'Anjou,* 1:112–13.

15. Blois B.D. MS 21 H 146, no. 5 (edited, CT 2:71–74, no. 343), and 2:83–85, no. 346.

16. Geoffrey of Vendôme, *Ep.* 1:8 (PL 157:46), and CT 2:203–4, no. 430.

17. CM p. 23, no. 13; p. 24, no. 14; p. 26, no. 15. Germund was named as obedientiary by 1040.

18. CM p. 37, no. 21, and p. 32, no. 18; land in Villiers, p. 26, no. 15, and p. 27, no. 16; land in Courtiras, p. 28, no. 17, and p. 34, no. 20; land in Courtozé, p. 55, no. 33, and p. 112, no. 71.

19. CT 1:362–63, no. 230, involved a tithe of horses in Gombergean; 2:51, no. 333, concerned tithes in Fontaines.

20. Geoffrey of Vendôme, *Ep.* 2:21–22 (PL 157:88–90) and 2:26 (PL 157:92), "qui sagittis rapinae et saecularis violentiae in nobis assidue jaculantur."

21. For donations to Marmoutier from the counts of Vendôme see CM p. 134, no. 86;

p. 334, no. 38A; p. 337, no. 40A; p. 197, no. 119. The Countess Euphronia brought a claim against the monks of Marmoutier at one point, but the charter is incomplete and difficult to evaluate, CM p. 269, no. 188.

22. CM p. 291, no. 12A, and p. 287, no. 11A. Several generations later the house of Lavardin was still acting as patrons of Marmoutier. See CM p. 325, no. 32A; p. 316, no. 27A; p. 323, no. 31A.

23. Gaimard, lord of Lavardin, seized some oxen of the abbey but made reparation, CM p. 316, no. 27A.

24. CM p. 8, no. 5, and p. 6, no. 4. The value of a church and its property was so great that it would have been financially worthwhile—although extremely aggravating—for the monks to have paid twice to obtain the church.

25. CT 1:140, no. 76 (JL 4147). "Quod si apud eos inveniri non poterit, quod absit, a Cluniaco vel a Majori-Monasterio vel undecumque melius poterunt monachi ibi congregati sibi eligant abbatem. . . ."

26. Garaud, L'Abbaye Sainte-Croix, p. 160, also mentions that Sainte-Croix had more unpleasantness with lay people than it did with other monasteries.

27. For a discussion of papal protection for monasteries see Camille Daux, "La Protection apostolique au moyen âge," Revue des questions historiques, NS 28, 72 (1902), 5–60, and Georg Schreiber, Kurie und Kloster im 12 Jahrhundert. Studien zur Privilegierung, Verfassung und besonders zum Eigenkirchenwesen der vorfranziskanischen Orden vornehmlich auf Grund der Papsturkunden von Paschalis II bis auf Lucius III (1099–1181), 2 vols. Kirchenrechtliche Abhandlungen, 65–68 (Stuttgart, 1910). Both these authors' specific discussions of la Trinité are flawed by their acceptance of all the abbey's papal privileges as authentic. For a treatment of all monasteries, churches, domaines, cities, states, and individuals who were under the papal protection see Paul Fabre, L'Etude sur le Liber censuum de l'église romaine (Paris, 1892).

28. See Guillot, Le Comte d'Anjou, 1:91–101, for the following discussion. Theodor Schieffer, Die päpstlichen Legaten in Frankreich, Historische Studien, 263 (Berlin, 1935), pp. 50–53, also cites Hildebrand's presence at Tours in 1054.

29. Geoffrey Barraclough, The Medieval Papacy (New York, 1968), p. 76.

30. Steven Kuttner, "Cardinalis: The History of a Canonical Concept," Traditio 3 (1945), 175.

31. The one indication that Oderic espoused reformist goals is CT 1:150, no. 80, in which celibacy is required of a parish priest.

32. Geoffrey of Vendôme, Ep. 1:8–9 (PL 157:46–51) and 1:14 (PL 157:55). Geoffrey describes his sufferings and disguise in letter eight: "Mala quae in itinere et in civitate passus sum, nostrorum per omnia, ne agnoscerer, factus famulus famulorum longum est enarrare."

33. René Crozet, "Le Voyage d'Urbain II et ses négociations avec le clergé de France (1095–1096)," Revue historique 179 (1937), 298. CT 2:121, no. 369 (JL 5782); 2:110, no. 364; 2:122–23, no. 370 (JL 5772).

34. Geoffrey of Vendôme, Ep. 1:18 (PL 157:58) and 1:7 (PL 157:42–46).

35. Ibid., 1:12 (PL 157:53).

36. David Knowles, "The Growth of Exemption in England, 1066 to 1216," Downside Review, 1 NS, 31 (1932), 206. Of Knowles's list of privileges enjoyed by exempt houses, la Trinité lacked only the explicit right to deny hospitality to bishops and exemption from episcopal visitation and correction.

37. Geoffrey of Vendôme, Ep. 2:7 (PL 157:74–77), dated 1106–7 by Wilmart, and 2:11 (157:79–80), dated 1107–10 by Wilmart recount the professio. Compain, L'Etude sur Geoffroi de Vendôme, pp. 157–59, advocates the theory of personal submission. The legal right of an abbot to compromise the privileges of his corporation in perpetuity is unclear to us and was certainly murky to the monks of la Trinité. The issue became confused because the abbot could act in two ways: individually for the abbey in all matters of vassalage, and as a corporate head in spiritual activities. We can not determine in what capacity

Geoffrey tendered his *professio*. The abbot defended his behavior in, Geoffrey of Vendôme, *Ep*. 2:11 (PL 157:80): "Professio, quam a me adhuc juvene et novitio extorsistis, regularis minime fuit. . . ." 2:7 (PL 157:75): "In professione siquidem illa consilio vestro nimia simplicitate acquievi. . . ."

38. De Pétigny, *Histoire archéologique du Vendômois*, pp. 395–97.

39. Geoffrey of Vendôme, *Ep*. 1:14 (PL 157:55). Geoffrey was ordained in Rome during his visit when he "saved" Urban. His youth at the time of consecration, "juvenis etate," is mentioned in the "Annales de Vendôme," p. 67. Ivo of Chartres, *Ep*. 195 (PL 162:204), is the bishop's reprimand to Geoffrey.

40. CT 2:111, no. 365 (JL 5499), "quia contra Romanae ecclesiae auctoritatem factam. . . ."

41. "Annales de Vendôme," p. 69. "Electus vero cum ab episcopo Carnotensi pro consuetudine benedictionem postularet, ipse autem econtra pro benedictione ab eo professionem exigeret, ille se nullatenus id facturum esse respondit: timere enim se di[cebat] ne, si pro benedictione contra dignitatem monasterii sui professionem faceret, maledictionem incurreret." Also see CT 2:308–9, no. 490.

42. Searle, *Battle Abbey*, pp. 28–29.

43. Geoffrey of Vendôme, *Ep*. 3:16 (PL 157:124). "Joannem caementarium, monachum nostrum, quem vobiscum habetis, propter iniquitatem suam a nobis excommunicatum indubitanter agnoscite." For instances of the abbatial need for episcopal powers, see 3:17 (PL 157:124) and 2:16 (PL 157:84).

44. "Annales de Vendôme," p. 67. The "Annales" must be using Easter dating, since the entry is recorded for February 26, 1095, although Urban was at la Trinité from February 19 through March 3, 1096. (In 1096, Easter fell on April 13.)

45. CT 1:130, no. 71, is an example of a confirmation by the bishop of Chartres of la Trinité's rights to the altar fees of churches donated to the abbey by lay men and women. Although Lemarignier cites examples of eleventh-century bishops of Orléans, le Mans, and Chartres giving *juridiction ecclésiastique* (episcopal powers over churches) to monasteries, la Trinité does not seem to have received such episcopal customs. Jean-François Lemarignier, *Etude sur les privilèges d'exemption et de jurisdiction ecclésiastique des abbayes normandes depuis les origines jusqu'en 1140*, Archives de la France monastique, 44 (Paris, 1937), pp. 84–90, and 116–17. See CT 1:130, no. 71, for relief and 1:158, no. 87, for customary relief in Maine.

46. CT 2:119–20, no. 368. Carl Joseph Hefele, *Conciliengeschichte*, 5 vols. (Freiburg, 1863), 5:193–202, tr. Henri Leclercq as *Histoire des conciles* (Paris, 1912), part 1, 5:401.

47. CT 2:94–97, no. 355. For another example of episcopal support see CS pp. 76–77, no. 42. See Ivo of Chartres, *Ep*. 41 (PL 162:52–53); 57 (PL 162:68); 82 (PL 162:103–4); 163 (PL 162:167), for supportive communications.

48. Geoffrey of Vendôme, *Ep*. 1:3 (PL 157:37); 3:16 (PL 157:124); 3:24 (PL 157:127–28); 3:25 (PL 157:128–29); 3:29 (PL 157:131); 3:30 (PL 157:131–32). No evidence survives to explain how John originally came to be working in le Mans. Probably, Bishop Hildebert had obtained his temporary assistance, and the trouble began when the work took longer than had been agreed on at the start.

49. Le comte P. de Déservillers, *Un Evêque au XIIᵉ siècle: Hildebert et son temps* (Paris, 1876), p. 232.

50. Geoffrey of Vendôme, *Ep*. 3:19 (PL 157:125–126) and 3:21 (PL 157:126), are letters seeking to galvanize Hildebert into action. *Ep*. 1:3 (PL 157:37–38) complains of Hildebert to Pope Pascal II.

51. Hildebert of Lavardin, *Ep*. 1:11 (PL 171:168).

52. Ct 2:157, no. 401, "et concilium et auxilium vestrum," and Geoffrey of Vendôme, *Ep*. 5:4 (PL 157:189). For the description of the election see 3:11 (PL 157:114). It was a "mulier publica" who proclaimed Rainald. Geoffrey wrote five letters seeking to stop Rainald's election: *Ep*. 4:8 (PL 157:55); 5:5 (PL 157:189–90); 4:9 (PL 157:155–56); 3:13 (PL 157:120–21); 3:14 (PL 157:121). To be elected a bishop, a candidate was supposed to be

at least thirty years of age and to have been a priest for four years. B. Haréau, "Une Election d'évêque au XIIe siècle: Rainaud de Martigné, évêque d'Angers," *Revue des deux mondes,* 2d series 88 (1870), 550.

53. Geoffrey of Vendôme, *Ep.* 3:2 (PL 157:105–6) and 3:7 (PL 157:109–10); 3:8 (PL 157:110–11) and 3:9 (PL 157:111–12).

54. CT 2:18, no. 419. Geoffrey of Vendôme, *Ep.* 3:5 (PL 157:107–8), c. 1107 urged Rainald to admit his error in a difference of opinion. The abbot may well have been alluding to the conflict over Toussaint, settled in 1108.

55. Ibid., 4:16 (PL 157:159–60).

56. Ibid., 3:11 (PL 157:112–18), expresses Geoffrey's genuine feelings of anger at the bishop but includes the conciliatory phrase: "pacem vobiscum feci. . . ."

CHAPTER FIVE

La Trinité's Contributions to Its Society

THE AIM of the first four chapters of this study has been to examine the community within which la Trinité functioned, to describe the interchanges of the abbey with its founders, personnel, patrons, and ecclesiastical confreres. This chapter will focus on the contributions la Trinité made to its society. These can be grouped in two parts: artistic contributions—both visual and literary—and the more elusive, but in no way less important, social and spiritual contributions.

Although historians usually leave a discussion of artistic artifacts to art historians, this investigation includes a section on the monastic arts of la Trinité to underscore their critical importance for a modern reconstruction of medieval social history. The physical form of a monastery affected not only its members but also outsiders who came in contact with the organization. Painting, stained glass, and illuminations enriched the interior life of the monastery, expressing something of the institution's concern with beautifying itself for its own inhabitants. The tracts, hymns, letters, and sermons written at the house instructed and stimulated members of the monastic community as well as passing to other literate people outside the abbey's walls. This discussion will not concentrate on evaluating the artistic worth of la Trinité's creative activity but rather on what we can learn of the monastery and its relations to the rest of society from the monks' literary and artistic work. A consideration of the abbey's charitable and spiritual outreach completes the picture of la Trinité's contributions to life in the Vendômois.

Part I: Artistic Contributions

The Plastic Arts

La Trinité brought together men who were interested in creating a suitable setting for the spiritual life in the monastic buildings and their decoration. The ordinary lay man or woman could appreciate the architecture, while the decoration of the interior of the abbey and of its manuscripts would have been enjoyed by a more restricted audience of religious and some of the monks' lay patrons.

The medieval architecture of the abbey of la Trinité and its priories conforms to the general regional style, although Lesueur has stressed the difficulty of identifying any unifying architectural themes for the area due to the diverse geological, political, and monastic influences represented there.[1] For instance, Vendômois churches include buildings erected under the auspices of religious from Tours, Beaugency, Blois, and Châteaudun. The greatest number of surviving churches in the Loir-et-Cher are Romanesque, dating from the energetic days of the eleventh and twelfth centuries; these early churches generally follow rough typologies according to size and importance. The large churches tend to have a central cupola over the transept, and a shallow choir with three levels; medium-sized buildings are usually cruciform; rural churches have no aisles and only tiny choirs with apses or flat chevets. Vaulting is unusual and generally portals are without tympani. The surviving evidence of la Trinité's buildings fits into this picture, yet defines the type more exactly for the subregion of the Vendômois.

Only a very limited number of la Trinité's buildings has survived. In addition to the mother church, some of the priories' churches remain, and in one case, a gateway of a priory has withstood the destructiveness of time and changes of taste. From the remnants of the abbey's extensive building program, three specific architectural features of the eleventh and twelfth centuries can be recognized which would have been familiar sights to anyone passing the early abbey's structures: Romanesque entry doorways, divided Romanesque windows, and bell towers. Of these three, it is the Romanesque portals that have best withstood the urge of later generations to rebuild their churches.

One of the earliest of the doorways exists at the church of the priory of Boisseau, the exterior of which survives almost in its original form. The Lady Adele gave the church to la Trinité in 1079, but it was probably rebuilt by the monks in the early days of the next century.[2] The monks designated Boisseau as an obedience in the list of la Trinité's dependents drawn in 1109 (CT 2:192, no. 423). The church is a small stone structure with a rectangular nave and flat chevet. The west facade is covered by a wooden porch, which although not twelfth-century, probably duplicates the original structure. The western doorway survives as a simple Romanesque entry. It is composed of a plain round inner arch and two unornamented archivolts finished off by a checkerboard stringcourse—the same motif that decorates the exterior of a capital on la Trinité's lady chapel. The archivolts rest on an abacus under which on each inner side stands a capital and column, although the column is missing from the south side. A stylized leaf decorates the capital on the north, and a crouching figure makes up the other capital. (See Plate 1.) This figure may well be a monk, as it seems to have its hands folded in prayer and to have the distinctive long sleeves of a monastic. Also, there is the suggestion of hair on either side of the head but not covering the crown of the head. This may represent a tonsured head, or it may be the result of obliteration caused by patching around the column. The entryway at Boisseau remains simple yet effective. Other, similar structures have survived at the dependent churches of Lisle, Pezou, and Coulommiers.

The church of Lisle was given to la Trinité in 1098 but was rebuilt in 1146 (CT 2:109, no. 363; 2:336, no. 512). (See Plate 1.) Restoration managed to do away with almost all of the early structure, but a Romanesque portal—now walled up—remains on the north side. An inner round arch inside two archivolts differs from those at Boisseau in that it is not decorated. The outer band carries a sawtooth and chevron pattern, while the inner archivolt has been redone, obliterating its original decoration. A stringcourse of rosettes, only the extremities of which survive,

Capital from the western portal of the priory church of Boisseau.

North doorway of the priory church of Lisle.

encircles the whole. The archivolts end on a horizontal support, serving as the abacus for a capital and column under the inner archivolt on either side of the door. (The columns are gone.) Two beasts, apparently drinking from a vase, ornament the northern capital, and the southern capital seems to be two birds face to face. The doorway of Lisle has the same organizational plan as does that of Boisseau but is more extensively ornamented.

A third example of an entryway from la Trinité's priory system can be seen at the church of Pezou which survives almost untouched. (See Plate 2.) This church was donated to la Trinité in 1079, but the doorway probably dates from the twelfth century.[3] Three archivolts encompass the plain central round arch. A projecting border of interlace next to incised double lines and a band of crossed ribbons edges the outer band. A sawtooth design decorates the second archivolt, and the third has a row of double bezants. This motif gave the designer some difficulty, for although two circles fit perfectly at the extremities of the archivolt, a partial third row had to be added as the arch rises to fill the widening gap. This results in a third row that waxes like the moon from a sliver at the bottom to a half circle at the top of the arch. The archivolts spring from a horizontal slab, which on the inside of the arch serves as the abacus for a pair of flanking capitals and columns. A leaf design covers the northern capital, and an animal incised in profile ornaments the southern capital. This doorway has greater depth than those of Boisseau or Lisle due to the addition of a third archivolt, and therefore the play of light and dark makes it more imposing than the other two.

By the late twelfth century, variations were being tried, one of which can be seen at the church of Coulommiers.[4] (See Plate 2.) The designers eliminated the central plain arch to broaden and aggrandize the doorway. Thus the portal has only two archivolts, bordered by a chevron stringcourse. A stylized plant—a motif also found on the portal of the church of Villetrun just a few kilometers to the east—decorates the outer archivolt, while the inner archivolt supports an acanthus leaf band. Both arches rest on a decorated abacus under which stand a pair of Corinthian capitals and plain columns which here immediately flank the opening instead of being next to the plain inner arch.

Western portal of the priory church of Pezou.

Western portal of the priory church of Coulommiers.

The evidence of these portals suggests that in the period under study la Trinité was experimenting with several decorative motifs yet beginning to vary the organization of the architectural elements. The universal appeal of these doorways is such that even when enthusiasm to renovate the old churches of the Vendômois became endemic in the nineteenth century, the doorways survived.

A second architectural feature present in la Trinité's buildings is their divided Romanesque windows. (See Plate 3.) Mention has been made in the first chapter of the surviving sections of the western wall enclosing the monastery. One of the untouched surviving windows in the north section of the enclosure wall (where the granary was probably located) has no ornamented archivolts. (See Plate 3.) It is divided into two round arches sharing as their inner support a slender colonette and capital. Over the colonette, the stone is pierced by a square hole, turned on end to present a diamond appearance.

The identical divided Romanesque window is present on the gatehouse of the priory of Courtozé. (See Plate 3.) Three knightly brothers gave the property of Courtozé to la Trinité before 1044, and it was designated an independent cell by 1109.[5] The gatehouse itself is probably twelfth-century. There are two second-story windows on the exterior facade of the gatehouse and one on the interior (now altered). The pattern is the same as that of the granary window: a divided round-arched window with central colonette and capital surmounted by a small square window on end. The execution of the design at Courtozé is slightly less refined than that of the window at the mother abbey, since Courtozé's windows have no overarching stringcourse and possess a sturdier colonette. The monks of la Trinité borrowed this organizational scheme for windows from Angevin prototypes. The window first appeared on the second tier of the tower of the abbey of Saint-Aubin in Angers. (See Plate 4.) This tower was built in one continuous campaign from 1130 to 1154.[6] The identical combination of elements was still being used when the granary building of the hospital of Saint-Jean was built in Angers after 1188.[7] The priory of Courtozé and the granary of la Trinité cannot be dated precisely, but the striking similarity of their win-

Granary window of la Trinité's western enclosure wall.

Gatehouse of the priory of Courtozé.

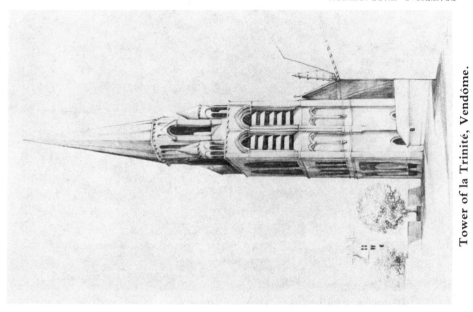

Tower of la Trinité, Vendôme.

Tower of Saint-Aubin, Angers.

dows to those of the Saint-Aubin tower suggests that the buildings of la Trinité were begun after 1130.

The third surviving architectural element is that of the bell tower—the most dramatic feature of medieval ecclesiastical architecture. (See Plate 4.) It has been noted that before the death of Abbot Rainald in 1044, the abbey had a wooden bell scaffold (*tristega signorum*) (CT 1:109, no. 54). Sometime early in the twelfth century, a stone bell tower was built to replace the wooden one. No documentary evidence survives from which to date this construction, but the possibility exists that it was to oversee the work on the tower that Geoffrey of Vendôme wrote urgent letters seeking to reclaim his monk, John the *caementarius,* from the bishop of le Mans.[8]

The tower of la Trinité is composed of five sections, the three bottom of which are square. Architectural emphasis increases in each section moving upward. The first segment is plain with only an attached buttress up the middle of each face and attached buttressing at each corner. The second level has a blind arcade of four paired arches on each face, which share a central colonette and capital. These windows are slightly pointed and are topped by a stringcourse of dogteeth. The third level has two tall, deeply set windows on each face. These are composed of three archivolts, the two inner of which are supported on both sides by acanthus leaf capitals and columns that run the height of the windows. The outer columns on either side of each window connect into columns that run down the building's second section. The line carries down through the base unit by means of the attached buttresses. This continuing line creates a unifying element, tying together the bottom three squares.

A stringcourse of dogteeth emphasizes the third-level windows, and a frieze of corbel heads delineates the top of the square. The fourth unit forms the transition from the square to the steeple, which is achieved by an octagonal drum. Round turrets soften the four corners of the drum, while behind the turrets an arcade of elongated round arches—the outer pair of which is blind and the inner pair pierced—carry the eye upward. The other four faces of the drum are taken up by one tall window— slightly pointed—under a steep gable. Another frieze of corbels edges the whole at the top. The spire forms the fifth unit, which together with the drum measures thirty-five meters in height. The total height of the tower is eighty meters.

The tower of la Trinité presents an extraordinarily harmonious whole. To appreciate how this tower achieves a successful resolution of the architectural difficulties, one has but to compare it with the contemporary tower of Saint-Aubin in Angers. (See Plate 4.) Four units make up this tower, the bottom one of which is taller than the second and third combined, giving a ponderous effect to the whole. The second and third levels use an arrangement of windows and turrets similar to that followed by la Trinité but without the long continuous accents of connecting columns. The height of the turrets precludes an intermediary level of arcades behind them, and the octagonal drum has only two accents instead of three. Saint-Aubin lacks the gables over the large windows of the drum that serve, at la Trinité, to unify the drum and the spire. Saint-Aubin's overall height measures 76.6 meters, slightly shorter than la Trinité. Abbé Plat argues that a vast porch connected the tower of la Trinité to the facade; Crozet points out, on the contrary, that the tower was made to be seen on every side, suggesting it was intended to be free-standing.[9]

The tower of la Trinité achieves a satisfying resolution of the geometric problem of unifying the square with the circle. Architectural details integrate the five sections, and corner towers soften the transition. A combination of window shapes varies the surface, alternating dark recesses with blind arcades. The tower is not only an architectural success, but also may have been an important inspiration for the builders at Chartres.[10]

The role of the bells of a monastery was to regulate the monastic *horarium,* yet the pealing must have also served the abbey's neighbors as a means of ordering their days. Most people in the environs, however, probably became so used to the bells that their ringing was hardly perceived on a conscious level. In this way, the monks' activities permeated their society whether or not lay people actively noticed them.

Bell towers played a role in the life of priories as well as at the mother abbey. One twelfth-century tower survives untouched at Broch, near Baugé. Since this church was not mentioned in 1109 when a list of priories was drawn up but was included in a list from 1157, it was probably built between these two dates (CT 2:400, no. 549). The tower is a square stone structure of three levels. The bottom and tallest unit has attached buttressing at the corners and an attached buttress up the middle of two faces. A cornice and corbels are at the top of this section. The second level has a pair of windows with slightly pointed arches and three deeply recessed archivolts. This arrangement of windows and the attached buttresses reproduce patterns from la Trinité. In fact, the design at Broch constitutes a simplified version of la Trinité's elaborate working out of its tower.

Although no documentary evidence can prove that the abbey had its own workshop of masons, characteristic shapes of windows and organization of the units of its towers suggest that the mother house disseminated men at least to oversee and plan work at its priories. The status of most of these men is unknown. However, Brother Albert certainly built the lady chapel at la Trinité (CT 1:356, no. 222), and Brother John—*caementarius*—was critically important for the construction of the cathedral at le Mans. The evidence of stylistic parallels in the designs found at priories and the work of Albert and John suggest the strong possibility of some centralized control over the abbey's building program directed by monks in the eleventh and early twelfth centuries. The sophistication of some of the designs suggests that the directors of the work were well versed in geometry and commanded basic engineering skills.

At the same time that the abbey was evolving its own architectural idiom, the variation of decorative motifs on church portals is evidence for the innovative spirit that balanced the centralized planning authority and kept the end products fresh and interesting. The finished work was not always, however, entirely satisfactory, when the planner, as at Pezou, for example, could not solve a problem inherent in combining his chosen elements. Yet when the abbey produced its finest work, like the eleventh-century capitals in la Trinité's transept, it is hard to fault the design or the workmanship. (see Frontispiece.)

La Trinité buildings had more than a visual impact on their neighbors. Each cell served as a focus for a burg, drawing people into a settlement which then had monks of la Trinité at its hub. The abbey and its priories may have purchased building materials and probably paid local laborers for each project, thereby infusing capital into the local economy. Donors of property to the abbey could proudly watch the building of a priory's church in which they had a particular interest, just as the peasants living in the vicinity of a priory could see it as a source of help in time of famine or other disaster. Peasants' houses were often built in the monastery's land around a priory's church (sometimes even within the cemetery), and people may well have used a protective porch, like the one at Boisseau, for shelter or various gatherings.[11] Perhaps the most significant message of the abbey's buildings to their lay neighbors was the comforting proximity of monastic spiritual support; la Trinité honeycombed the Loire basin with the physical presence of its monastic buildings—a visible statement of the abbey's power and prestige.

Much of the artistic activity of la Trinité's inhabitants would have been outside the common person's ken. A great portion of the interior decoration of the abbey as well as most manuscript illuminations would have been viewed only by other religious or by a small circle of important lay patrons. A large part of these products of la Trinité's artistic skills is gone—vestments, hangings, precious metalwork, sculpture—but there are some surviving examples of painting and one panel of stained glass.

Although manuscript illumination provides most of our knowledge of medieval painting, monumental painting was definitely part of the medieval arts, and fresco painting flourished in the valleys of the Loire and the Loir. The Romanesque church of la Trinité may well have been extensively painted—much as we find the nearby churches of Areines and of Saint-Gilles in Montoire. Only one example of fresco, located in the chapter house, has survived at la Trinité. A fourteenth-century partition hid the south wall until renovation removed it in 1972, revealing five unretouched but partially mutilated fresco scenes.[12] The second from the left is the most complete, representing ten apostles in a boat casting their nets. The pigments are all earthen, and the blues are ground lapis lazuli. Artists employed an elaborate painting technique, building their colors over a bottom layer. This procedure was well known in the eleventh century at la Trinité, where Abbot Oderic wrote, "in a picture the color black is painted underneath so that white and red will be shown more vividly. . . ."[13]

Evidence for the identity of the painters of this series eludes us. Taralon points out that the style of the work can be dated to about 1100 and resembles that of the illuminated miniature in manuscript no. 193 at Vendôme.[14] The library of Vendôme may have supplied inspiration for the fresco painter in the same way as Joan Evans posits the library of Cluny furnished ideas for the wall painter of the Cluniac cell of Berzé.[15] At the same time, the large number of surviving fragments of fresco in the area, together with the presence of two painters (pictor) in the late twelfth century in the Vendômois, indicates that local lay artisans were available (CT 2:498, no. 619). The possibility therefore exists that this fresco could have been executed either by monks or by secular artists.

Fresco painting would have been viewed within the abbey by some lay people who came as donors or litigants to the chapter house and even probably by the poor who were received for alms and for the mandatum (liturgical washing of feet). Manuscript illumination would have been seen by a more limited group of religious and perhaps by prominent lay patrons on special occasions. The collection of books that has survived from the monastic library includes eighty-five eleventh- and twelfth-century texts. The discussion of this library constitutes in itself, therefore, a field rich enough for a detailed monograph. For the purpose of this study, three individual artists working at la Trinité in the period provide an indication of the artistic range of which la Trinité's monks were capable.

One extremely productive artist and copyist, whom I have dubbed "the lion artist," worked at la Trinité in the second decade of the twelfth century. He copied and embellished manuscript no. 26, Origen's *Homilies on Numbers and Matthew*. At the end of the work, he appended a list of nineteen works as "an inventory of books of la Trinité, Vendôme, made in the year of our Lord, 1119, at the command of Lord Abbot G., in the twenty-sixth year of his abbacy."[16] The list includes fifteen works by Augustine, one by John Chrysostom, and three Bible sections. Twelve of the Augustinian works are extant in the library of Vendôme: nos. 35, 37, 39, 40, 45, 122, 129 (two works), 139, 140, 192 (two works). A comparison of these twelve with no. 26 reveals that they are all by the same hand. This is also true of nos. 27, 41, and 138, bringing to sixteen the total number of manuscripts executed at la Trinité by the lion artist.

The lion artist delighted in incorporating lions' bodies or heads into his compositions. His work is essentially linear, based on brown ink drawing to which color is added only secondarily.[17] The palette for MSS 26 and 27 (which have more historiated capitals than any of his other works) is muted: brown, soft blue and green, and light orange predominate. The drawing is crisp and quick; no gold leaf is used. Several illuminations in these two works share an identical organization. Both have a historiated uncial d filled with interlace and terminating in a human torso holding an upright flower in his right hand (Vendôme B.M. MS 26, fol. 16v; MS 27, fol. 96r). Within the d of MS 26 are two lions rampant holding interlace vines in their mouths. The lion motif is repeated in a capital I shaft in MS 27, wrapped in interlace vines with a dragon's head sprouting a leaf at the bottom and a lion's head at the peak of the letter from whose mouth two parrots' heads emerge (Vendôme B.M. MS 27, fol. 45v). A full lion serves as a capital N in MS 26 (Vendôme B.M. MS 26, fol. 5v).

The lion artist worked with a notable delicacy, humor, and imagination. His drawing is sprightly and unstudied and provides a sharp contrast to the work of the miniaturist who did a full-page frontispiece of Abbot Geoffrey of Vendôme kneeling before Christ (Vendôme B.M. MS 193, fol. 2v). (See Plate 5). This miniature opens a collection of Geoffrey's works that must have been produced after his death in 1132, since the abbot wears a halo in the picture.[18] Geoffrey, tonsured and bearded, kneels on Christ's right hand; he is labeled "the sinner, Geoffrey," and wears a green chasuble over a red tunic while saying to Christ, "in You will I hope, even if You kill me." The bearded, barefoot Christ, sitting on a circular mandorla, holds the abbot by his left wrist. Behind the two figures is a Romanesque architectural background terminating in capitals and columns. Since the scribe

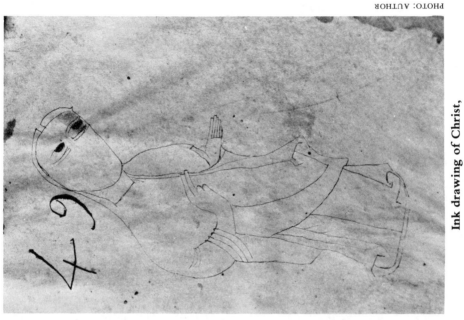

Ink drawing of Christ,
Vendôme B.M. MS 49, front flyleaf.

Illuminated frontispiece,
Vendôme B.M. MS 193, fol. 2v.

who copied the manuscript also did the lettering in the illumination, he probably executed the drawing as well. The figures are richly colored, and the architectural drawing is done in brown ink. There are careful white highlights on the figures, which are outlined in black. Because the artist did not center the figures within the architectural frame, the composition seems as awkward as do the stylized poses of the figures. The miniaturist worked with careful precision, unlike the lion artist, and had good command of the use of color. But he was limited to stiff, hierarchic poses and had difficulties with composition.

A third notable artist working at la Trinité in the twelfth century produced two manuscripts, nos. 23 and 34, rich in the use of gold; this penchant earns him the title of the "gold leaf artist." A colophon in no. 34 is undated, but a twelfth-century hand identifies the work as a "book of la Trinité, Vendôme."[19] In this manuscript there are two elaborate historiated initials, one of which shows St. Augustine seated within a capital F. The saint holds his work in his left hand and points at it with his right. The letter is of gold-leaf interlace on a rich background. A bird being caught by a weasel-like creature and by a man is entwined within the letter F. Augustine has black hair and a beard and wears a pink robe and hat together with a green cape; his undergarment is gray. Parts of the F are filled in with dark green embellished with tiny white starbursts. The gold leaf artist used color lavishly to produce elegant, rich work.[20] He did not employ the graceful line of the lion artist but far outstripped the miniaturist in handling the composition and colors of his work.

The evidence of these three artists' work suggests that although no "school" was in evidence, a lively and innovative artistic atmosphere prevailed at la Trinité in the twelfth century. Nevertheless, it would be difficult, indeed, to justify the art of the scriptorium as contributing in a significant manner to the abbey's environment. Illuminated manuscripts were a highly personal art form, executed usually by a single artist and appreciated by one reader at a time. Despite this limited audience, the illuminated work in no way lacks energy and creativity. In fact, the quality of the work, expense of the materials, and time expended by the artists underline the recognition by the monks of the importance of embellishing religious texts. Since the private art of manuscript decoration aided the inner spiritual life of the monks, such emphasis seemed appropriate. Illuminations supplied part of the artistic counterbalance to the architectural public art, such that within the abbey's artistic activity, we can discern one aspect of the tension between personal spiritual goals and social responsibility.

The high quality of la Trinité's artistic efforts is borne out by the one small but important survival of twelfth-century stained glass, a panel of the Virgin and Child enthroned, now in la Trinité's axis chapel. No evidence indicates the original location of the panel and therefore whether it had a more or less restricted audience. As the window is only 2.40 meters by .63 meters, it may either have been part of a larger work or have filled a lancet window.

The Christ child sits in his mother's lap, and both figures within a double pointed mandorla are borne up by two angels in the bottom corners. Two other angels at the top of the panel cense the holy figures. The colors are cool and subdued: blue, yellow, and white predominate with a small, rich red accent in the background. Stylistically, the V folds in the Virgin's robe resemble work done in the three surrounding cities of le Mans, Poitiers, and Angers. The biggest debt is, however, to Angevin work.[21] The elegance of the composition points to the sure hand of a superior craftsman.[22]

One other work of art needs to be mentioned, as it vividly underscores the interrelation of monks and laity and the fashion in which an artistic object could be involved in monastic patronage. This was a reliquary that disappeared in the French Revolution but was one of a quartet of boxes that for many centuries contained the *Sainte Larme* (tear of Christ shed over Lazarus).[23] The relic and reliquary were said to have been given to Geoffrey Martel by the Byzantine emperor, Michael Paleologus, in thanks for the Angevin's services fighting the Saracens.[24] Less dramatic but more likely donors would be the son-in-law of Geoffrey and Agnes, Henry III, and his wife Agnes.

The reliquary was a small rectangular box resting on four animals' forequarters. Both long sides bore four figures, each pair divided by a column: Isaiah, Ezechiel, Jeremiah, and Daniel were on one side with the Lamb of God in the center, over the words "Happy Freising, observe your protectors." On the reverse were ranged Tertullian and Sts. Corbin, Maurice, and George with a dove in the middle. One more saint's name was later added over the dove: St. Eutropus. The subscription ran, "O Christ, four holy ministers recount Your mortal life." On one end of the casket was Christ in a mandorla and on the other end a large, stylized eye with the words "King Henry, Bishop Notker" underneath. The cover was ornamented with the four figures of Abraham, Melchisedech (who had an eye in place of his head), Moses and Aaron. The subscription was, "Notger gives this to Henry." The whole was encrusted with jewels.

Between 1039 and 1052 the bishop of Freising was Notger, and between 1026 and 1056 the emperor was Henry III; this box, which served as a portable altar, was probably given by the bishop to the emperor.[25] Henry had married Agnes of Burgundy's daughter and namesake, and both Agnes senior and Geoffrey Martel were with the young empress' court in 1045–46 when they may have received the altar from the imperial couple. The adaptations of adding Europus' name and the eye imagery were carried out sometime between the reliquary's acquisition and 1175, by which date la Trinité was exhibiting the relic of the tear (CT 2:438, no. 572). Its inscriptions indicate that the box came from the hands of German craftsmen and not those of the Loir Valley. Its importation may have had an artistic impact on artisans at la Trinité; at the very least, it certainly emphasized the important patronage enjoyed by the abbey—patronage that reaffirmed the benefactors' prestige and added to the importance of the client abbey.

In sum, la Trinité was artistically alive and productive in its first 150 years of existence. Decorative innovation balanced the development of a stylistic architectural idiom. The designers of the first church had a sound knowledge of geometry and were capable of erecting a tower that still stands as a marvelous solution to the problem of the marriage of the square and the circle. Fresco, stained glass, and manuscript illumination flourished within the abbey during the same period. A variety of talents worked within the scriptorium, but no one style or "school" prevailed. Nevertheless, when la Trinité's artists looked for inspiration, they imitated the abbey's political and personal orientation toward the counts of Anjou and borrowed styles from Angevin craftsmen. For this stylistic legacy, the secular patronage tie again acted more magnetically on the abbey than did ecclesiastical ties to the diocesan and Chartres. Seymour observed a comparable pattern for the cathedral of Noyon which was influenced architecturally by Paris and its political tie to the Capetians more than by Tournai, to which it had an ecclesiastical bond.[26]

La Trinité probably contributed to its larger society by functioning as a patron and hiring artists and artisans. At the same time, the abbey expressed the sense of its own importance in the size and elegance of its buildings. These visually symbolized the help the abbey brought to its neighbors. Monastic buildings housed grain supplies for the hungry, as well as sheltering the sick and tired travelers. A magnificent physical plant attracted oblates and impressed prospective donors; it pleased its patrons by reflecting their generosity. The physical remains of the abbey still emphasize the self-confidence it felt and the strong secular support it enjoyed.

Literary Activity

La Trinité's monks produced a variety of written work that was available to a literate audience. Since the Rule (*RB*:48) required monks to labor at *lectio divina*—an activity that increased in importance during Lent—indigenous treatises must have circulated at least within the cloister and may have been copied for a larger reading public. Medieval letters were often collected, so that they reached a wider audience than just the recipient. Liturgical writing and sermons had an immediate impact on all monks participating in the abbey's spiritual exercises and may have been disseminated in copies for other readers. Thus, the literary output of la Trinité's monks must have affected their fellows as well as sometimes reaching a larger educated audience.

A treatise by la Trinité's second abbot, Oderic, survives in the form of a group of short essays, or meditations.[27] The first six folios have been mostly destroyed, and the original title is lost. At some point, the work was entitled *De virtutibus et vitiis,* although this may not have been the original title. The form resembles a *florilegium,* but the content is mostly original. Some of the essays are brief paragraphs; others extend for a dozen folios. The topics vary and can be roughly grouped as moral issues and theological discussions. The work is notable for its moderate and humane tone.

One essay discusses the virtue of monastic silence (MS 203, fols. 12v–17r). Oderic urges his readers to restrain from idle talk, which can lead the unwary into indiscretions. The man who talks continuously lets loose a flood of words that can destroy the peace and order of his surroundings. Yet, Oderic continues, too great an adherence to the rule of silence can lead to evil, because when one dams up thoughts, errors multiply. He who keeps the silence too rigorously may fall into the sin of pride in his own achievement, leading him to feel superior to those who have been less exacting about their silence. His pride will be a far worse sin than the loquaciousness of others. Rigorous silence can also cause a man to refrain from speaking out to denounce some evil, thus allowing it to become inflamed like an infected wound. Oderic quotes Solomon: "There is a time to be silent and a time for speaking" (Eccl. 3:7). To develop the ability to make moral discriminations is to gain the key to controlling one's own faults.

Oderic uses the image of water in his essay. Water when flooding can destroy all around it, but when controlled and dammed becomes useful—indeed, indispensable. He relates this image to the reader: "for the human spirit, like water, rises when confined."[28] The image marvelously evokes the very spirit of monasticism. Men and women voluntarily cloister themselves to intensify their abilities to reach God, like the Loir, whose waters when dammed create power.

La Trinité's fifth abbot, Geoffrey of Vendôme, left a large body of writing: letters, sermons, and a few tracts (2–5 and 7 of the *opuscula* in Migne are actually letters). Geoffrey was probably educated in Angers under William and the archdeacon Garnier, and his Latin is good, although hackneyed.[29] He repeats characteristic phrases and images: "one could [not] and one should

[not]"; "we ask by warning and we warn by asking." The wolf symbolizes any prelate in Geoffrey's disfavor; Christ is the medicine for our sins; the Virgin and Christ child are the star and its rays; the good thief is the symbol for the penitent's hope of salvation.

Geoffrey's nonepistolary writings deal most frequently with the subject of human sin and penitence, the sacraments, and reform and right governance of the church; he weaves together the recurring themes of sin, penitence, forgiving grace, and salvation in his sermon on the good thief, *De latrone salvato in cruce*—one of his most effective works.[30] Geoffrey reminds his audience that the thief on Christ's left side received eternal damnation, which he merited. The thief on the right side, however, came to believe while he suffered. With his eyes, he saw a dying man next to him but with faith and the Holy Spirit, he recognized the immortal, majestic Christ and praised and confessed his Lord. Thereby, a thief sentenced to death received eternal life, becoming a martyr and confessor. Geoffrey then explains that the dying thief could be saved without receiving the sacraments, since he was baptized by Christ on the cross and partook of the other sacraments by faith.

In the second part of the sermon, Geoffrey emphasizes the importance of the thief's faith, which actually placed him above the apostles. The thief found his faith on the day that Peter denied his, despite the apostle's personal relationship to Christ. A comparison of the thief and Peter follows. Peter was called and elect; he was an apostle and a martyr. He does miracles and binds and looses. The thief had no prior experience of Christ yet recognized divine truth. The thief was elected although not called; he was a martyr and confessor. Peter faltered as a warning to all against presumption, whereas the thief's salvation brings hope to sinners. Geoffrey avoids concluding that the thief exceeded Peter spiritually but cautions that at least the thief possessed no lesser faith than did Peter.

The sermon functions on two levels. First, it offers hope to every sinner that "the last shall be first," with the vivid example of that lowest of human failures—the condemned criminal—dramatically saved at the last moment. On the other hand, the ser-

mon seems to have political overtones, as it raises the thief almost to challenge Peter, the first bishop of Rome and symbol of
the papacy. Wilmart dates this sermon between 1124 and 1129,[31]
which overlaps with the reign of two popes: Calixtus II, who
died on December 13, 1124, and Honorius II, who reigned December 15, 1124, to February 13, 1130. However, the tone of
this work seems inappropriate for the reign of either man. Geoffrey had mostly warm exchanges with Calixtus, and although
sometimes he saw fit to chide the pope gently, the abbot avoided
any acrimonious confrontations; his interchanges with Honorius
were uniformly amicable.[32] If we question Wilmart's dating for
this sermon, its internal evidence points to the possibility that it
might have been written in 1111 when Geoffrey was furious with
Pope Pascal II for his investiture agreement with the emperor,
Henry V. At the time when the abbot had heard of Pascal's actions, he had written him an angry letter attacking the papal
compromise.[33] Christ had given the rule of the church to Peter
and Paul, wrote Geoffrey, and Peter rules the faith in this world
while Paul controls doctrine and the next world. If a pope es-
pouses lay investiture, he falls into heresy and can no longer be
shepherd, since "he is no longer pastor but an adversary." Geoffrey minces no words and emphasizes that Peter symbolizes Pascal. When the two works are compared, the sermon on the good
thief easily accords with the tone of this chastising letter and may
be from the same time. In the miniature at the front of his works
(MS no. 193) we see Geoffrey represented as a sinner putting his
trust in Christ. Did Geoffrey like to associate himself with the
good thief rather than with Peter, who in a moment of crisis
might—and in fact did—betray his sacred trust?

In addition to the writing of Oderic and Geoffrey, anonymous
monks at la Trinité penned liturgical works, some in honor of
saints with particular significance for the abbey. Bound into the
end of the *Lives of the Fathers* is a hymn to St. Eutropus, noted
in neumes in an eleventh-century hand (Vendôme B.M. MS 162,
fols. 119r–120v). Métais discovered the rest of the office in a thirteenth-century breviary and argued that the two parts had been
composed together in the eleventh century by a monk of la Trinité.[34] St. Eutropus was, according to tradition, a first-century
martyred bishop of Saintes whose relics were said to have been

preserved at the church of Saint-Eutrope in Saintes. Although no documentary evidence exists, the tradition continues that when Geoffrey Martel seized Saintes after defeating his wife's two stepsons between 1033 and 1039, he removed the relics of Eutropus as well as those of St. Léonce from Saintes and gave them to la Trinité.[35] Métais also notes that the office, as he reconstructs it, is clearly Benedictine and that there were no Benedictines at the church of Saint-Eutrope until 1081. However, a chapel was begun at la Trinité in 1060 and dedicated in 1070 to (among others) the two saintly bishops of Saintes: Eutropus and Léonce. During the next few centuries the celebration of St. Eutropus' feast increased and expanded at la Trinité to a *festum duplex* in the thirteenth century and eventually to a *festum subannuale* in the sixteenth century. Together with the chapel dedication, this would suggest that some relics might have found their way to Vendôme in the eleventh century, generating a purely local cult and office that developed from the veneration of the relics.

An office for St. Beatus was also composed at la Trinité and appears in the thirteenth-century breviary.[36] St. Beatus was traditionally supposed to have been a hermit living in a grotto beneath the castle walls of Vendôme. About 1040, a church was dedicated to the saint in Vendôme, and the canons of Laon sent an arm relic of the saint to la Trinité in 1164 (CT 1:99, no. 46; 2:425, no. 562). Métais argues that an eleventh-century monk of la Trinité probably wrote the office, a theory that fits all the available evidence. These two offices for Eutropus and Beatus— one connected with local relics, the other commemorating a native saint—must have given an impetus to cults in the Vendômois and thereby heightened regional pride.

Two of Geoffrey of Vendôme's works were liturgical hymns, one to the Virgin and one to Mary Magdalen.[37] Neither hymn is particularly original; the one celebrating the Magdalen reiterates Geoffrey's fascination with a sinner *par excellence* who, like the good thief, embodies hope for all other sinners. The first verse sums up Geoffrey's prayer:

Mary of repentance,
The formula for sinners, the hope of grace,
Keep us so that the author of goodness
Will now revive us lying buried in our sins.[38]

The liturgical literary activity at la Trinité also produced an anonymous twelfth-century hymn to the Virgin. This is not in Geoffrey's rhymed style and is less cliché-ridden and more sophisticated. The Virgin is portrayed as the greatest intercessor—the mediatrix of the incarnation and our salvation, and closes with the plea:

> Be for me the hope of grace
> You who bears the wealth of the world.[39]

The actual liturgical life at la Trinité can only be partly reconstructed because the customary is not complete. La Trinité probably had its customary in two volumes, as did Cluny;[40] what survives is part of the liturgical volume that indicates the care with which the liturgy was planned, the importance given to commemorating the stages in Christ's life, and the impressiveness of the ceremonies. The festival mass on Good Friday, celebrated in midafternoon, was the peak of Holy Week services (CT 4:353–57). After reading the Gospel and collect, all the monks, unshod, adored the cross. Two monks vested in red chasubles then carried a large, empty, wooden cross from a side altar to the high altar, where, facing the congregation, they held out the cross by its arms and sang the antiphon *Ecce lignum*. The cross was then fastened behind the altar, and the figure of Christ was covered ceremonially with a clean linen cloth.

The abbey's intellectual life grew out of its library and scriptorium. The only contemporary inventory is the one recorded by the lion artist, which suggests that in 1119 Augustine's writings were seen as the essential backbone for the library. Appropriately for an abbey dedicated to the Holy Trinity, the Augustinian work heading the list is his *De trinitate*. Jean Vezin, who has studied the scriptoria of Angers in the eleventh century, argues that there was a clear relationship between the manuscripts of the second half of the century produced in Angers, Tours, and Vendôme.[41] He states that the similarities can be found in most works written in areas under Geoffrey Martel's control: the Loire basin shared a characteristic use of dark brown inks, thick writing with pronounced clubbing and distinctive ligatures from *R* to following vowels. Today's reader still notices these features in the lion artist's works, produced at la Trinité as late as the second decade of the twelfth century.

Although only a small sample of the artistic and literary life of the monks of la Trinité survives today—mostly anonymous— there seems to have been a definite creative spirit at work. It flowed out of its formal boundaries and can be seen in sponta- neous works like the quick ink sketch or study of Christ on the binding leaf of one manuscript.[42] (See Plate 5) The Christ figure bends in a soft S curve and raises his right hand in a blessing. The gentle pose creates an interesting contrast to the angularity of the line. The figure's large head inclines to the right, and his huge eyes, which are the only facial features, seem full of power. This same creative energy flowed from a scribe's pen as he added a verse at the end of the *Life of St. Gregory*.[43] The work has left him spiritually naked in the recognition of his own deficiencies. He humbly begs the saint to clothe him and allow him joy by accepting his love and admiration. The climate at la Trinité in the eleventh and twelfth centuries was such that men expressed their creativity with verve and feeling, if not always in pure clas- sical forms.

Part II: Social and Spiritual Contributions

Improving the Quality of Life

The monks of la Trinité had an artistic and literary impact on their neighbors. A donor coming to the chapter house to place his gift on the altar and receive the thanks of the assembled monks saw the frescoes, vestments, and candles and may have participated in the liturgy. Laborers were involved in building monastic buildings, and patrons shared in the glory of the fin- ished products. Priories became economic foci for the growth of burgs. Angevin artistic styles followed Angevin patronage into the Vendômois to underscore the importance of the foun- ders. Literate men and women read the collections of abbots' let- ters, while offices celebrating local saints and their relics fostered regional pride. Nevertheless, those people receiving benefits from monastic creativity still constituted only a small percentage of the total population of the area. Did the community at large experience other positive results from the monks' activities? This question can be answered in the affirmative, since it can be argued that la Trinité did improve the quality of life for a diverse cross section of its neighbors by alleviating suffering in this world and by offering hope for salvation in the next world. The monks provided services for the poor, the sick, and the needy of the Vendômois.

To meet the most immediate need of the poor for food, la Trinité was actively involved in providing sustenance to the hungry. Much of this monastic charity was woven into the liturgy, like the *mandatum* of the poor on Maundy Thursday.[44] After the morning chapter meeting, the poor were selected for the service. One person was picked for each monk as well as one for each monk who had died during the year, and two for the abbot. This group of poor people attended mass with the monks but received only the unconsecrated host. After mass, a substantial meal of bread, wine, and vegetables was given to the poor. Later in the day after none, a procession formed, and with a great pealing of bells and singing of psalms entered the church through the galilee. The entire congregation communicated at the festival mass that followed. At the end of the service, the deacon and celebrant for the week escorted the poor into the cloister where they were all seated. Each monk took his place before a seated poor person. The monks sang an antiphon after the sounding of three gongs. Then each monk genuflected and proceeded to wash the feet of the person before him. The washing was followed by kissing the feet of the poor person and then offering him wine. Finally, each monk knelt before his partner in the liturgy, offered him two pennies, and kissed his hands. Afterwards when the monks entered the church for vespers, the poor were escorted out of the cloister.

The ceremony follows the New Testament model (John 13:4–5) and serves to remind each religious to act humbly and to imitate Christ in his daily life. Although the poor served as objects of the footwashing ceremony, their physical needs were not forgotten, and they were well fed before the long festival mass—

but not until after they had heard the early mass while still fasting. Humane concerns were balanced against ceremonial forms.

Another festival marked with a major distribution of food was All Saints' Day, when the monks fed one hundred hungry people (CT 4:360). Since the fundamental purpose of such liturgical charity was to emphasize corporate monastic almsgiving, on the first Sunday in Lent at the beginning of the most austere penitential season of the church, the monks went without an extra portion of food and donated it to the almoner for the poor. Liturgical charity could also be instituted by lay individuals. When Richilde and Hugo of Alluyes made a donation to the abbey, their spiritual benefits included the daily feeding of a poor person by the monks for as long as the donors should live (CT 1:383, no. 242).

The importance of this charity interconnected with the liturgy should not be underestimated either for the extent of its pragmatic worth or for its heightening of community awareness of the needy. Monastic charity, however, went beyond its ceremonial aspect to indicate a genuine response to social need. The monks could couple their concern for the hungry with the settling of litigation. After a woman had broken into a priory of la Trinité with her followers and despoiled it to enforce her right to procuration, she was brought to account by the monks and forced to return an equivalent amount of foodstuffs. The monks then gave this food to the hungry (CT 2:431, no. 566). In another case, the chronicle of the abbey describes a crisis situation in 1161 and mentions, in passing, that the abbey had assumed the responsibility of maintaining a daily dole.

> However, later such a famine began that mothers cast their babies at the doors of monasteries. Burghers, who previously had stood out as rich men, fled to other regions seeking sustenance, leaving their little gardens, vineyards, and farms behind. For indeed at that time a sester of wheat sold in Angers for twenty-five solidi and for fifteen solidi in Vendôme. Then Abbot Girard of la Trinité arranged that from the beginning of Lent to the Feast of St. John the Baptist, three sesters of grain would be given daily to the poor according to the customary daily alms distribution. Bread and cheese or vegetables shall be transported to the poor who live in the suburbs and cleared fields up to St. John's Day.[45]

The abbey went beyond limiting itself to symbolic liturgical charity by distributing food on a daily basis to the needy. Then when severe famine struck the area, the monks responded vigorously by transporting food to peasants who were too weak from malnutrition to travel into Vendôme.

The monks of la Trinité combined a concern for the sick with their caring for the hungry. They had access to some general medical knowledge, since the monastic library contained at least three medical manuscripts.[46] Abbot Oderic uses physiological metaphors in his treatise, indicating a sound understanding of fever and the infectious process, while from Geoffrey of Vendôme's many letters about his illnesses, we hear of purgatives, the lancing of a boil, and oil treatments for contractures.[47] Monastic efforts to care for the sick tend to go unnoted in the documents, although one case is mentioned indirectly during the discussion of Count Fulk Rechin's mistreatment of the abbey. The count seized and had prepared for himself some finely ground flour (*piscisgranum*), which the monks were preparing for a sick man in Houssay (CT 1:301, no. 173).

The monastery maintained a *hospitium* for wealthy sick people. In 1145, the lord of Beaugency generously endowed the abbey for its care of one of his knights who had died in the monastic *hospitium* (CT 2:330, no. 508). This facility was hospice as well as hospital, serving as an accommodation for mounted guests.[48] In addition, the abbey had a hospice (*domus elemosine*) in which the poor were received both as indigents and when traveling. The facility's revenues were increased in the last year of the twelfth century when the institution was described as having been in existence for some time (CT 2:495, no. 618). The almshouse was certainly active at la Trinité from the abbey's earliest days, for in 1058 the abbey accepted into its community two brothers who were serfs after they had been blinded by Geoffrey Martel for traitorous behavior (CT 1:219, no. 122). Although the men made a donation of five *mansurae* of land to the abbey, the monks were still performing an act of charity in taking blind men into the monastic *familia,* since the sightless would have proved a substantial burden to the monks.

The abbey offered solutions to people trapped by social or economic conditions. Orphaned or fatherless children, like Magnelin, were given a home and training (CT 1:55, no. 34); families ruined by inflation could commend themselves as serfs to the monastery and receive secure support. (See Chapter Two.) When rapidly escalating costs in the 1070s forced one noblewoman to turn to her relatives for aid, they refused to help her (CT 1:365, no. 233). The monks, however, were willing to grant her and her husband a lifetime income in exchange for a piece of her property, thereby insuring them a secure old age. In the light of David Herlihy's persuasive argument for a continuous downward trend of social mobility in the Middle Ages, monastic charity and support played an important part in social welfare and became critical for the excess daughters of the petty nobility who could not sally forth to repair their fortunes with the sword.[49]

La Trinité, in short, functioned as a medieval social service institution supplying charitable, medical, and economic assistance to its neighbors. These services, whether specifically linked to the liturgy or not, usually still were part of the religious life of the monks. Even in the reception of a visitor to the abbey, prayers were offered with him as an integral part of the hospitality (CT 1:451, no. 295).

The monks accepted the command to love their neighbors as a serious charge, but even this took second place to their primary purpose of working to achieve their own salvation and through their prayers to help others to gain the rewards of eternity. One way in which la Trinité actively pursued spiritual goals was by implementing reform ideas. During the eleventh and twelfth centuries, many proprietary churches were being returned to ecclesiastical ownership (usually monastic), which could act to improve the quality of parish life. In one such case the monks recorded an agreement reached in the 1040s between Abbot Oderic and the priest of Mazé.[50] The priest was to promise to give up his wife and live chastely. He became the man of the abbot and received some vineyards as a fief. The parish revenues were carefully enumerated so that it would be clear what income went to the priest and what was owed to the abbey. In this way, Oderic attempted to improve the care accorded the souls of the parishioners who were indirectly in the abbey's care.

Monastic suffrages lay at the heart of the abbey's spiritual life. These prayers were offered for both the rich and the poor, although the large number of documents dealing with benefits received by the prosperous and prominent tends to obscure spiritual concern for the poor. The lady chapel had been specifically constructed in Vendôme to serve the poor and the monastery's servants (CT 1:356, no. 222). In Angers the church of Toussaint was acquired by la Trinité in 1049 (CT 1:165, no. 92); this church had been built for the poor such that its priest was to pray for and bury poor people and to visit them in their homes. A few years later after the construction of l'Evière, la Trinité gave up the care of Toussaint. Bienvenu defends this action, stressing that although charity formed part of monastic activity, it was not central to the monastic ideal.[51] Equally, from a practical point of view, la Trinité could not deal with all social needs in the area. Once committed to the responsibilities of l'Evière, the monks may have decided to give up Toussaint so as to concentrate their charitable efforts in Angers within a monastic environment—their accustomed sphere.

Monastic spiritual benefits could take various forms. One could become a member of the prayer fellowship during one's lifetime or have commemorations of one's death by masses, a feast, or be included in the monastery's martyrology. Each of these undertakings insured monastic prayers for the recipient. Pilgrims about to leave for Rome might come on the eve of departure to solicit the monks' prayers because when danger loomed, the prayers of the religious proved comforting (CT 1:280, no. 162). The shoemaker, Thibald, was distraught when his son died participating in pagan games on the vigil of St. John the Baptist, since the boy had died without confessing his sins or receiving communion (CT 1:411, no. 261). Abbot Oderic comforted the father with the promise of thirty masses for the boy's soul.

La Trinité's monks could exercise great power because of the awe and respect accorded them for their pious lives. The relics in their possession enhanced their position. The first evidence of a cure connected with la Trinité's relics comes from the second half of the twelfth century. A child developed an eye disease that drove him to beg his father to cease molesting the monks of la Trinité (CT 2:450, no. 580). When the father complied, his son improved; the entire family then went to the abbey into the sanctuary of the *Sainte Larme* where "the boy John received the original health of his eyes by the grace of God."[52]

The spiritual power felt to emanate from the abbey and its inhabitants led lay men and women to prize the guarantee of burial within the monastic confines. Important lay people could be buried in one of the abbey's chapels, or in the galilee or cloister, and women as well as men received the privilege of monastic burial.[53] Generally, monastic burial seems to have been accorded to those from knightly families, although occasionally commoners were interred in the abbey, as was Raimbert, a pelterer. Sometimes people arranged before their death for their own burial or the family made arrangements at the time of a death. It was also common for a lord to assume the responsibility of planning and paying for the monastic burial of one of his own knights.[54] In dealing with requests for burials, la Trinité does not seem to have resorted to the questionable tactics that did Sainte-Croix, whose monks pushed their neighbors to make wills, and sometimes even refused burial to those who died intestate.[55]

As a corporate body the monks affected, supported, and comforted their lay neighbors. Even more, an individual monk choosing to lead a particularly austere eremetical life could make an especially strong impression on the secular community. Hervé—mistakenly said to be of Chalonnes—was one such monk of la Trinité. As a young man, Hervé had temporarily been a member of Robert Arbrissel's pious band in the forest of Craon. Later, around 1102, he entered the cell of Saint-Eutrope attached to the priory of l'Evière in Angers where he was joined in the eremetical life by Eve, a young English ascetic.[56] Geoffrey of Vendôme addressed them a letter just after the two were established in Angers, celebrating the beauties of the holy life; the two anchorites must have truly lived above all reproach, since the abbot had sharply criticized Robert Arbrissel for living in just such questionable closeness with women religious.[57] Although the two lived an austere life, it was enriched by books borrowed from l'Evière and la Trinité, and at some point, Eve had the comfort of being joined by her niece, Ravenissa. The two women added an intermarginal note to a Gospel book of the abbey's,

> Eve, a recluse made this sign of the cross in memory of her constancy to her vow and Ravenissa her niece [made] that one.[58]

Hervé deeply impressed those seeking after the monastic life and served as an informal recruiter of novices for la Trinité. Two letters of Abbot Geoffrey to Hervé deal with oblates sent to the abbey by the hermit.[59] Apparently Geoffrey proved understanding and receptive when Hervé encouraged men from simple backgrounds to enter the monastery despite their lack of dowry. Etienne Delaruelle suggests that the eremetical life in the twelfth century was consistent with the concept of the Christian church as the Gregorian Reformers wanted to shape it.[60] Therefore, it was logical for Abbot Geoffrey to support the recluses out of sympathy for reform goals.

In sum, the abbey of la Trinité had a creative existence that can be seen in its artistic, literary, social, and spiritual activity. Monks produced lasting works of great merit like the bell tower, the bells of which and of each priory continually touched the daily lives of the monastery's neighbors. The monks fashioned liturgical hymns and reached out to help the poor by reenacting charitable works in imitation of Christ's acts. La Trinité's religious prayed for travelers and gave them shelter; they commissioned work by artists as well as creating works of their own; they accepted society's damaged members and buried its dead. Life in the Vendômois in the eleventh and twelfth centuries would have been bleaker and harder to bear if the monks had not been there to improve the quality of earthly existence and to increase the hope for salvation.

Notes

1. See Frédéric Lesueur, *Les Eglises de Loir-et-Cher* (Paris, 1969), pp. 7–13, for the following discussion of stylistic similarities in the department.
2. CT 1:439, no. 282. Lesueur, *Eglises de Loir-et-Cher*, p. 80, dates the structure to the twelfth century.

3. CT 1:437, no. 280, and Lesueur, *Eglises de Loir-et-Cher,* p. 287.

4. Ibid., p. 140. Although this doorway has been extensively restored, it reproduces the original carefully. The lands of Coulommiers were given to the abbey in 1080 (CT 1:455–61, no. 299), and the church as it exists now was built in the latter part of the twelfth century.

5. CT 1:111, no. 57, and 2:192, no. 423. Although only the gatehouse remains now, Launay drew another of the buildings that stood just inside the gate and was built in the same style as the gate. Vendôme B.M. Gervais Launay, *Vendôme,* 3 vols. (Vendôme, n.d.), vol. 1, unnumbered plate of Courtozé.

6. L. De Farcy, "La Tour Saint-Aubin," *Bulletin monumental* 70 (1906), 552.

7. Mussat, *L'Architecture gothique dans l'ouest de la France,* pp. 213–21.

8. Abbot Geoffrey wrote the first of his letters seeking to bring John back to la Trinité between 1102 and 1104, *Ep.* 3:16 (PL 157:122–24), and the last in the years 1116–18, *Ep.* 3:30 (PL 157:131–32). Plat, *L'Eglise de la Trinité,* p. 50, suggests John's connection with the tower.

9. Plat, *L'Art de bâtir en France,* p. 123. Crozet, "Le Clocher de la Trinité de Vendôme," p. 145.

10. Plat, *L'Eglise de la Trinité,* p. 69, suggests that the tower of la Trinité influenced the towers of Chartres.

11. "Dedit etiam dimidium censum domorum quae sunt in cymiterio, domum suam propriam, quae juxta ecclesiam erat cum furno, puteo, orto, curte, quae in circuitu est," CT 1:415, no. 265. "Dedit et quinque arpennos terrae, circa ecclesiam ipsam extra cimiterium, ubi domos aedificarent tam monachi quam rustici eorum," CT 1:439, no. 282.

12. Taralon, "Découverte de peintures," 31–35.

13. Vendôme B.M. MS 203, fol. 19v, "in pictura niger color substernitur, ut supiectus alb et rubeus pulchrior ostendatur. . . ."

14. Taralon, "Découverte de peintures," p. 34.

15. Joan Evans, "La date des peintures murales décorant la chapelle des moines" *Annales de l'académie de Mâcon,* 3d series, 42 (1954–55), 88–89.

16. Vendôme B.M. MS 26, fol. 240v, "brevis librorum Sanctae Trinitatis Vindocinensis, factus anno incarnationis Dominice M. C. XVIIII., jubente domno G. abbate, anno ordinationis sue XX. VI." (The inventory is edited, CT 2:210, no. 435.)

17. The one exception is MS 35, whose historiated capitals have been brightly and somewhat clumsily colored—perhaps by someone other than the lion artist.

18. It was standard iconographical usage to depict a living person with a square halo (or nimbus) and to reserve the circular halo for dead saints. George Ferguson, *Signs and Symbolism in Christian Art* (New York, 1959), pp. 89–90.

19. Vendôme B.M. MS 34, fol. 146. This is Augustine's *Contra Faustum* and *Enchiridion.* The miniature of the author is fol. 90v.

20. See, for example, the three historiated capitals of MS 23, also by the gold leaf artist. One depicts St. Paul within the bowl of a letter *P.* Paul has a halo and is sitting behind a desk writing on a parchment with quill and knife. The saint wears a blue tunic and pink robe and is within an architectural frame. Just outside the frame, a tonsured monk, wearing a pink robe and gray cape, holds a manuscript. The bowl of the *P* is made of a fanciful blue bird with pink wings. The letter's ascender is of pink interlace, incorporating a man being grabbed by a bird. The background of the letter is of intense blue with little white star bursts; the whole is on a gold leaf field.

21. Anne Pascaud-Granboulan, "Le Vitrail de la vierge à la Trinité de Vendôme," *l'Information d'histoire de l'art* 16 (1971), 130. Also see Louis Grodecki, *Les Vitraux des églises de France* (Paris, 1947), p. 16.

22. Pascaud-Granboulan, "Le Vitrail," p. 129. A witness list from the last quarter of the eleventh century of CT 2:60, no. 338, includes "Lisoius, vitrearius."

23. Gagnières made a watercolor of the reliquary, B.N. Cabinet des Estampes, V A 81 Topographie de la France, Loir-et-Cher, Vendôme. The drawings are reproduced by

A. de Rochambeau, "Voyage à la Sainte-Larme de Vendôme," *Bull. Vend.* 12 (1873), 183–186.

24. *Histoire veritable de la Sainte Larme que notre Seigneur pleura sur le Lazare. Comme et par qui elle fut apportée au monastère de la Sainte Trinité de la ville de Vandôme* (Vendôme, 1672), pp. 18–22.

25. René Crozet, "Le Monument de la Sainte Larme à la Trinité de Vendôme." *Bulletin monumental* 121 (1963), 171–72. See similar portable altars made in Germany in the eleventh and twelfth centuries. Hanns Swarzenski, *Monuments of Romanesque Art: The Art of Church Treasures in North-Western Europe* (Chicago, 1953), plates 85, 234, and 242.

26. Seymour, *Notre-Dame of Noyon*, p. 175.

27. Vendôme B.M. MS 203. Five different hands are evident in the script, all of which can be dated only generally to the second half of the eleventh or early twelfth century. The manuscript is small, 160 by 112 mm, has a modern binding, and simple rubrications to mark the beginning of each section.

28. Ibid., fol. 14r, "humana etenim mens aquae more et circumclusa ad superiora colligitur." The monks dammed water behind locks, which in the case of the locks of Courtozé, they opened periodically for the fishing, CT 1:405, no. 257.

29. Geoffrey of Vendôme addressed letters to his former teachers: *Ep.* 5:14 (PL 157:196); 5:12 (PL 157:195); 5:16 (PL 157:199). Jean Vezin, *Les Scriptoria d'Angers au XIe siècle* (Paris, 1974), p. 11, mentions that there was a Garnier serving as archdeacon of Angers c. 1084–1110.

30. The subjects of Geoffrey of Vendôme, *Op.* 13–16, and *Ser.* 1–3, 5–10, are sin and penitence. The sacraments are dealt with in *Op.* 1, 8, 9, and *Ser.* 10. Reform and governance are the subjects of *Op.* 2, 3–6 (addressed to Pope Calixtus), and 11–12 and *Ser.* 11. Geoffrey of Vendôme, *Ser.* 10 (PL 157:274–76), is *De latrone salvato in cruce.*

31. André Wilmart, "La Collection chronologique des écrits de Geoffroi abbé de Vendôme," *Revue bénédictine* 43 (1931), 244.

32. Geoffrey of Vendôme wrote Calixtus: *Ep.* 1:10 (PL 157:51–52); 1:11 (PL 157:52–53); 1:12 (PL 157:53–54); 1:13 (PL 157:54–55); to Honorius 1:14 (PL 157:55); 1:15 (PL 157:55–57). Also CT 2:239, no. 452, 2:243–47, no. 458; 2:248, no. 459; 2:249, no. 460; 2:249, no. 461, are all Honorius' bulls supporting la Trinité. Geoffrey did have a difference of opinion with one papal legate, Umbald of Lyons (legate during 1126–28) over attendance at a council in Orléans: Geoffrey of Vendôme, *Ep.*, 1:29 (PL 157:69).

33. Ibid., 1:7 (PL 157:42–46). "Super his autem si quis aliter senserit, non est catholicus, manifestetur, et veritatis argumento probabitur esse hereticus. Tolerandus quidem est pastor, ut canones dicunt, pro reprobis moribus; si vero exorbitaverit a fide, jam non est pastor, sed adversarius. . . ."

34. Vendôme B.M. MS 17 E, fols. 382r–386. The office is printed and discussed by Charles Métais, "Un Office de Saint Eutrope au XIe siècle," *Bull. Vend.* 25 (1886), 253–84; reprinted in *Etudes et documents,* 3 vols. (Vendôme, 1888), 1:1–27. See p. 11 for author's discussion of Benedictines at Saint-Eutrope and pp. 4–5 for development of the feast day.

35. Guillot, *Le Comte d'Anjou,* 1:52–53, deals with Geoffrey's campaigns in Aquitaine. Simon, *Histoire de Vendôme,* 1:47, and de Pétigny, *Histoire Archéologique du Vendômois,* p. 262, both recount the story of the translation of the saints' relics to Vendôme.

36. Vendôme B.M. MS 17 E, fols, 391r–394v, printed by Métais, "Saint Bienheuré de Vendôme: Vie et offices inédits XIe–XIIIe siècles," *Bull. Vend.* 27 (1888), 255–97, and reprinted by Métais, *Etudes et documents* (Vendôme, 1888), 1:1–45. See p. 7 for author's theory on dating its composition.

37. Geoffrey of Vendôme, *Op.* 17 (PL 157:234–35), and 18 (PL 157:235–38).

38. Ibid.:

Maria poenitentiae
Formula lapsis, spes veniae,
Ut nos auctor bonitatis

Jam sepultos in peccatis
Resuscitet, obtine.

39. Vendôme B.M. MS 60, fols. lv–3v:

Spes mihi sis veniae
Quae vehis orbis opem.

40. Hunt, *Cluny under St. Hugh*, p. 34.
41. Jean Vezin, *Les Scriptoria*, pp. 2, 102, 128. For inks see p. 113, for clubbing see p. 127, for ligatures see p. 212.
42. Vendôme B.M. MS 49, on recto side of unnumbered front binding leaf.
43. Vendôme B.M. MS 52, fol. 110v:

Ludere me libuit variabilis ordine campi,
Postquam prosa fugit musa jocosa redit,
Haec mihi tu tribuis doctor pretiose Gregori,
Qui bona das famulis sed mala nulla tuis;
Vestitus coepi nudus tua munia dixi.
Indue me factis velleribusque tuis;
Et quia mortalis desunt commertia carnis
Da mihi sub pedibus posse jacere tuis.

44. See CT 4:347–53, for the following discussion of the liturgical customs at la Trinité for Maundy Thursday. Lester K. Little, *Religious Poverty and the Profit Economy in Medieval Europe* (Ithaca, N.Y., 1978), p. 67, speaks of monastic charity as being secondary to as well as comfortably integrated with the liturgy.
45. "Annales de Vendôme," p. 72. "Tanta autem postea fames exorta est, ut matres projicerent infantulos ad portas monasteriorum; burgenses, qui ante divites extiterant, relictis hortulis, vineis et prediis, in alienas regiones fugiebant victum querentes: quippe tunc enim vendebatur sextarium frumenti apud [civitatem] Andegavam xxv solidis, Vindocino xv solidis. Tunc abbas Girardus instituit ut cotidie a principio quadragesime usque ad festivitatem sancti Johannis Babtiste darentur pauperibus iii sextaria annone preter consuetum beneficium; pauperibus jacentibus in vicis et plateis portabatur panis et caseus vel legumen usque ad eandem festivitatem." Niermeyer believes that this use of *beneficium* can best be translated as "alms." J. F. Niermeyer, *Mediae Latinitatis Lexicon Minus* (Leiden, 1976), p. 96, col. 1.
46. Vendôme B.M. MS 109, Galen, *Opuscula medica;* MS 174, Constantine of Africa, *Opuscula medica;* and MS 175, an anonymous medical work.
47. Vendôme B.M. MS 203, fol. 15v. "Vulnera enim clausa plus cruciant, quia cum putredo que intrinsecus fervet eicitur, ad salutem dolor aperitur." Also Oderic continues to use accurate medical metaphors, fol. 16r. Geoffrey of Vendôme, *Ep.* 4:25 (PL 157:168), mentions an overstrong dosage, "qua dum corpus purgare debui, pene me corporis vita purgavi." *Ep.* 4:32 (PL 157:173) tells of the nuns of Fontevrault lancing a boil on Geoffrey's back. In *Ep.* 4:11 (PL 157:156–57) Geoffrey sarcastically recommends oil for shriveled hands—"shriveled," in this case, by lack of caring, not by physical injury.
48. Emile Lesne, *Histoire de la propriété ecclésiastique en France*, Les Eglises et les monastères: centres d'accueil, d'exploitation et de peuplement, 6 Mémoires et travaux, pub. by Facultés de Lille 53 (Lille, 1943), p. 126. For the *domus elemosine*, see p. 142. At Cluny this same discrimination was apparent with mounted travelers received at the guesthouse and pedestrians in the almonry. Hunt, *Cluny under St. Hugh*, p. 65.
49. David Herlihy, "Three Patterns of Social Mobility in Medieval History," *Journal of Interdisciplinary History* 3 (1973), 646. "Because of differences in rates of replacement across the social spectrum, families in favored positions produced more heirs and successors than those on the less advantaged levels of society. The dominant trend of social mobility in this traditional society was therefore consistently downward."

50. CT 1:150–51, no. 80. Also see C. van de Kieft, "Une Eglise privée de l'abbaye de la Trinité de Vendôme au XIe siècle," *Moyen âge* 69 (1963), 157–68, in which this transaction is examined.

51. Bienvenu, "Pauvreté, misères et charité," p. 15.

52. "Ibi Johannes praedictus puer, pristinam sanitatem oculorum suorum Dei gratia recepit."

53. CT 2:488, no. 612, is a burial in a chapel; 2:31, no. 323, and 2:474, no. 600, are burials in the galilee; 2:429, no. 565, and 2:516, no. 636, are burials in the cloister. Examples of the burials of women within the abbey are found in 1:314, no. 182, and 2:279, no. 476. For Raimbert's burial, see CT 1:294, no. 168.

54. CT 2:43–45, no. 329; 2:125, no. 374; 2:364–65, no. 526.

55. Garaud, *L'Abbaye Sainte-Croix*, p. 31.

56. See André Wilmart, "Eve et Goscelin," *Revue bénédictine* 50 (1938), 428. Etienne Delaruelle, "Les Ermites et la spiritualité populaire," *La Piété populaire au moyen âge* (Turin, 1975), p. 127, points out that medieval hermits cannot be defined exactly, since they could practice *inclusio* singly, in groups, under a rule or independently, in the wilderness or near a monastery.

57. Geoffrey of Vendôme, *Ep.* 4:48 (PL 157:184–86), is to Eve and Hervé; 4:47 (PL 157:181–84) castigates Robert Arbrissel.

58. Vendôme B.M. MS 2, fol. 1r, "hoc signum crucis istius fecit Eva reclusa ob memoriam stabilitatis suae et istud Ravenissa neptas eius."

59. Geoffrey of Vendôme, *Ep.* 4:49 (PL 157:186) and 4:50 (PL 157:186–88).

60. Delaruelle, "Les Ermites," p. 152.

Conclusion

THE CONFLICT in monastic life between, on the one hand, the spiritual isolation from the world exhorted by the Rule and, on the other, the social responsibility and care of material possessions demanded by lay patrons, created enormous tensions in the history of the abbey of la Trinité. Before the Gregorian Reform, these contradictory impulses led all monasteries to an interdependence and identification with the world in an absorption of religious houses by secular society that was part of what Norman Cantor has termed "the medieval equilibrium."[1] Bifocal monastic concerns with material as well as spiritual matters both embedded the monastery in its environment as a living institution, interacting on many practical levels with its neighbors, and constrained it to remain spiritually aloof. The fragile balance of these ambivalent goals and the integral membership in its wider society that la Trinité maintained in its early years began to shift near the beginning of the twelfth century.

Abbot Oderic exercised restraints calculated to maintain the equilibrium between a "strong grasp on the things of this world, and an ardent desire for the rewards of eternity."[2] During the years of his abbacy, la Trinité grew rapidly in numbers and wealth, as benefactors from all social levels donated property to the monks. The geographical dispersion of these gifts necessitated an organizing system involving outlying cells. Monastic professions increased so rapidly that by 1080 one hundred monks assisted at an important chapter, while the number of servants also had to grow proportionately larger. Apparently, Oderic felt no need to limit this expansion of manpower and material holdings. Nevertheless, he attempted to contain the growth within

169

appropriate limits: functionaries numbered no more than the apostolic twelve; monastic oblates seem to have been only adults; and outlying cells were kept dependent and designated as *obedientiae* (the same word used to describe the vow of monastic obedience). Oderic attempted to define the abbey's expansion within the spiritual boundaries of the regular life—a life in which the humble and obedient adherence to the Rule was a foremost concern.

Although his elevation to the cardinalate placed him among the great prelates of the church, Oderic confined his energies to the directing of the abbey and its development, without losing sight of the Benedictine goals. Except for his support of the Gregorian Reform on the local level (e.g., enforcing celibacy among the parish clergy), he avoiding meddling in ecclesiastical or secular politics. Rather, he interpreted the Rule in such a way that the abbey involved itself in the needs of the county without weakening its own fabric. In a period of rapid inflation, the abbot accepted commendations of starving families. The abbey established a hospice to operate as almshouse and travelers' resthouse. The monks distributed alms to and offered prayers for the poor; they built a lady chapel next to the chevet of the monastic church to insure a ministry to the lower levels of society. The prestige and piety of the cardinal-abbot added enormously to the renown of the abbey, so that Oderic's program was rewarded by and interconnected with the lay community, a cross section of which, commoners and lords, actively supported the abbey.

The role of both abbot and abbey changed subtly during the thirty-nine years of Geoffrey of Vendôme's abbacy. The social groups from which the abbey drew its support contracted so that by the late eleventh century the abbey's lay patrons were almost exclusively noble. Growth at the abbey was allowed to continue, but the spiritual restraints—although mostly symbolic—were allowed to fall into desuetude. Children joined the ranks of adult oblates; the larger obediences were elevated to the status of partially independent priories; monastic officials proliferated beyond the original twelve; and the organization of the abbey's affairs became increasingly bureaucratic. La Trinité's expansion and growth paralleled the burgeoning organizational complexity of the lives of its patrons, the counts of Anjou, as well as of other great secular families.

Abbot Geoffrey entered enthusiastically into the affairs of the entire world as he knew it. He supported reformist goals and was vocal in attacking lay investiture and simony. He lectured popes, lords, abbots, and bishops; he traveled extensively, wrote, and oversaw the increasingly dispersed priories. Geoffrey rejected Oderic's restricted sphere of influence for a larger world. This extension of the abbot's interests far from home hurt the abbey's organic involvement with the Vendômois; and when Geoffrey was active locally, it was most often confronting the house of Vendôme which tended to damage local harmony.

Each abbot had to make personal decisions about his style and role in the chapter and the world outside the cloister. Oderic had a homely personal style. Although the acquisition of a cardinalate from Hildebrand raised him to the rank of a prince of the church, Oderic continued to function as abbot-father for his monks. In contrast, Geoffrey affected a more showy abbatial manner, acting as an ecclesiastical lord both within the abbey and outside its walls. He often appeared at public occasions with his own crucifer, and usually eschewed the humble mule to travel on horseback like a noble, sometimes with a large entourage.[3] Geoffrey treated his monks sternly, stressing their obligation to obey him in every particular. The leadership of la Trinité became in Geoffrey's time more a position of worldly power than of monastic virtue. This change was not unique to la Trinité; for example, the same shift in outward appearances can be detected between the practices of Abbot Hugh of Cluny and those of his successor in roughly the same time period.[4]

The many changes in size, organization, and style evident during the abbacy of Geoffrey constituted the beginning of the loss of the careful balance of spiritual and secular involvements that Oderic had been able to maintain. A number of factors upset this delicate juggling act: political changes, a general religious trend that can be seen as a crisis of monastic prosperity, new lay institutions, and the personality of the fifth abbot.

La Trinité both affected and was affected by the major political shifts occurring locally and across Europe. Wars, usurpations, dynastic marriages—all left their mark on the abbey. In 1030 the county of Vendôme was a small, independent unit with only a nominal tie to the bishop of Chartres. After ousting its count a year later, Geoffrey Martel controlled the Vendômois, and since Vendôme fell thereby to the control of the Angevin heir, this initiated the abbey's dependent relationship with Anjou. The most important long-term result of this patronage for the monastery was that it precluded linking the abbey with the French monarchy. At one time Louis VII had confirmed some of la Trinité's monastic holdings (when his marriage to Eleanor of Aquitaine had brought Poitou and Saintonge within his purview). But after Louis and Eleanor's marriage was dissolved, la Trinité slipped out of the Capetian sphere of influence. In direct contrast, the abbey of Marmoutier, which enjoyed royal protection, managed to outstrip la Trinité and attain monastic hegemony in the Loire basin. La Trinité also suffered a loss when the quality of Angevin patronage shifted so that the counts of Anjou no longer could maintain their original personal intimacy with their client abbey but assumed instead the position of impartial rulers and judges. The changes felt by the abbey in this period of divided loyalties and expanded political horizons belonged to a much larger process—the breakdown of localism.

Other forces affecting secular society also touched the abbey. In 1185 Henry II's articulation of the customs of the abbey effected a peaceful settlement between abbey and count. In accepting the customs, which clearly stated that la Trinité had a vassal's responsibility of aid to its overlord (the count of Vendôme), the abbey lost its political immunity; it fell victim to the feudalization of its society. The abbey itself had often resorted to establishing feudal ties with recalcitrant patrons to effect peaceful settlements of disagreements, and in 1185 the strong Angevin hand imposed the same solution on the monastery's relationship with the house of Vendôme.

Religious reform movements generated by the church and the laity also had an impact on the abbey. From the mid-eleventh century, the papacy inaugurated an active program to gain a position of preeminence. The Gregorian Reform sought to break secular control over ecclesiastical property and privileges and to subordinate the bishops to Rome. The papal reform initiative—despite its setbacks—was generally successful, as is evident in the increased flow of lawsuits to the papal courts and of demands for papal grants of exemption. La Trinité was one of many monastic bodies that carried their litigation to Rome and petitioned exemptions. Although the abbey received almost total *de jure* freedom from episcopal authority, the monks of la Trinité continued to rely heavily on local bishops for support in the monastery's daily affairs.

Two abbots were caught up, albeit to different degrees, in their enthusiasm for the reformists' cause. Abbot Oderic probably received his cardinalate to enlist him in the active ranks of the reformers. After Hildebrand became pope and pushed his claims to extremes, Oderic seems to have withdrawn quietly from the body of Gregorian supporters because their demands had exceeded reasonable bounds. Geoffrey of Vendôme also espoused a reforming position. Yet he too withdrew support from Pope Pascal II when the latter carried the Gregorian program to its logical but extremist end. Both abbots were concerned with the spiritual reform of the church, but always within moderate boundaries compatible with the spiritual as well as the worldly involvement of the monastic life. In this instance, Geoffrey showed the same basic concern as Oderic not to upset the equilibrium between the spiritual and the secular.

Sentiment for religious reform flowed upward from the laity in this period, particularly in west-central France. The enthusiasm engendered by Robert Arbrissel serves as some indication of popular feelings. Lay spirituality reached a high level, as did support for the reformed monastic orders like that of Cîteaux. Between 1050 and 1150 criticism of the great Benedictine houses, of their wealth and litigiousness, became general, and by 1100 the Benedictine monopoly was broken.[5] Despite this, the new orders had little success in the Vendômois; for instance, no Cistercian abbeys appeared in the area during the twelfth century. There were two causes for la Trinité's lack of new rivals. On one hand, most of the available property and resources had already been apportioned among la Trinité, Marmoutier, and other Benedictine houses in the area, while the movement of assarting had left little unoccupied land in which a new order might have taken root. At the same time, la Trinité had maintained a pious reputation through the sanctity of men like Abbot Oderic, the hermit Hervé, and two monks who became bishops (Arrald, who became bishop of Chartres, and Arnulf, later bishop of Gap). These men, probably in concert with others whose names are now unknown, perpetuated the image of high Benedictine spirituality that sustained la Trinité's popularity into the first half of the twelfth century.

Nevertheless, la Trinité still experienced negative ramifications of its prosperity. The increasing accumulation of property made it more and more difficult for the monks to maintain a balance between their divergent responsibilities. A departmentalization of money and men developed to handle the abbey's extensive holdings. The cloistered family that lay at the heart of Benedict's precepts was expanded and complicated beyond a workable size; monks were dispersed throughout the countryside to oversee property; wealth and a lordly style of living tended increasingly to isolate the abbot from his monks. The care of things grew to overbalance the care of souls as the crushing weight of the material side tipped the monastic scales. La Trinité took part—albeit unwillingly—in the general shift from gift to profit economy that Lester Little defines for eleventh-century Europe.[6]

The same period saw the beginning of the movement for secular individuals and societies to undertake charitable and civic good works that had formerly been the province of the monks. The first local evidence for this development was the foundation of the hospice of Saint-Jacques in Vendôme in the first half of the twelfth century.[7] Increasingly during the thirteenth century, social welfare passed from monastic to secular hands—a shift that eventually diminished monastic social and spiritual welfare concerns.

The final factor in disrupting the equilibrium was the personality of Geoffrey of Vendôme. Although the counts of Vendôme had felt little love for la Trinité from the time of its founding, Geoffrey's combativeness and arrogant claims of privilege visibly embittered the relationship between the local rulers and the abbey. It took decades before the memories faded enough to allow the abbey to accept its local lordly family in the place of that of Anjou as chief monastic supporter, a change that occurred at the expense of the abbey's immunity. The counts of Vendôme were never to share the intimacy with the abbey that had its Angevin patrons in the mid-eleventh century. However, after 1185, when the abbey accepted the obligations of vassalage, the counts of Vendôme did assume a seigneurial role. Abbot Geoffrey also affected the abbey's direction by involving himself and his monks in an enlarged political sphere, thus eroding some of the former sense of community la Trinité had shared with its neighbors. Finally, it was Geoffrey, unaware of the possible impact of his actions, who dispensed with the early restraints that had served as reminders of the abbey's dual responsibilities.[8]

By the end of the twelfth century, la Trinité had mostly lost its ability to balance piety and property. The "medieval equilibrium" came to an end at the abbey, not because the monks withdrew from the world to pursue a more ascetic life,[9] but because the abbey's expansion, the replacing of localism by regionalism, and divisive political events caused the abbey's organic bond to its environment to fail. When the increasingly exaggerated care for material possessions and prestige was offset by a diminishing social responsibility, the monks could no longer live in *sancta simplicitas*. La Trinité's contributions to its world receded in proportion as its worldly possessions increased, to the diminution of its role in its social environment.

Nevertheless, la Trinité had functioned mostly in harmony with and to the advantage of its community for a century and a half—a long time for any institution to contribute positively to society. The abbey's strength grew out of the important bond it had with its patrons, a bond that worked well because of its mutual benefits for both monks and patrons.

Geoffrey Martel and Agnes of Burgundy had founded la Trinité to satisfy their own needs and ambitions. The site chosen reflected their economic and defensive considerations; the dedication and the choice of the first abbot expressed Geoffrey's rivalry with his father; and the timing of the foundation pointed to the founders' urgent need to legitimize their marriage and their overlordship of Vendôme. In a general way, moreover, the founders could bask in the reflected glory and piety of their rich, well-ordered foundation, which centered around a church whose height, dimensions, and monumental sculpture expressed its self-confidence. Moreover, the monastery consciously did its part to help its founders by supplying tangible aid during periods of military need.

In addition to their rich endowment (primarily of landed property), Agnes and Geoffrey exercised pressure to encourage lesser barons and knights to support the abbey. Geoffrey could command the loyalty of his men—foresters, officials, and castellans—who sought to imitate their lord's generosity, while Agnes persuaded others to become patrons. Not only did Geoffrey and Agnes enlist other benefactors, but they also acted as the monks' protectors. The extent to which Geoffrey's reputation kept the abbey free of depredations became apparent only when a spate of attacks and claims hit the abbey after his death.

The founders did not include privileges in their original endowment. In 1056, however, reacting to papal pressure, Geoffrey reinstated Fulk Oison in Vendôme, which necessitated a change to protect la Trinité from Fulk's jealousy and belligerence. Although Agnes and Geoffrey were no longer married, their common concern compelled them to act jointly, donating la Trinité and l'Evière to the pope, and thereby creating the base for the abbey's subsequent exemption. The monks' desire for complete exemption was such that they did not stop at falsifying charters to that end. However, in practice they repeatedly called upon the local bishops for services and support.

Patronage often embroiled the abbey in the worldly affairs of its patrons. In a society where armed conflict was a commonplace, this meant that support for the monks could become a political issue. The counts of Anjou and Poitou continually fought each other through the second half of the eleventh century. During one such confrontation, the hard-pressed Angevin count was forced to petition divine aid, promising to right la Trinité's wrongs if he won the battle. He was successful and made good his vow. Later, the political rivalry of the two rulers led to the count of Poitou's decision to block the entry into his lands of la Trinité's monastic competitor, the abbot of Saint-Aubin. In both cases, no hesitation was shown by the rulers who saw such interchanges with the abbey as a natural extension of their secular rights and activities.

La Trinité's Angevin origins predisposed the monks to turn to Anjou for artistic inspiration. They incorporated Angevin architectural styles in their buildings (like the Romanesque divided window found on the abbey's granary and at Courtozé) and used a design suggested by Angevin prototypes in the axis chapel's stained-glass lancet window of the Virgin and Child. Angevin influence is also readily apparent in the script used in Vendôme during the second half of the eleventh and first part of the twelfth century. The monks, in their turn, affected the society in which they lived. Their art and architectural styles were available to influence other building projects in the area; their liturgies encouraged local cults; and their treatises and letters were available for la Trinité's confreres as well as for literate lay people.

The creative activity of the monks was made possible through lay patronage. It required extensive resources to free monks to write, illuminate manuscripts, design sculptural programs, or direct architectural work. An endowment allowed the monks to support a large *familia,* which exploited the demesne and undertook much of the upkeep of the monastery and its possessions. The economic resources of the abbey also made it possible to fund the building of the monastery's fabric.

Lay patrons tended to orient their support along feudal and family lines. Geoffrey Martel's officials supported la Trinité both as a way of expressing their loyalty to their lord and to help their own social standing through association with this important monastic community. When a knight owing loyalty to the lord of Beaugency fell ill, he was cared for by the monks of la Trinité because the castellans of Beaugency were patrons of the abbey. At the man's death, his lord made a donation to the monks to insure his follower's burial in the abbey's precincts. Patronage for la Trinité followed lineages as it did feudal dependencies. Noble families continued their benefactions to the abbey over three and four generations, although marriages sometimes diluted loyalties by introducing women with new benevolent concerns into a family group. Patronage was strengthened by a family member's entrance into la Trinité as an oblate or a monk *ad succurren-dum*, as well as by the care the monks extended to a sick relative or the burial of a family member within the monastery's walls. In addition, a lineage became involved with la Trinité when a relative received a corrody or a mortgage from the monks, and a family may have felt special warmth for the monks when they prayed for a relative leaving on crusade or said masses for a dead family member.

The monks of la Trinité showed concern for the simple folk of the Vendômois as well as for the nobility. La Trinité took in orphans, like Magnelin, for training and protection. The abbey's granary housed grain supplies that were used for a daily dole to the poor as well as for emergency rations in times of famine. The monks accepted and cared for the humble sick and accommodated nonnoble travelers. The abbey provided spiritual comfort for the poor in the lady chapel and in liturgical charity like the *mandatum*.

Despite the benefits they often received, lay men and women could cause trouble for the abbey. This was done intentionally when members of a donor's family regretted an alienation of property and tried by legal or even violent means to reclaim a gift. A contentious tendency was growing during the period, as can be seen in the 23 percent increase in litigation experienced by la Trinité. The abbey's most continually abrasive neighbors were the counts of Vendôme, who resented the monks as usurpers and interlopers. Most of the points contested by the abbey and the comital family were finally settled in the customs of 1185.

Periodically, lay people generated friction indirectly for la Trinité by gifts whose title or jurisdiction was unclear. Some-times these haphazard donations triggered bitter battles between la Trinité and other monastic communities. Lay patronage did not inevitably lead to hostilities but could be a means of express-ing secular antagonisms that polarized families like those of Montoire and Lavardin to support either la Trinité or its rival, Marmoutier. Occasionally, lay patrons even took sides actively in quarrels between abbeys, as did the count of Poitou, who barred the abbot of Saint-Aubin from his lands. However, pa-trons did not figure in all conflicts between monasteries, since many clashes were triggered by interactions involving only the two communities, as when fugitives were accepted or hospitality was denied.

The monks sought to deal with lay people's claims by various means, including compromise settlements and legal procedures. In addition, la Trinité used feudal pressures and sometimes relied on the spiritual sanctions of excommunication and interdict. In one third of the cases, the monks gave gifts to claimants as part of the settlement. The abbey's most potent weapon, however, was its spiritual power, which became most apparent to a claimant when faced with death. Juliana of Pray came to the abbey to settle a long-standing conflict with the monks only after the death of her daughter forced her to enlist the monks' prayers for the child's soul.

The depredations of secular people were insignificant in comparison with the positive benefits the abbey received from its lay patrons. By protecting la Trinité and endowing it with economic resources, the founders and other benefactors created and enriched the monastic community so that it became the central institution of its society. If we imagine the Vendômois in 1100 divested of the abbey, we see a greatly depleted society. Gone would be the economic focus: the major employer, technical training center, agricultural exploiter, and resource from which people could secure a loan or mortgage. Gone would be the monastic social services: the travelers' accommodations, hospitals, reception of monks *ad succurrendum,* and cemeteries. There would be no monastery gates at which the poor could gather assured of a daily ration, or where a desperate mother could leave a starving baby. The bells of la Trinité's tower would no longer regulate the day's activities for the abbey or its neighbors. Gone would be the artistic presence of the abbey. No pope would visit Vendôme; a meeting of barons could not take place in the abbey's hospice. The local people would lack offices celebrating special saints, and la Trinité's important relics would not protect the populace. Twenty-seven other communities would also have lost the focus and enrichment of housing a cell of la Trinité. Indeed, the inhabitants of the Vendômois would have missed the abbey's most important contribution, its energy and vitality.

La Trinité was a living social, economic, artistic, and spiritual

180   PRAYER, PATRONAGE, AND POWER

force in its society, made possible and sustained by the economic and political power of its lay patrons. A donation might be for the purpose of the reception of a child as an oblate, to secure an old-age pension, or to effect the burial of a relative. Often, however, the abbey's return to the patron was of relative insignificance economically, or the donor received no visible benefit at all. Nevertheless, patronage continued as a recognition of the importance of monastic suffrages. In a world where people feared the fires of the Last Judgment and yearned for salvation, the monks' intercessions were highly valued. Sooner or later even the worst of the abbey's tormentors was faced with his or her own mortality or that of a relative. The sobering effects of such a realization usually resulted in a settlement with and/or donation to the monks. Thus, a yearning for spiritual comfort and reassurance could result in temporal leverage and tangible rewards for la Trinité. It might, in fact, be argued that the prayers of the monks constituted the abbey's greatest temporal power, although worldly success was not the ostensible goal of monastic suffrages.

Lay patronage supported la Trinité, and prayer constituted the power that attracted that patronage. Reliance on and interaction with secular benefactors created many problems for the monks; but, at the same time, la Trinité drew its strength from its patrons, so that "from sea to sea," Geoffrey of Vendôme could boast, "there is no better instituted monastery than ours." [10]

Notes

1. Cantor, "The Crisis of Western Monasticism," pp. 55–61.

2. Southern, *Western Society and the Church*, p. 216.

3. CT 2:200, no. 427, lists Stephen, Geoffrey's crucifer, attending the abbot at a large gathering. Geoffrey of Vendôme, *Ep.* 4:32 (PL 157:173), describes traveling on horseback and by water. In *Ep.* 4:19 (PL 157:161), he pointedly requests a mule from a friend for a trip to Rome, which suggests that he was not in the habit of riding such a lowly animal. See *Ep.* 4:7 (PL 157:152) in which a cellarer grudgingly agrees to put up a dozen of the horses in Geoffrey's train.

4. Hunt, *Cluny under St. Hugh*, p. 171.

5. Jean Leclercq, "La Crise du monachisme aux XIᵉ et XIIᵉ siècles," *Bullettino dell' Instituto storico Italiano per il medio evo a Archivio Muratoriano* 70 (1958), 21–30; also printed in translation in *Cluniac Monasticism in the Central Middle Ages*, ed. Noreen Hunt (London, 1971), pp. 217–37.

6. Little, *Religious Poverty and the Profit Economy*, pp. 3–69. The "unthinking acceptance of this transition was costly for the old monastic order." P. 68.

7. CT 2:406, no. 553. See discussion of the general trend by Suzanne Roberts, "Charity and Hospitality in the Rouergue, 1100–1350." Diss. Harvard 1975.

8. "Monasticism, for example, did not exist in the abstract; it existed only through the actions and beliefs of individuals, and, when the consciousness of those individuals changed over time, monasticism changed as well." Charles Radding, "Evolution of Medieval Mentalities: A Cognitive-Structural Approach," *American Historical Review* 83 (1978), 595.

9. Leclercq, "La Crise du monachisme," pp. 25–41.

10. Abbot Oderic warned: "Sed sancti viri cum mundi huius potestate fulciuntur, tanto sub maiori mentis disciplina se redigunt, quanto sibi per impatientiam potestatis suaderi illicita quasi licentius sciunt." Vendôme B.M. MS 203, fol. 31v. Geoffrey of Vendôme, *Ep.* 1:13 (PL 157:54), "quod a mari usque ad mare monasterium melius ordinatum sit quam nostrum."

Appendix I

The Forgeries

The propensity of medieval monks to revise or fabricate charters, familiar to modern scholars, was known to their contemporaries as well.[1] The motivations for this practice must have varied in individual cases, although most monks involved in falsifying charters probably justified their distortions as defensible statements. There had been a long tradition of forgery, which could be defended as truthful—even if not accurate—since the intention of the falsified document remained the key issue. Many cloistered religious saw society as peopled with immoral men and women, while even within the secular church unjust men often controlled events. How could monks live within such a wicked world without losing their privileges and goods to rapacious neighbors? One possible method of protecting themselves was to articulate their rights and list their possessions in the forms they felt had been originally intended, even if no documents existed to prove their claims. Forging a charter was a compromise by monks attempting to live piously within a wicked world.

Whether or not such actions were moral, they constituted a powerful manipulation of the environment. Monasteries kept records and harbored literate men within a generally unlettered world; the monks, therefore, could often falsify records without detection. La Trinité was responsible for a number of spurious charters, all of which sought to improve the abbey's situation to the detriment of some other individual or group. Even the purest of articulated monastic motives cloaked the real purpose that generated the forgeries—la Trinité wanted more power.

Five scholars have considered the authenticity of la Trinité's charters. (See Figure 6.) Launoy first seriously questioned the documents on the part of Henri-Louis d'Allongny, marquis of Rochefort and baron of Craon, who was embroiled in litigation with the abbey over contested rights.[2] Although Launoy approached his study with scholarly care, his

Figure 6. Designations of la Trinité's Forgeries.

Charter	Launoy	Métais	Halphen	Meinert	Guillot
10		a			f
35	f	a	a	i	a
36	f	a	f	f	f
37	f	a	a	f	f
38	f	a	f	f	f
39	f	a		f	f
40	f	a		i	f
48	f	a			f
75	f	a		f	
76	f	a	f	f	
95	f	a		f	f
105	f	a	a—fr	a	a?
106	f	a	a—fr	a	
107	f	a	a	f	
146	f	a	f	f	
164	f	a	a	f	
165	f	a	a	a	
238	f	a		f	
252	f	a	a	f	
344	f	a		a	
366	f	a		f	
367	f	a		f	
	Also forgeries: nos. 364, 365, 369, 370, 436, 470, 472, 473.				

Key: f = forgery
a = authentic
i = interpolated
fr = fragmentary

criticisms must be treated cautiously as those of a partisan employed in the service of an adversary of the monks. The arguments in his *Inquisitio* are mostly inconclusive, constructed as they are on theological bases and grounded in a strong nationalistic desire for Gallic independence from Rome.

In sharp contrast to Launoy who attacked the authenticity of twenty-nine charters, Abbé Métais defended the validity of these as well as of all the other documents he edited in the cartulary.[3] Métais' defense should be approached with some skepticism too, since his partisanship often overpowered his scholarly judgment. Louis Halphen considered some of the documents in two articles, the latter of which revised some of his earlier opinions.[4] His analysis remains valuable but is superseded by the careful, detailed investigation of Hermann Meinert.[5] Meinert's extensive knowledge of diplomatic formulae makes his analysis particularly keen. His work remains the final word on the authenticity of la Trinité's documents in all but three cases—that of no. 35, one of the reputed foundation documents; no. 105; and nos. 9 and 10.

I am not in full agreement with Meinert's analysis of no. 35, a particularly crucial document for the reconstruction of la Trinité's history. Meinert states categorically that the wording in no. 35, "potestatis suae et honoris dignitate careat," can only be an interpolation.[6] This phrase, he claims, belongs only in late eleventh-century papal documents. Meinert also questions other phrases in the eschatocol: "absque consuetudine vel cuiuslibet hominis exactione," and "absque ulla calumnia successorum nostrorum sive contrarietate . . . nec aliquid sucessores nostri pro rebus praedicto loco a quibuslibet hominibus donatis deposcant." He insists that these are later interpolations from 1094–95.[7]

Meinert's attack is refuted by Olivier Guillot, who defends no. 35 as the original foundation text.[8] Guillot cites evidence of phraseology similar to that of no. 35 in other mid-eleventh-century Angevin documents. A charter of Countess Agnes drawn after the dedication of Saint-Jean d'Angély uses words strikingly similar to those held by Meinert to be the prime proof of interpolation: "et honoris nostri dignitate perpetuo careat."[9] Guillot adduces contemporary examples similar to Meinert's other suspect phrases. However, Guillot goes beyond the refutation of Meinert's stylistic criticism in seeking to prove no. 35 the original.

A donation in no. 35 of seven arpents of land by a priest, Letgerius, is scratched out in no. 37. Guillot questions the purpose of the deletion and locates a possible explanation in another charter relating to an illegitimate gift. Letgerius, a priest, had illegally given to la Trinité a quarter of a mill, which was subsequently reclaimed by its rightful owner, Mathias, sometime between 1040 and 1070.[10] This information about Letgerius leads Guillot to the conclusion that the priest's donation in no. 35 must predate the reclamation by Mathias, which occurred in 1070 at the latest. The scratching out of Letgerius' donation in no. 37 proves that when the mill had been returned to Mathias, the abbey had no further interest in keeping a record of property it had forfeited. The story unearthed by Guillot of the Letgerius donation would refute Meinert's claim that no. 35 is a document interpolated during the abbacy of Geoffrey of Vendôme (1093–1132).

But Guillot's argument is flawed. He assumes that the seven arpents given by Letgerius in no. 35 and the one quarter of a mill given illegally by Letgerius in no. 210 belong to one original gift—a likely supposition but one that cannot be proved. Indeed, if the mill was not located on the seven arpents, Guillot's entire argument collapses. Leaving the Letgerius evidence to one side as interesting but inconclusive, the most telling evidence for the authenticity of no. 35 lies in its totality. The foundation charters of Fulk Nerra and Hildegarde for their two Angevin foundations, Saint-Nicolas, in 1020, and Ronceray, in 1028, closely resemble no. 35, the foundation document of la Trinité, which was established by their son, Geoffrey Martel, and his wife, Agnes.[11] Fulk's charters contain no extraordinary privileges, and the endowments consist primarily of fields and vineyards. Geoffrey is named with his parents as cofounder of both houses, so the terms must have been familiar to him. Because of the rivalry between Geoffrey and his father, Geoffrey sought to outdo his father in generosity, but retained the familiar type of endowment. This pattern held true for both of the major foundations of Geoffrey and Agnes, la Trinité in 1040 and Notre-Dame of Saintes in 1047.[12] Both houses were liberally endowed with lands, vineyards, woods, and churches but were not accorded sweeping exemptions and major privileges like those that crop up in la Trinité's forged foundation documents, nos. 36 and 37. These two spurious foundation charters incorporate extensive and unlikely privileges: the abbot's election is to be free; no legate shall have any control over the abbey; the abbot need attend only councils held by the pope; and the abbot's court shall have precedence over the count's court. Nos. 36 and 37 present these privileges as if they were grants by Agnes and Geoffrey, although secular lords had no jurisdiction over ecclesiastical exemptions such as freedom from legatine and episcopal interference. In the legitimate foundation document, the founders give la Trinité secular privileges: the right to assart in one forest and the right to half the pannage and all the wax from the forest of the Gâtines. Notre-Dame receives the privilege of assarting woods; some limited rights for hunting and wood gathering; and one extraordinary privilege, that of minting money in Saintes. Geoffrey and Agnes' two foundations exhibited their wealth, prestige, and power, exceeding Fulk and Hildegarde in extent but not in form. This consistency of form combined with Guillot's defense of no. 35's language suggest strongly that in this instance Meinert's judgment may be inaccurate, so that no. 35 should be considered as authentic.

No. 105 is a charter existing in two parts and accepted as fully authentic by Meinert. It was issued by the founders in 1056 and recapitulates the foundations of la Trinité in Vendôme and l'Evière in Angers; it donates the two houses *in tuitione* to the papacy.[13] There is little doubt that the first half represents the authentic document; the second half of no. 105 uses the phrase "in patrocinium et ditionem beati Apostolorum principis Petri," which Meinert defends as known to eleventh-century abbeys.[14] However, no other genuine eleventh-century charters issued by la Trinité use "in patrocinium," while the forgeries incorporate "alodium et patrimonium" routinely. Even more conclusively, the first part of the charter ends with a standard closing, date, and indiction; the charter is over. But the second part begins again awkwardly after this eschatocol, expanding and emphasizing the strength of the monasteries' ties to the papacy, their indissolubility, and adding sanctions for interference with the abbeys. Finally, Abbé Gaignières, one of the most painstaking and exacting of the ancien–régime copyists, recorded only the first part, suggesting that he was working from a document written earlier than the interpolated second half of no. 105, printed by Métais.[15]

One other problem not considered by Meinert involves charters nos. 9 and 10, which are too inconsistent for both to be regarded as authentic. No. 9 contains two separate pieces of evidence lumped together by Métais. First is a French summary by Simon of a charter of the sale of a mill by Erfred Rufus and Ivo, the deacon, to la Trinité. This is dated 1033 and took place in the *galilea monasterii*. It carried the marks of Geoffrey, Agnes, and Abbot Rainald. Second is a Latin extract for a document recording the purchase by Agnes of a mill from a certain Erfred and signed by Abbot Rainald. No. 10 gives the Latin text of a charter in which Geoffrey and Agnes bought a mill from Erfred Rufus in 1033 in the abbey's galilee with Abbot Oderic (abbot from 1045 to 1082) as a witness. Since the foundation document, no. 35, does not list this mill in the inventory of possessions, it was probably acquired after 1040. Also, it is unlikely that the galilee could have been built as early as 1033. The first part of no. 9 and all of no. 10 are probably efforts to backdate Agnes' purchase, which actually took place after the dedication of May 31, 1040, but before Abbot Rainald's death in 1044. The purchase is authentically recorded in part two of no. 9.[16]

Meinert establishes that Geoffrey of Vendôme perpetrated most of the forgeries of la Trinité's charters.[17] He even questions whether the actual writing may not have been by the abbot. The identity of the falsifier of the documents, however, has little bearing on an understanding of la Trinité's role within its environment. More to the point, each spurious parchment responded to some stimulus from the surrounding society.[18] When the return of Count Fulk Oison threatened the abbey's security, no. 95 appeared. As trouble loomed with Count Geoffrey Preuilly over customary comital privileges, no. 37 was concocted, probably in 1097. At the time of bad feeling between the monks and Count Geoffrey Grisegonelle, the monks produced nos. 76 and 107. To attempt to forestall any repetition of the *professio* requirement by the bishop of Chartres, no. 36 uses the term *consilio* in the abbatial election formula. La Trinité's spurious charters, like other overt weapons of excommunication, feudal pressures, and monastic spiritual benefits, were apparently used by the monks to manipulate the larger society in which they functioned.

Notes

1. CT 2:82, no. 345. L. C. Hector, *Paleography and Medieval Forgery* (London, 1959), pp. 6–10. Eleanor Searle, "Battle Abbey and Exemption: The Forged Charters," *English Historical Review* 83 (1968), 449–80.

2. Jean de Launoy, *Inquisitio in chartam fundationis et privilegia Vindocinensis monasterii* (n.p., 1661).

3. Charles Métais, "De l'authenticité des chartes de fondation et bulles de l'abbaye de la Trinité de Vendôme," *Moyen âge* 2d series, 8 (1904), 1–44. Also see CT *passim* in notes.

4. Louis Halphen, "Etude critique sur les chartes de fondation et les principaux privilèges pontificaux de la Trinité de Vendôme," *Moyen âge* 5 (1901), 69–112. Also the revised discussion in "Les Chartes de fondation de la Trinité de Vendôme et de l'Evière d'Angers," *Moyen âge* 2d series, 8 (1904), 401–11.

5. Hermann Meinert, "Die Fälschungen Gottsfrieds von Vendôme," *Sonderabzug aus dem Archiv für Urkundenforschung*, 10 (Berlin, 1928), 232–25.

6. Ibid., pp. 237–38: "Diese Wendung kann in Nr. 35 nur eine Interpolation sein." The reference is to CT 1:59, no. 35.

7. Ibid., pp. 238 and 303.

8. Guillot, *Le Comte d'Anjou*, 2:67–69.

9. Ibid., 2:69.

10. CT 1:341–42, no. 210. Also see Guillot, *Le Comte d'Anjou*, 2:69.

11. Ibid., 2:39, no. C 33, for charter of foundation of Saint-Nicolas. *Cartulaire de l'abbaye du Ronceray*, pp. 1–5.

12. *Cartulaire de Notre-Dame de Saintes*, pp. 1–5.

13. Guillot, *Le Comte d'Anjou*, 2:121, and Meinert, "Die Fälschungen," p. 324.

14. Ibid., pp. 250–51.

15. B.N. MS 17049, p. 699.

16. Guillot also argues that no. 9, part one, and no. 10 are forgeries. Guillot, *Le Comte d'Anjou*, 2:293.

17. Meinert, "Die Fälschungen," p. 301.

18. Ibid., pp. 301–15, for the relations of spurious documents to the next four actual events.

Appendix II

Abbots and Priors

There is doubt about the existence of William, who appears in no charters and is skipped over in one document, which relates, "Girardus abbas V. Roberto successerat." CT 2:426, no. 563. The "Annales de Vendôme," p. 71, also state that Girard succeeded Robert. However, William appears as ninth abbot in the death roll edited in *Rouleaux des morts,* ed. Léopold Delisle (Paris, 1856), p. 387, and in the abbey's necrology, CT 4:427.

Priors:

Rainald?	(became first abbot)
Fulk	prior under Rainald and Oderic
Albert	prior under Oderic
Haimo	prior under Oderic
Hildrad	prior under Oderic
Berno	prior under David (became fourth abbot)
Archembald	prior under Berno
Frotmund	prior under Berno and Geoffrey
Bernier	prior under Geoffrey
Rivallon	prior under Geoffrey
Fromond	prior under Geoffrey (became sixth abbot)
Hubert	prior under Geoffrey and Fromond (became seventh abbot)
Fulcher	prior under Hubert
Rivallon	prior under Robert
Hugo	prior under Robert
Guarin	prior under Robert
John	prior under Girard
William	prior under Girard
Lucas	prior under Girard (became tenth abbot?)

Appendix III

Genealogies

The Counts of Anjou

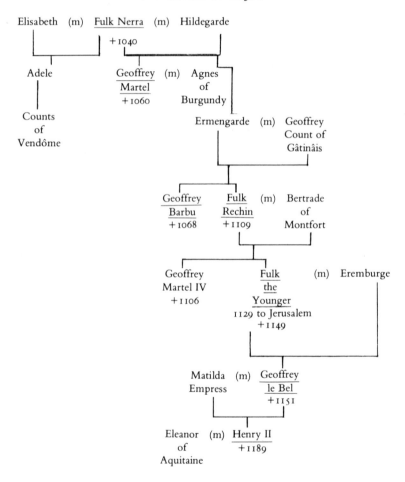

The Counts of Vendôme

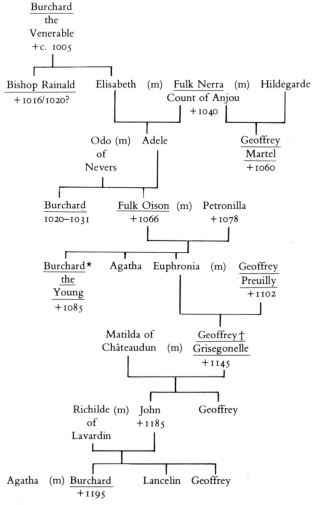

*Regency of Guy of Nevers for minor heir, 1066–1075.
†Regency of Euphronia for minor heir, 1102–1105.

Castellans of Montdoubleau

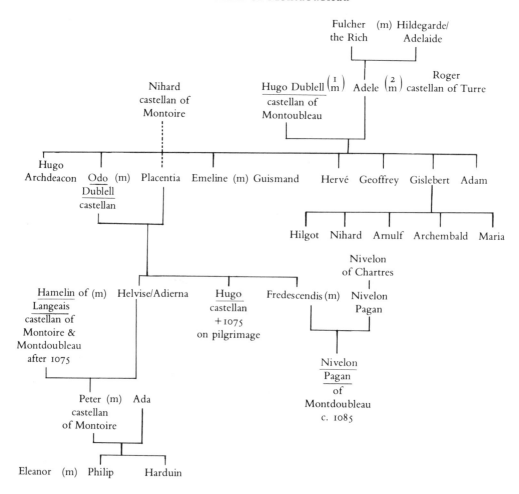

Knightly Lineage of Ingelbald Brito

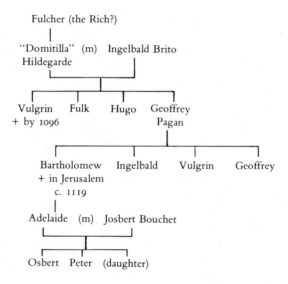

Fulcher (the Rich?)
|
"Domitilla" (m)   Ingelbald Brito
Hildegarde

Vulgrin   Fulk   Hugo   Geoffrey
+ by 1096   Pagan

Bartholomew   Ingelbald   Vulgrin   Geoffrey
+ in Jerusalem
c. 1119
|
Adelaide   (m)   Josbert Bouchet

Osbert   Peter   (daughter)

Bibliography

Sources: Unpublished

Angers, Bibliothèque Départementale de Maine-et-loire fonds H 360.
Blois, Bibliothèque Départementale de Loir-et-Cher MSS 21 H 1, 21 H 40, 21 H 54, 21 H 69, 21 H 80, 21 H 94, 21 H 110, 21 H 124, 21 H 128, 21 H 137, 21 H 144, 21 H 146, 21 H 163, 21 H 164, 21 H 173, 21 H 183, 21 H 198.
Paris, Bibliothèque Nationale, Latin MSS 5419, 5956A, 11819, 11834, 12688, 12700, 12780, 13070, 13071, 13758, 13820, 16996, 17049.
Nouvelle Acquisition Latine MSS 1935, 1939, 2415.
Nouvelle Acquisition Française MSS 7433, 20225.
Collection Baluze MSS 47, 139.
Collection Touraine MSS 2_1, 2_2, 13_1, 30.
Supplement Grec MS 278.
Vendôme, Bibliothèque Municipale, MSS 2, 14, 17C, 17E, 18, 20, 23, 26, 27, 28, 29, 30, 31, 33, 34, 35, 37, 38, 39, 40, 41, 42, 44, 45, 46, 47, 48, 49, 52, 53, 54, 55, 56, 58, 60, 61, 91, 98, 99, 100, 103, 109, 113, 113^2, 114, 115, 115^2, 117, 120, 122, 123, 124, 125, 126, 127, 128, 129, 130, 132, 133, 134, 135, 136, 137, 138, 139, 140, 141, 143, 144, 145, 146, 147, 148, 156, 160, 161, 162, 174, 175, 184, 190, 192, 193, 203, 213.
Campion, R. Le Vendômois. n.p. 1920.
Launay, Gervais. Vendôme. 3 vols. Vendôme: n.d.
London, British Library, Harley MS 270, Sloane MS 3103.
New Haven, Conn., Beinecke Library, Marston MS 25.

Sources: Published

Archives d'Anjou: Recueil de documents et mémoires inédits sur cette province, ed. Paul Marchegay. 2 vols. Angers: 1843.

Cartulaire blésois de Marmoutier, ed. Charles Métais. Chartres/Blois: 1891.

Cartulaire de l'abbaye cardinale de la Trinité de Vendôme, ed. Charles Métais. 5 vols. Paris: 1893–1904.

Cartulaire de l'abbaye du Ronceray d'Angers, 1028–1184, ed. Paul Marchegay. Paris: 1900.

Cartulaire de l'abbaye royale de Notre-Dame de Saintes. Vol. 2 Cartulaires inédits de la Saintonge, ed. Thomas Grasilier. Niort: 1871.

Cartulaire de Marmoutier pour le Dunois, ed. Emile Mabille. Châteaudun: 1874.

Cartulaire de Marmoutier pour le Vendômois, ed. de Trémault. Paris/Vendôme: 1893.

Cartulaire ae Saint-Aubin d'Angers, ed. Bernard de Broussillon. 3 vols. Angers: 1903.

Cartulaire de Saint-Jean d'Angély, ed. Georges Musset. *Archives historiques de Saintonge et d'Aunis*, 30 and 33. Paris: 1901–1904.

Cartulaire du chapitre de Saint-Laud d'Angers, ed. A. Planchenault. *Documents historiques sur l'Anjou*, 4. Angers: 1903.

Cartulaire saintongeais de la Trinité de Vendôme, ed. Charles Métais. *Archives historiques de la Saintonge et de l'Aunis*, 22 (1893), 1–431.

Catalogus codicum hagiographicorum latinorum antiquiorum saeculo XVI qui asservantur in bibliotheca nationali parisiensi. 3 vols. Brussels: 1889–93.

"Chartes de l'abbaye de Vendôme concernant le Poitou et la Saintonge," ed. Giry. *Archives historiques de la Saintonge*, 12 (1884), 378–82.

Chartes et documents pour servir à l'histoire de l'abbaye de Saint-Maixent, ed. Alfred Richard. 2 vols. *Archives historiques du Poitou*, 16. Poitiers: 1887.

Chroniques d'Anjou, ed. Paul Marchegay and André Salmon. 2 vols. Paris: 1856.

Chroniques des comtes d'Anjou, ed. Paul Marchegay and André Salmon. Paris: 1856–71.

Chroniques des comtes d'Anjou et des seigneurs d'Amboise, ed. Louis Halphen and René Poupardin. Paris: 1913.

Chroniques des églises d'Anjou, ed. Paul Marchegay and Emile Mabille. Paris: 1869.

Consuetudines monasticae, ed. Bruno Albers. Vol. 1. Stuttgart/Vienna: 1900.

Corpus consuetudinum monasticarum, ed. Kassius Hallinger. 7 vols. Siegburg: 1963– .

Court, Household and Itinerary of King Henry II, ed. and tr. R. W. Eyton. New York: 1974.

Epistolae vagantes of Pope Gregory VII, ed. and tr. H. E. J. Cowdrey. Oxford: 1972.

Fulbert of Chartres. *The Letters and Poems of Fulbert of Chartres,* ed. and tr. Frederick Behrends. Oxford: 1976.

Geoffrey of Vendôme. *Epistolae, opuscula, sermones. PL* 157: 33–290.

Goscelin. *Liber confortatorius,* ed. C. H. Talbot. Analecta monastica. Vol. 3. Studia Anselmiana. Rome: 1955.

Le guide du pèlerin de Saint Jacques de Compostelle, ed. and tr. Jeanne Vielliard. Mâcon: 1963.

Hildebert of Lavardin. *Epistolae. PL* 171:141–312.

Ivo of Chartres. *Epistolae. PL* 162:11–288.

Libellus de diversis ordinibus et professionibus qui sunt in aecclesia, ed. and tr. Giles Constable and B. Smith. Oxford: 1972.

Marbod of Rennes. *Epistolae. PL* 171:1465–92.

Recueil d'annales angevines et vendômoises, ed. Louis Halphen. Paris: 1903.

Recueil de chroniques de Touraine, ed. André Salmon. Société Archéologique de Touraine. Tours: 1854/6.

Recueil des actes de Henri II, roi d'Angleterre et duc de Normandie concernant les provinces françaises et les affaires de France, ed. Léopold Delisle. 3 vols. Paris: 1920.

Recueil des historiens des Gaules et de la France, ed. Michel-Jean-Joseph Brial. Paris: 1808.

Regesta pontificum romanorum ab condita ecclesia ad annum post Christum natum 1198, ed. Philip Jaffé, F. Kaltenbrunner (to A.D. 590), P. Ewald (590–882), S. Loewenfeld (882–1198). 2 vols. Leipziq: 1885–88.

Rouleaux des morts du IXe au XVe siècle, ed. Léopold Delisle. Paris: 1864.

Some Useful Secondary Sources

Atlas historique français: le territoire de la France et de quelques pays voisines: Anjou. Ed. L'Institut géographique national. Directed by F. Michel, B. Angliviel, G. Laclauère. 2 vols. Monumenta historiae Galliarum. Paris: 1973.

Balon, J. "L'Eglise de France au haut moyen âge dans le centre et l'ouest de la France et spécialement à Bourges." *Revue historique de droit français et étranger,* 45 (1967), 5–33.

Becquet, Jean. "L'Erémitisme clérical et laïque dans l'ouest de la

France." *L'Eremitismo in Occidente nei secoli XI e XII.* Settimana internazionale di studio, 2d, Passo della Mendola, 1962. Miscellanea del Centro di studi medioevali, 4. Milan: 1965, 182–202.

Beech, George. *A Rural Society in Medieval France: The Gâtine of Poitou in the Eleventh and Twelfth Centuries.* Baltimore: 1964.

Berlière, Ursmer. "Les Archidiaconés ou exemptions privilégiées de monastères." *Revue bénédictine,* 40 (1928), 116–22.

———. "Les Confraternités monastiques au moyen âge." *Revue liturgique et monastique* (1926), 134–42.

———. "Les Confréries bénédictines au moyen âge." *Revue liturgique et monastique* (1927), 135–45.

———. "Les Ecoles claustrales au moyen âge." *Bulletins de la classe des lettres et des sciences morales et politiques.* Académie royale de Belgique (1921), 550–72.

———. "Les Elections abbatiales au moyen âge." *Mémoires de l'académie royale de Belgique,* 2d series (1927), 3–100.

———. "L'Exercice du ministère paroissial par les moines dans le haut moyen âge." *Revue bénédictine,* 39 (1927), 227–50.

———. "Le Nombre des moines dans les anciens monastères," *Revue bénédictine,* 41 (1929), 231–61, and 42 (1930), 19–42.

Berthet, B. "Abbayes et exploitations: l'exemple de Saint-Claude et des forêts jurassiennes." *Annales E.S.C.,* 5 (1950), 68–74.

Bienvenu, Jean-Marc. "Les Caractères originaux de la réforme grégorienne dans le diocèse d'Angers." *Mémoires de l'académie des sciences, belles-lettres et arts d'Angers,* 9th series 2 (1968), 141–57.

———. "Pauvreté, misères et charité en Anjou aux XIe et XIIe siècles." *Moyen âge,* 72 (1966), 389–424, and 73 (1967), 5–34 and 189–216.

———. "Recherches sur les péages angevins aux XIe et XIIe siècles." *Moyen âge,* 12 (1957), 209–40 and 437–67.

Bloch, Marc. *Les Caractères originaux de l'histoire rurale française.* Paris: 1955.

———. "Champs et villages." *Annales d'histoire économique et sociale,* 6 (1934), 467–89.

Bonenfant, P. and G. Despy. "La Noblesse en Brabant XIIe–XIIIe siècles." *Moyen âge,* 64 (1958), 27–66.

Boussard, Jacques. *Le Comté d'Anjou sous Henri Plantagenet et ses fils (1151–1204).* Paris, 1938.

———. "L'Eviction des tenants de Thibaud de Blois par Geoffrey Martel, comte d'Anjou, en 1044." *Moyen âge,* 69 (1963), 141–49.

———. "L'Origine des familles seigneuriales dans la région de la Loire moyenne." *Cahiers de civilisation médiévale,* 5 (1962), 303–22.

————. "La Vie dans le comté d'Anjou aux XIe et XIIe siècles." *Moyen âge*, 56 (1950), 29–68.

Boyer, Marjorie. "A Day's Journey in Medieval France." *Speculum*, 26 (1951), 597–608.

Brooke, Christopher. "Princes and Kings as Patrons of Monasteries: Normandy and England." *Il monachesimo e la riforma ecclesiastica (1049–1122)*. Settimana internazionale di studio, 4th, Passo della Mendola, 1968. Miscellanea del Centro di studi medioevali, 6. Milan: 1971, 125–44.

Büttner, H. "Frühmittelalterliches Städtewesen in Frankreich, vornehmlich im Loire und Rhonegebiet." *Studien zu den Anfängen des europäischen Städtewesens*. Constance/Lindau: 1965.

Cantor, Norman. "The Crisis of Western Monasticism." *American Historical Review*, 66 (1960), 47–67.

Capitani, Ovidio. "La Lettera di Goffredo II Martello conte d'Angiò a Ildebrando (1059)." *Studi Gregoriani*, 5 (1956), 19–31.

Carrière, Victor. *Introduction aux études d'histoire ecclésiastique locale*. 3 vols. Paris: 1934.

Chartrou, Josèphe. *L'Anjou de 1109 á 1151*. Paris: 1928.

Chédeville, André. *Chartres et ses campagnes XIe-XIIIe siècles*. Paris: 1973.

————. "Etude de la mise en valeur et du peuplement du Maine au XIe siècle, d'après les documents de l'abbaye de Saint-Vincent du Mans." *Annales de Bretagne*, 67 (1960), 209–25.

————. "Les Restitutions d'églises en faveur de l'abbaye de Saint-Vincent du Mans." *Cahiers de civilisation médiévale*, 3 (1960), 209–17.

Compain, Luc. *Etude sur Geoffroi de Vendôme*. Bibliothèque de l'Ecole des Hautes-Etudes, 86. Paris: 1891.

Conant, Kenneth J. "Medieval Academy Excavations at Cluny." *Speculum*, 29 (1954), 1–45.

Constable, Giles. " 'Famuli' and 'Conversi' at Cluny." *Revue bénédictine*, 83 (1973), 326–50.

————. "Monastic Possession of Churches and 'Spiritualia' in the age of Reform." *Il monachesimo e la riforma ecclesiastica (1049–1122)*. Settimana internazionale di studio, 4th, Passo della Mendola, 1968. Miscellanea del Centro di studi medioevali, 6. Milan: 1971, 304–31.

————. *Monastic Tithes: From Their Origins to the Twelfth Century*. Cambridge, England: 1964.

————. "The Study of Monastic History Today." *Essays on the Reconstruction of Medieval History*. Ed. Vaclav Mudroch and G. S. Couse. Montreal/London: 1974.

Cousin, Patrice. *Précis d'histoire monastique*. Paris/Tournai: 1959.

Crozet, René. "Le Clocher de la Trinité de Vendôme." *Bulletin monumental*, 119 (1961), 139–48.

————. "Le Monument de la Sainte-Larme à la Trinité de Vendôme." *Bulletin monumental*, 121 (1963), 171–80.

————. "Le Vitrail de la crucifixion à la cathédrale de Poitiers." *Gazette des beaux-arts*, 1 (1934), 218–31.

————. "Le Voyage d'Urbain II et ses négociations avec le clergé de France (1095–1096)." *Revue historique*, 179 (1937), 271–310.

————. "Le Voyage d'Urbain II en France (1095–1096) et son importance au point de vue archéologique." *Annales du Midi*, 49 (1937), 42–69.

Daux, Camille. "La Protection apostolique au moyen âge," *Revue des questions historiques*, 28 NS, 72 (1902), 5–60.

De Farcy, L. "La Tour Saint-Aubin." *Bulletin monumental*, 70 (1906), 550–67.

Delaruelle, Etienne. "Les Ermites et la spiritualité populaire." *La Piété populaire au moyen âge*, Turin: 1975, 125–54.

de Pétigny, J. *Histoire archéologique du Vendômois*. Vendôme/Blois: 1882.

————. "Robert d'Arbrissel et Geoffroi de Vendôme." *Bibliothèque de l'école des chartes*, 3d series 5 (1854), 1–30.

de Rochambeau, A. "Voyage à la Sainte-Larme de Vendôme." *Bull. Vend.*, 12 (1873), 157–212.

de Saint-Venant, R. *Dictionnaire topographique, historique, biographique, généalogique et héraldique du Vendômois et de l'arrondissement de Vendôme*. 2 vols. Vendôme/Blois: 1969.

Déservillers, le comte P. de. *Un Evêque au XIIᵉ siècle: Hildebert et son temps*. Paris: 1876.

d'Espinay, G. *Les Cartulaires angevins: étude sur le droit de l'Anjou au moyen âge*. Angers: 1864.

Devailly, Guy. *Le Berry: du Xᵉ siècle au milieu du XIIIᵉ. Etude politique, réligieuse, sociale et économique*. Paris: 1973.

Dhondt, Jan. *Etudes sur la naissance des principautés territoriales en France (IXᵉ–Xᵉ siècles)*. Bruges: 1948.

————. "Henri Iᵉʳ, l'empire et l'Anjou." *Revue belge de philologie et d'histoire*, 25 (1946/7), 87–109.

Dillay, Madeleine. "Le Régime de l'église privée du XIᵉ au XIIIᵉ siècle dans l'Anjou, le Maine, la Touraine." *Revue historique de droit français et étranger*, 4th series 4 (1925), 253–94.

―――. "Le Service annuel en deniers des fiefs de la région angevine." *Mélanges Paul Fournier*. Paris: 1929, 143–50.

Dimier, Marie-Anselme. "Observances monastiques." *Analecta cisterciensia*, 11 (1955), 149–98.

―――. "Quelques légendes de fondation chez les cisterciens." *Studia monastica*, 12 (1970), 97–105.

Dubois, Jacques. "Les Moines dans la société du moyen âge (950–1350)." *Revue d'histoire de l'église de France*, 60 (1974), 5–37.

―――. *Un Sanctuaire monastique au moyen âge: Saint-Fiacre–en–Brie*. Geneva: 1976.

―――. "La Vie des moines dans les prieurés du moyen âge." *Lettre de Ligugé*, 1, no. 133 (1969), 10–33.

Duby, Georges. "Economie domaniale et économie monétaire: le budget de l'abbaye de Cluny entre 1080 et 1155." *Annales E.S.C.*, 7 (1952), 155–71.

―――. "Géographie ou chronologie du servage? Note sur les 'servi' en Forez en Mâconnais du Xᵉ au XIIᵉ siècle." *Hommage à Lucien Febvre*. 2 vols. Paris: 1953. 1:147–49.

―――. "Un Inventaire des profits de la seigneurie clunisienne à la mort de Pierre le Vénérable." *Petrus Venerabilis*. Ed. Giles Constable and James Kritzeck. Rome: 1956, 128–40.

―――. "Lignage, noblesse et chevalerie au XIIᵉ siècle dans la région mâconnaise. *Annales E.S.C.*, 27 (1972), 803–27.

―――. "Le Monachisme et l'économie rurale." *Il monachesimo e la riforma ecclesiastica (1049–1122)*. Settimana internazionale di studio, 4th, Passo della Mendola, 1968. Miscellanea del Centro di studi medioevali, 6. Milan: 1971, 336–49.

Dumas, Auguste. "Le Régime domanial et la féodalité dans la France du moyen âge." *Le Domaine*. Recueil de la société Jean Bodin, 4. Brussels: 1949, 149–64.

Dupré, A. "Etude locale sur les lettres de Geoffroy, 5ᵉ abbé de la Trinité de Vendôme." *Actes du 39 congrès archéologique de France. 1872, Vendôme*. Paris: 1873, 171–94.

Esmein, M. "La Question des investitures dans les lettres d'Yves de Chartres." *Etudes de critique et d'histoire*. 1. Section des sciences réligieuses de l'Ecole des Hautes Etudes. Paris: 1889, 139–78.

Evans, Joan. *Cluniac Art of the Romanesque Period*. Cambridge, England: 1950.

Figueras, Caesáro M. "Acerca del rito de la professión monástica medieval 'ad succurrendum.' " *Liturgica*, 2 (1959), 359–400.

Fossier, Robert. *La Terre et les hommes en Picardie jusqu' à la fin du XIIIᵉ siècle*. 2 vols. Paris: 1968.

Galbraith, Vivian H. "Monastic Foundation Charters of the Eleventh and Twelfth Centuries." *Cambridge Historical Journal*, 4 (1934), 205–22.

Garaud, Marcel. *L'Abbaye Sainte-Croix de Talmond en Bas-Poitou c. 1049–1250*. Poitiers: 1914.

Gaussin, Pierre-Roger. *L'Abbaye de la Chaise-Dieu (1043–1518)*. Paris: 1962.

Génestal, Robert. *Rôle des monastères comme établissements de crédit*. Paris: 1901.

Genicot, Léopold. "L'Erémitisme du XIᵉ siècle dans son contexte économique et social." *L'Eremitismo in Occidente nei secoli XI e XII*. Settimana internazionale di studio, 2d, Passo della Mendola, 1962. Miscellanea del Centro di studi medioevali, 4. Milan: 1965, 45–69.

Gougaud, Louis. *Anciennes coutumes claustrales*. Ligugé: 1930.

———. *Dévotions et practiques ascétiques du moyen âge*. Paris: 1925.

Graham, Rose. "The Annals of the Monastery of the Holy Trinity at Vendôme." *English Historical Review*, 13 (1898), 695–700.

Grégoire, Réginald. "La Place de la pauvreté dans la conception et la pratique de la vie monastique médiévale latine." *Il monaschesimo e la riforma ecclesiastica (1049–1122)*. Settimana internazionale di studio, 4th, Passo della Mendola, 1968. Miscellanea del Centro di studi medioevali, 6. Milan: 1971, 173–92.

Grodecki, Louis. *Les Vitraux des églises de France*. Paris: 1947.

Guilloreau, Léon. "L'Anjou et ses établissements monastiques." *Revue de l'Anjou*, NS 37 (1898), 173–212 and 431–66.

Guillot, Olivier. *Le Comte d'Anjou et son entourage au XIᵉ siècle*. 2 vols. Paris: 1972.

Hallinger, Kassius. "Woher kommen die Laienbrüder?" *Analecta sacri ordinis cisterciensis*, 12 (1956), 3–104.

Halphen, Louis. "Les Chartes de fondation de la Trinité de Vendôme et de l'Evière d'Angers." *Moyen âge*, 2d series 8 (1904), 401–11.

———. *Le Comté d'Anjou au XIᵉ siècle*. Paris: 1906.

———. "Etude critique sur les chartes de fondation et les principaux privilèges pontificaux de la Trinité de Vendôme." *Moyen âge*, 14 (1901), 69–112.

———. *Les Institutions judicaires en France au XIe siècle: région angevine.* Angers: 1902.

———. "Prévôts et voyers du XIe siècle (région angevine)." *Moyen âge,* 15 (1902), 297–325.

Haréau, B. "Une Election d'évêque au XIIe siècle: Rainaud de Martigné, évêque d'Angers." *Revue des deux mondes,* 2d series 88 (1870), 548–62.

Hector, L. C. *Paleography and Medieval Forgery.* London: 1959.

Herlihy, David. "Church Property on the European Continent, 701–1200." *Speculum,* 36 (1961), 81–105.

———. "Three Patterns of Social Mobility in Medieval History." *Journal of Interdisciplinary History,* 3 (1973), 623–47.

Histoire veritable de la Sainte Larme que notre Seigneur pleura sur le Lazare. Comme et par qui elle fut apportée au monastère de la Sainte Trinité de la ville de Vandôme. Vendôme: 1672.

Hill, Bennett D. *English Cistercian Monasteries and Their Patrons in the Twelfth Century.* Urbana, Ill./London: 1968.

Hockey, Frederick Stanley. *Beaulieu: King John's Abbey.* Old Woking, Surrey: 1976.

———. *Quarr Abbey and Its Lands, 1132–1631.* Leicester: 1970.

Hunt, Noreen, ed. *Cluniac Monasticism in the Central Middle Ages.* London: 1971.

———. *Cluny under Saint Hugh, 1049–1109.* Notre Dame, Ill.: 1967.

Johnson, Penelope D. "Pious Legends and Historical Realities: The Foundations of la Trinité, Vendôme, Bonport, and Holyrood." Forthcoming in *Revue bénédictine,* 91 (1981).

Jones, Leslie W. "The Art of Writing at Tours from 1000 to 1200 A.D." *Speculum,* 15 (1940), 286–98.

———. "The Library of St. Aubin's at Angers." *Classical and Mediaeval Studies in Honor of Edward Kennard Rand.* New York: 1938, 143–61.

Kieft, C. van de. "Les 'Colliberti' et l'évolution du servage dans la France centrale et occidentale, X^e–XIIe siècles." *Tijdschrift voor Rechtsgeschiedenis,* 32 (1964), 363–95.

———. "Une Eglise privée de l'abbaye de la Trinité de Vendôme au XIe siècle." *Moyen âge,* 69 (1963), 157–68.

King, Edmund. *Peterborough Abbey, 1086–1310: A Study in the Land Market.* Cambridge, England: 1973.

Knowles, David. *Christian Monasticism.* New York: 1969.

———. "The Growth of Exemption in England 1066 to 1216." *Downside Review,* 1 NS 31 (1932), 201–31 and 396–436.

————. *The Monastic Order in England.* Cambridge, England: 1966.

Koch, A. C. F. "L'Origine de la haute et de la moyenne justice dans l'ouest et le nord de la France." *Tijdschift voor Rechtsgeschiedenis,* 21 (1953), 420–58.

Kuttner, Stephen. *"Cardinalis:* The History of a Canonical Concept." *Traditio,* 3 (1945), 129–214.

Latouche, Robert. "Un Aspect de la vie rurale dans le Maine au XIe et au XIIe siècle: l'établissement des bourgs." *Moyen âge,* 8 (1937), 44–64.

————. "Défrichement et peuplement rural dans le Maine, du IXe au XIIIe siècle." *Moyen âge,* 54 (1948), 77–87.

————. *Histoire du comté du Maine pendant le Xe–XIe siècles.* Paris: 1910.

Launoy, Jean. *Inquisitio in chartam fundationis et privilegia vindocinensis monasterii.* n.p. 1661.

Leclercq, Jean. "La Crise du monachisme aux XIe et XIIe siècles." *Bullettino dell' Istituto storico italiano per il medio evo a archivio muratoriano,* 70 (1958), 19–41.

————. "Deux opuscules sur la formation des jeunes moines." *Revue d'ascétique et de mystique,* 132 (1957), 387–99.

————. "Documents sur la mort des moines." *Revue Mabillon,* 45 (1955), 165–80, and 46 (1956), 65–81.

————. "Pierre le Vénérable et l'érémitisme clunisien." *Petrus Venerabilis.* Ed. Giles Constable and James Kritzeck. Rome: 1956, 99–120.

————. "La Vêture 'ad succurrendum' d'après le moine Raoul." *Analecta monastica.* Studia Anselmiana, 3d series 37 (1955), 158–68.

Lemarignier, Jean-François. "Aspects politiques des fondations de collégiales dans le royaume de France au XIe siècle." *La vita comune del clero nei secoli XI e XII.* Settimana internazionale di studio, 1st, Passo della Mendola, 1959. Milan: 1962, 19–49.

————. *Etude sur les privilèges d'exemption et de jurisdiction ecclésiastique des abbayes normandes depuis les origines jusqu' en 1140.* Archives de la France monastique, 44. Paris, 1937.

————. "L'Exemption monastique et les origines de la réforme grégorienne." *A Cluny: Congrès scientifique. Fêtes et cérémonies liturgiques en l'honneur des saints abbés Odon et Odilon 9–11 juillet, 1949.* Dijon: 1950, 288–340.

Lepage, Yves. "Recherches sur les chevaliers dans le comté de Vendôme de 1030 à 1150." *Bull. Vend.* (1970), 140–50.

————. "Recherches sur le comté de Vendôme de la fin du Xe au milieu de XIIe siècle." Diss. Faculté des lettres et sciences humaines de Tours 1969–70.

Le Pelletier, Laurent. *Breviculum fundationis et series abbatum S. Nicolai andegavensis.* Angers: 1616.

———. *Rerum scitu dignissimarum a prima fundatione monasterium S. Nicolai andegavensis.* Angers: 1635.

Lesne, Emile. *Les Eglises et les monastères: centres d'accueil, d'exploitation et de peuplement.* Histoire de la propriété ecclésiastique en France, 6. Mémoires et travaux des facultés catholiques de Lille, 53. Lille: 1943.

———. *Les Livres "scriptoria" et bibliothèques du commencement du VIIIe à la fin du XIe siècle.* Histoire de la propriété ecclésiastique en France, 4. Mémoires et travaux des facultés catholiques de Lille, 46. Lille: 1938.

Lesueur, Frédéric. *Les Eglises de Loir-et-Cher.* Paris: 1969.

Little, Lester K. *Religious Poverty and the Profit Economy in Medieval Europe.* Ithaca, N.Y.: 1978.

Lot, Ferdinand. "La Vicaria et le vicarius." *Nouvelle revue de droit français et étranger,* 17 (1893), 281–301.

Lynch, Joseph. *Simoniacal Entry into Religious Life from 1000 to 1260.* Columbus, Ohio: 1976.

Mabillon, Jean. *Lettre d'un benedictin à monseigneur l'evesque de Blois touchant le discernement des anciennes reliques, au sujet d'une dissertation de M. Thiers, contre la Sainte Larme de Vendôme.* Paris: 1700.

Martène, Edmond. *Histoire de Marmoutier.* Mémoires de la société de Touraine, 24. Tours: 1874.

Meinert, Hermann. "Die Fälschungen Gottfrieds von Vendôme." *Sonderabzug aus dem Archiv für Urkundenforschung,* 10 (1928), 232–325.

Métais, Charles. *Chartes Vendômoises.* Vendôme: 1905.

———. "De l'authenticité des chartes de fondation et bulles de l'abbaye de la Trinité de Vendôme." *Moyen âge,* 2d series 8 (1904), 1–44.

———. "Du titre cardinalice des abbés de Vendôme." *Bull. Vend.,* 43 (1904), 12–32.

———. *Etudes et documents.* 2 vols. Vendôme: 1891–94.

———. *Urbain II et Geoffrey Ier cardinal du titre de Sainte-Prisce, 5e abbé de la Sainte Trinité de Vendôme, 1093–1099.* Blois: 1882.

Molinier, Auguste. *Les Obituaires français au moyen âge.* Paris: 1890.

Mollat, Guillaume. "La Restitution des églises privées au patrimonie ecclésiastique en France du IXe au XIe siècle." *Revue historique de droit français et étranger,* 4th series 27 (1949), 399–423.

Mollat, Michel. "Les Moines et les pauvres, XIe–XIIe siècles." *Il mona-chesimo e la riforma ecclesiastica (1049–1122)*. Settimana interna-zionale di studio, 4th, Passo della Mendola, 1968. Miscellanea del Centro di studio medioevali, 6. Milan: 1971, 193–215.

Morin, Germain. "Rainaud l'ermite et Ives de Chartres: un épisode de la crise du cénobitisme au XIe–XIIe siècle." *Revue bénédictine, 40* (1928), 99–115.

Mussat, André. *L'Architecture gothique dans l'ouest de la France aux dou-zième et treizième siècles*. Paris: 1963.

Niderst, R. *Robert Arbrissel et les origines de l'ordre de Fontevrault*. Rodez: 1952.

Olivier-Martin, F. "Les Liens de vassalité dans la France médiévale." *Les Liens de vassalité et les immunités*. Recueil de la société Jean Bodin, 1. Brussels: 1958, 217–22.

Omont, Henri. *Catalogue des manuscripts latins et français de la collection Phillips acquis en 1908 par la Bibliothèque Nationale*. Paris: 1909.

Oury, Guy M. "La Vie monastique selon Hildebert de Lavardin évêque du Mans." *La Province du Maine*, 76 (1974), 115–25.

Paschaud-Granboulan, Anne. "Le Vitrail de la Vierge à la Trinité de Vendôme." *Information d'histoire de l'art*, 16 (1971), 128–32.

Petot, Pierre. "L'Evolution du servage dans la France coutumière du XIe au XIVe siècle." *Le Servage*. Recueil de la société Jean Bodin, 2. Brussels: 1937, 155–64.

———. "Sur une charte-notice vendômoise." *Mélanges d'histoire du moyen âge dédiés à la mémoire de Louis Halphen*. Paris: 1951.

Plat, Gabriel. *L'Art de bâtir en France des romans à l'an 1100, d'après les monuments anciens de la Touraine, de l'Anjou et du Vendômois*. Paris: 1939.

———. *L'eglise de la Trinité de Vendôme*. Paris: 1934.

———. "L'Eglise primitive de la Trinité de Vendôme." *Bull. Vend.* (1925), 95–135.

———. "Notes pour servir à l'histoire monumentale de la Trinité." *Bull. Vend.* (1906), 226–54.

Portel, Charles. "Chapiteau de la Trinité." *Bull. Vend.* (1955), 43–44.

———. "Vers une résurrection monumentale de l'abbaye de la Trin-ité." *Bull. Vend.* (1949), 14–16.

Poupardin, René. "Généalogies angevines du XIe siècle." *Mélanges d'archéologie et d'histoire de l'école française de Rome*, 20 (1900), 206–8.

Raftis, J. A. "Western Monasticism and Economic Organization." *Comparative Studies in Society and History*, 3, no. 4 (1961), 452–69.

Raison, L. and R. Niderst. "Le Movement érémetique dans l'ouest de la France à la fin du XIe siècle et au début du XIIe siècle." *Annales de Bretagne,* 55 (1948), 1–46.

Renouard, Y. "Essai sur le rôle de l'empire angevin dans la formation de la France et de la civilisation française aux XIIe et XIIIe siècle." *Etudes d'histoire médiévale,* 2 (1968), 849–61.

Richard, Alfred. *Histoire des comtes de Poitou.* 2 vols. Paris: 1903.

Riché, Pierre. "L'Enfant dans la société monastique au XIIe siècle." *Pierre Abélard/Pierre le Vénérable.* Paris: 1975.

Roberts, Suzanne. "Charity and Hospitality in the Rouergue 1100–1350." Diss. Harvard 1975.

Roby, Douglas. "Philip of Harvengt's Contribution to the Question of Passage from One Religious Order to Another." *Analecta Praemonstratensia,* 49 (1973), 69–100.

Salmon, Pierre. *The Abbot in Monastic Tradition.* Tr. Claire Lavoie. Washington, D.C.: 1972.

Schieffer, Theodor. *Die päpstlichen Legaten in Frankreich.* Historische Studien, 263. Berlin: 1935.

Schreiber, Georg. *Kurie und Kloster im 12 Jahrhundert. Studien zur Privilegierung, Verfassung und besonders zum Eigenkirchenwesen der vorfranziskanischen Orden vornehmlich auf Grund der Papsturkunden von Paschalis II bis auf Lucius III (1099–1181).* 2 vols. Kirchenrechtliche Abhandlungen, 65–68. Stuttgart: 1910.

Schreiner, Ludwig. *Die frühgotische Plastik Südwestfrankreichs, Studien zum Style Plantagenet 1170 und 1240 mit besonderer Berücksichtigung der Schlussssteinzyklen.* Cologne: 1963.

Searle, Eleanor. "Battle Abbey and Exemption: The Forged Charters." *English Historical Review,* 83 (1968), 449–80.

———. *Lordship and Community: Battle Abbey and Its Banlieu, 1066–1538.* Studies and Texts, 26. Toronto: 1974.

Seymour, Charles, Jr. *Notre-Dame of Noyon in the Twelfth Century.* New York: 1968.

Simon, Michel. *Histoire de Vendôme et de ses environs.* 3 vols. Vendôme: 1834–35.

Swarzenski, Hanns. *Monuments of Romanesque Art: The Art of Church Treasures in North-Western Europe.* Chicago: 1953.

Taralon, Jean. "Découverte de peintures murales romanes dans la salle capitulaire de l'ancienne abbaye de la Trinité de Vendôme." *Bulletin de la société nationale des antiquaires de France,* 9th series 8 (1973), 31–35.

Thiers, Jean B. *Dissertation sur la Sainte Larme de Vendôme.* Paris: 1699.

Trouillard, Guy Jules. *Inventaire et sommaire des archives départementales antérieures à 1790*. Blois: 1936.

Urseau, Charles. "La Grande salle des malades de l'hôpital Saint-Jean d'Angers." *Bulletin monumental*, 81 (1922), 369–79.

Vanuxem, J. "The Theories of Mabillon and Montfaucon on French Sculpture of the Twelfth Century." *Journal of the Warburg and Courtauld Institutes*, 20 (1957), 45–58.

Verriest, L. "Les Faits et la terminologie en matière de condition juridique des personnes au moyen âge: serfs, nobles, vilains, sainteurs." *Revue de Nord*, 25 (1939), 101–27.

Vezin, Jean. *Les Scriptoria d'Angers au XIe siècle*. Bibliothèque de l'Ecole des Hautes Etudes, 322. Paris: 1974.

White, Stephen D. *"Pactum . . . Legem Vincit et Amor Judicium.:* The Settlement of Disputes by Compromise in Eleventh-Century Western France." *American Journal of Legal History*, 22 (1978), 281–308.

Wilmart, André. *Auteurs spirituels et textes dévots du moyen âge latin*. Paris: 1932.

———. "La Collection chronologique des écrits de Geoffroi abbé de Vendôme." *Revue bénédictine*, 43 (1931), 239–45.

———. "Eve et Goscelin." *Revue bénédictine*, 46 (1934), 414–38, and 50 (1938), 42–83.

———. "Les Ouvrages d'un moine du Bec: Un débat sur la profession monastique au XIIe siècle." *Revue bénédictine*, 44 (1932), 21–46.

Wood, Susan. *English Monasteries and Their Patrons in the Thirteenth Century*. Oxford: 1955.

Yver, Jean. "Les caractères originaux du groupe de coutumes de l'ouest de la France." *Revue historique de droit français et étranger*, 4th series 29 (1952), 18–79.

Index